QUALITY

MANAGEMENT

E S S

L S

QUALITY
MANAGEMENT
ESSENTIALS

David Hoyle

AMSTERDAM • BOSTON • HEIDELBERG • LONDON • OXFORD • NEW YORK
PARIS • SAN DIEGO • SAN FRANCISCO • SINGAPORE • SYDNEY • TOKYO

Butterworth-Heinemann is an imprint of Elsevier

Butterworth-Heinemann is an imprint of Elsevier
Linacre House, Jordan Hill, Oxford OX2 8DP, UK
30 Corporate Drive, Suite 400, Burlington, MA 01803, USA

First edition 2007

British Library Cataloguing in Publication Data
A catalogue record for this book is available from the British Library

Library of Congress Cataloguing in Publication Data
A catalogue record for this book is available from the Library of Congress

ISBN 10: 0-75-066786-9
ISBN 13: 978-0-75-066786-9

For information on all Butterworth-Heinemann publications
visit our website at http://books.elsevier.com

Typeset by Charon Tec Ltd (A Macmillan Company), Chennai, India
www.charontec.com
Printed and bound in Great Britain

07 08 09 10 11   10 9 8 7 6 5 4 3 2 1

Contents

Preface

If we follow the evolution of quality management from its early beginnings, we find that the foundations were laid centuries ago but developed along different strands. Focusing initially on checking final product against standards in an ever-increasing quest to eliminate product failure, quality management thinking moved upwards from the work place through all disciplines until it could go no further. For many years, the supporting functions were excluded if they did not directly contribute to the achievement of product quality. But when it arrived in the boardroom it became more difficult to distinguish quality issues from non-quality issues. There emerged the concept of little "q" and big "Q". Little "q" is only concerned with the saleable goods and services and the directly related processes, functions, customers, suppliers and costs. Big "Q" is concerned with business outputs and all processes, functions, stakeholders and costs. It became apparent that every function of the business contributes to business outcomes (outputs + impacts) and that every function influenced in some way the ability of the organization to create and retain satisfied customers. It was soon realized that business survival depended on its relationships with employees, suppliers, shareholders, and society in general – that these parties all have an interest in the business and that their needs and expectations are important in the quest to create and retain satisfied customers for its products and services.

Throughout this evolution the terminology has lagged behind the thinking. Inspection evolved into quality control, which evolved into quality assurance. But this was not enough, along came Total Quality Management in an attempt to focus on big "Q" while quality assurance focused on little "q". Unfortunately TQM was not well understood and resulted in many misconceived but well meaning initiatives. It did not quite bridge the intellectual gap between quality management and general management so remained the interest of a few specialists. The EFQM Excellence Model has to some extent bridged this gap but this is an assessment framework rather than a management philosophy.

The question is whether we really need to use the word "quality" at all and that prolonging its use is detrimental to our quest. Every time we use the term quality, our listeners or readers may be thinking little "q" not big "Q".

This book attempts to take the reader on several journeys in order to explain the concepts, principles and thinking behind the tenets of quality management and the practical methodologies that have emerged to implement them. We weave a path that embraces both little q and big Q and take a detour or two to address misconceptions and alternative theories but maintain a focus on big Q. Throughout the book there is an armoury of questions, tools and techniques to enable students, practitioners and managers to build a case for change and convince top management of a need for change.

Chapters 1–3 provide an appreciation of the basic concepts that constitute the body of knowledge of quality management. Starting with stakeholders and their needs putting quality in context we then examine the meaning, relationships and dimensions of quality. We go on to examine how quality is managed, presenting the two opposing theories of managing success and managing failure and introduce the principles that underpin the management of quality. Aspects and fundamental principles of quality control, assurance and improvement are examined next including a study of variation and six sigma. Chapter 3 comprises an examination of quality management systems, the philosophy on which they are based, including misconceptions and a look at the current fad, integrated management systems, the myths and alternative theories.

Chapters 4 and 6 put forward two very different approaches to managing quality. The first in Chapter 4 shows how ISO 9000 can be used, firstly explaining its origins and putting it in context and then outlining the requirements in a way that shows how they work together to define a management system capable of producing outputs that satisfy customer requirements.

ISO 9000 and its derivatives has come to dominate discussions on quality often with adverse effects. Therefore Chapter 5 takes a look at various perceptions and misconceptions that have grown up around ISO 9000 since 1987 and the associated infrastructure. Such an appreciation is needed for anyone contemplating ISO 9000 certification.

A different approach to managing quality is addressed in Chapter 6. This is the process approach and although critics might argue that ISO 9000:2000 has been based on the process approach, the difference arises from the way the approach is defined in ISO 9000. There the approach is defined as the systematic identification and management of processes and their interactions. This definition was felt to be unhelpful as it failed to define the primary focus of effective process management. In this Chapter the process approach is an approach to managing work in which the activities, resources and behaviours function together in such a relationship as to produce results consistent with the process objectives. It is shown how the process approach to management can be used to develop the organization's mission, its strategic objectives and the processes for achieving these objectives. After explaining the characteristics of a process in detail and the principles of process management, the steps to be undertaken in developing a process based management system are described.

No excuse is made for devoting more space to process management than to ISO 9000 because in due course ISO 9000 will evolve to embrace all the tenets of process management.

A change in style greets the reader in Chapter 7. We follow the journeys of four people who discover a need for change in their organization. We derive the objectives relevant to each case and examine how top management might challenge each individual in proving the need for change. We then look at the factors involved in assessing the feasibility of change and in preparing a presentation that deals with different learning styles. Guidance is provided on the content of a presentation that is intended to gain management commitment for a project that will bring about improvement in some aspect of performance. Guidance is also provided on what to do before, during and after the presentation including help with dealing with challenges.

There are two Appendices. The first contains a list of questions that should provide food for thought and the second is a glossary of terms used in the field of quality management.

Chapters 1–6 were first published in the 5th edition of my ISO 9000 Quality Systems Handbook as background information but it was felt that they could stand alone as a general introduction to quality management. They have been revised and updated and new material added.

If you read the book from cover to cover you will discover a degree of repetition in one form or another. Hopefully this is not too irritating but it is done for a reason, that of changing perceptions. We rarely learn by a chance observation and it often requires frequent exposure to ideas presented in different forms and context before our beliefs or perceptions are changed.

My hope is that this book may reach a different audience to that of my ISO 9000 Quality Systems Handbook, possibly an audience that is more concerned with big Q than little q. We gain knowledge by asking questions and if a few executives stumble across this book and start using the principles and asking the many questions within it, it will have been worthwhile.

David Hoyle
Monmouth

hoyle@transition-support.com

Chapter 1
Introduction to quality

By three methods we may learn wisdom: First, by reflection, which is noblest;
Second, by imitation, which is easiest; and third by experience, which is the
bitterest.

Confucius (551 479 BCE) Chinese philosopher

Principles or prescription

One of the great problems in our age is to impart understanding in the minds of
those who have the ability and opportunity to make decisions that affect our
lives. There is no shortage of information – in fact there is too much now we can
search a world of information from the comfort of our armchair. We are bombarded with information but it is not knowledge – it does not necessarily lead to
understanding. With so many conflicting messages from so many people, it is difficult to determine the right thing to do. There are those whose only need is a set
of principles from which they are able to determine the right things to do. There
are countless others who need a set of rules derived from principles that they can
apply to what they do and indeed others who need a detailed prescription
derived from the rules for a particular task. In the translation from principles to
prescription, inconsistencies arise. Those translating the principles into rules or
requirements are often not the same as those translating the rules into a detailed
prescription. Rules are often an imperfect translation of principles and yet, they
are enforced without regard to or even an understanding of the principles they
were intended to implement. This is no more prevalent than in local government
where officials behave like robots, enforcing rules without regard to what the
rules were intended to achieve.

The principles in the field of quality management have not arisen out of academia but from life in the work place. Observations from the work place have
been taken into academia, analysed, synthesized and refined to emerge as

universal principles. These principles have been expressed in many ways and in their constant refreshment the language is modernized and simplified, but the essence is hardly changed.

Without a set of principles, achieving a common understanding in the field of quality management would be impossible. Since Juran, Deming and Feigenbaum wrote about quality management in the 1950s there has been considerable energy put into codifying the field of quality management and a set of principles from which we can derive useful rules, regulations and requirements has emerged. This chapter addresses these principles in a way that is intended to impart understanding not only in the minds of those who prefer principles to prescription, but also in the minds of those who prefer prescriptions. There is nothing intrinsically wrong with wanting a prescription. It saves time, it's repeatable, it's economic and it's the fastest way to get things done but it has to be right. The receivers of prescriptions need enough understanding to know whether what they are being asked to do is appropriate to the circumstances they are facing.

The concepts expressed in this book embody universal principles and have been selected and structured in a manner that is considered suitable for those wishing to get some clarity in a field of knowledge that often appears contradictory. It is not intended as a comprehensive guide to quality management – some further reading is given in the Bibliography. ISO 9000:2000 also contains concepts some of which are questionable but these will be dealt with as they arise. The aim is to give the reader a balanced view and present a logical argument that is hoped will lead to greater understanding. As the book is supposed to be about the management of quality, there is no better place to start than with an explanation of the word *quality*.

Needs, requirements and expectations

Organizations are created to achieve a goal, mission or objective but they will only do so if they satisfy the needs, requirements and expectations of their stakeholders. Their customers, as one of the stakeholders, will be satisfied only if they provide products and services that meet their needs, requirements and expectations. Their other stakeholders (shareholders, employees, suppliers and society) will only be satisfied if the products and services provided to customers are produced and supplied in a manner that satisfies their needs, requirements and expectations – in other words, it makes a profit, does no unintentional harm, and is conceived and produced with due regard to prevailing legislation.

We all have needs, wants, requirements and expectations. Needs are essential for life, to maintain certain standards, or essential for products and services, to fulfil the purpose for which they have been acquired. According to Maslow,[1] man is a wanting being; there is always some need he wants to satisfy. Once this is accomplished, that particular need no longer motivates him and he turns to another, again seeking satisfaction. Everyone has basic physiological needs that

Figure 1.1   Hierarchy of needs

are necessary to sustain life. (Food, water, clothing, and shelter). Maslow's research showed that once the physiological needs are fulfilled, the need for safety emerges. After safety come social needs followed by the need for esteem and finally the need for self-actualization or the need to realize ones full potential. Satisfaction of physiological needs is usually associated with money – not money itself but what it can buy. The hierarchy of needs is shown in Figure 1.1.

These needs are fulfilled by the individual purchasing, renting or leasing products or services. Corporate needs are not too dissimilar. The physiological needs of organizations are those necessary to sustain survival. Often profit comes first because no organization can sustain a loss for too long but functionality is paramount – the product or service must do the job for which it is intended regardless of it being obtained cheaply. Corporate safety comes next in terms of the safety of employees and the safety and security of assets followed by social needs in the form of a concern for the environment and the community as well as forming links with other organizations and developing contacts. Esteem is represented in the corporate context by organizations purchasing luxury cars, winning awards, superior offices and infrastructures and possessing those things that give it power in the market place and government. Self-actualization is represented by an organization's preoccupation with growth, becoming bigger rather than better, seeking challenges and taking risks. However, it is not the specific product or service that is needed but the benefits that possession brings that is important. This concept of benefits is the most important and key to the achievement of quality.

Requirements are what we request of others and may encompass our needs but often we don't fully realize what we need until after we have made our request. For example, now that we own a mobile telephone we discover we really need hands-free operation when using the phone while driving a vehicle. Our requirements at the moment of sale may or may not therefore express all our needs. By focusing on benefits resulting from products and services, needs can be converted into wants such that a need for food may be converted into a want for a particular brand of chocolate. Sometimes the want is not essential but the higher up the hierarchy of needs we go, the more a want becomes essential to maintain our social standing, esteem or to realize our personal goals. Our requirements may therefore include such wants – what we would like to have but are not essential for survival.

In growing their business organizations create a demand for their products and services but far from the demand arising from a want that is essential to maintain our social standing, it is based on an image created for us by media advertising. We don't need spring vegetables in the winter but because industry has created the organization to supply them, a demand is created that becomes an expectation. Spring vegetables have been available in the winter now for so long that we expect them to be available in the shops and will go elsewhere if they are not. But they are not essential to survival, to safety, to esteem or to realize our potential and their consumption may in fact harm our health because we are no longer absorbing the right chemicals to help us survive the cold winters. We might want it, even need it but it does us harm and regrettably, there are plenty of organizations ready to supply us products that will harm us.

Expectations are *implied needs* or *requirements*. They have not been requested because we take them for granted – we regard them to be understood within our particular society as the accepted norm. They may be things to which we are accustomed, based on fashion, style, trends or previous experience. One therefore expects sales staff to be polite and courteous, electronic products to be safe and reliable, policemen to be honest, coffee to be hot, etc. One would like politicians to be honest but in some countries we have come to expect them to be corruptible, dishonest or at least, economical with the truth! As expectations are also born out of experience, some people might expect businessmen to be corruptible and selfish and it comes as no surprise to read about long drawn out court cases involving fraud and deceit.

> **Expectations**
>
> It is easy to exceed customer expectations when your usual performance is well below the norm

Likewise, after frequent poor service from a train operator, our expectations are that the next time we use that train operator; we will once again be disappointed. We would therefore be delighted if, through some well focused quality initiative, the train operator exceeded our expectations on our next journey.

The stakeholders

Organizations depend on customers because without them there is no business. However, in order to satisfy these customers, organizations also depend on a number of other parties that provide them with resources and sanction their operations. There are parties other than the customer that have an interest or stake in the organization and what it does but may not receive a product. The term quality is not defined relative to customers but to requirements and these interested parties do have requirements. ISO 9000:2000 defines an interested party as *a person or group having an interest in the performance or success of an organization*. But, the organization may not have an interest in all of them and on reflection perhaps the word *interest* is not quite appropriate. Consider for instance, competitors, criminals and terrorists. None of these has put anything into the organization and their interest is more likely to be malevolent than benevolent so in these cases the organization fights off their interests rather than satisfies them. A better word to *interest* would be *stake* but in some cultures this translates as a bet that you place on a horse to win a race. However, it is common in the west for the term stakeholder to be used in preference to the term interested party, as it implies benevolence unlike the term interested parties which might be benevolent or malevolent.

> **Interested party**
>
> A person or group having an interest in the performance or success of an organization – primarily includes:
>   Customers, shareholders, employees, suppliers, and society but can also include competitors, criminals, and terrorists

Parties with a benevolent interest (stakeholders) are customers, owners, employees, contractors, suppliers, investors, unions, partners and society. They all expect something in return for their stake and can withdraw it should the expected benefits not be returned. When you produce products you are producing them with the intent that all these parties benefit but particularly

> **Stakeholder**
>
> A person or organization that has freedom to provide something to or withdraw something from an enterprise. Primarily customers, shareholders, employees, suppliers and society.

for the benefit of customers. The other parties are not particularly interested in the products and services themselves but may be interested in their effects on their investment, their well-being and the environment.

The term interested party is also being used[2] to refer to anyone significantly affecting or affected by someone else's decision-making activity but the danger in this definition is that it places terrorists, criminals and competitors into the same category as those parties that the organization seeks to satisfy. Any statement that implies organizations have a duty to satisfy their interested parties would be invalid as they should only strive to satisfy those with a benevolent interest. We will therefore use the word stakeholder from here on.

The customer

A product that possesses features that satisfy customer needs is a quality product. Likewise, one that possesses features that dissatisfy customers is not a quality product. So the final arbiter on product quality is the customer. The customer is the only one who can decide whether the quality of the products and services you supply is satisfactory and you will be conscious of this either by direct feedback or by loss of sales, reduction in

> **Customer**
>
> Organization that receives a product or service – includes:
>   Purchaser, consumer, client, end user, retailer or beneficiary

market share and, ultimately, loss of business. This brings us back to benefits. The customer acquires a product for the benefits that possession will bring. Therefore if the product fails to deliver the expected benefits it will be considered by the customer to be of poor quality. So when making judgements about quality, the requirement should be expressed in terms of benefits not a set of derived characteristics. In the foregoing it was convenient to use the term customer but the definition of *quality* does not only relate to customers. Dissatisfy your customers and they withdraw their stake and take their business elsewhere.

Clearly the customer is the only stakeholder that brings in revenue and therefore meeting their needs and expectations is paramount but not at the expense of the other stakeholders. The trick is to satisfy customers in a way that will satisfy the needs of other stakeholders. (See the section on quality management principles in chapter 2.)

The internal customer

We tend to think of products and services being supplied to customers and in the wake of Total Quality Management (TQM), we are led to believe there are internal and external customers. A customer is a stakeholder; they have entered into a commitment in return for some benefits that possession of a product or experience of a service may bring. The internal receivers of products are not stakeholders (they are part of the process) therefore they are not strictly customers. Normally the customer is external to the organization supplying the product.

However, if we consider for a moment the notion of an internal customer, the operator who receives a drawing from the designer would be regarded as a customer. But the operator doesn't pay the designer for the drawing, has no contract with the designer, does not pass the output of his work to the designer, does not define the requirements for the drawing and cannot choose to ignore the drawing so is not a customer in the excepted sense but a user of the drawing. If the operator provides a test piece to a laboratory and receives the test results, one might regard the operator as the laboratory's customer but once again, there is no contract and no money passing between the two parties. In fact the operator, the designer and laboratory all have the same customer – the person or organization that is paying for the organization's output and specifying the requirements the organization must satisfy. The notion of internal customers and suppliers is illustrated in Figure 1.2. In the upper diagram, requirements are passed along the supply chain and if at each stage there is some embellishment or interpretation by the time the last person in the chain receives the instructions they may well be very much different than what the customer originally required. In reality each stage has to meet the external customer requirement as it applies to the work performed at that stage not as the person performing the previous or subsequent stage wants. This is shown in the lower diagram where at each stage there is an opportunity to verify that the stage output is consistent with the external customer requirement.

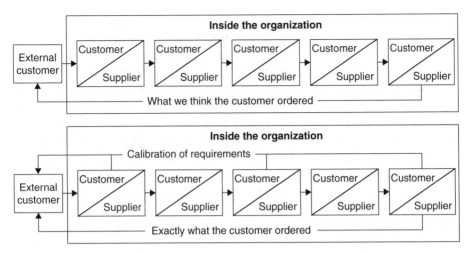

Figure 1.2 The internal customer-supplier chain

In a well-designed process, individuals do not impose their own requirements on others. The requirements are either all derived from the customer requirements or from the constraints imposed by the other stakeholders.

If instead of the label internal customers and suppliers, individuals were to regard themselves as players in a team that has a common goal, the team would achieve the same intent. In a team, every player is just as important as every other and with each player providing outputs and behaving in a manner that enables the other players to do their job right first time, the team goal would be achieved. The observation by Phil Crosby that quality is ballet not hockey[3] is very apt. In hockey, the participants do not treat each other as customers and suppliers but as team members each doing their best but the result on most occasions is unpredictable. In ballet, the participants also do not treat each other as customers and suppliers but as artists playing predetermined roles that are intended to achieve predictable results. Organizational processes are designed to deliver certain outputs and in order to do so individuals need to perform specific roles in the process in the same relationship that ballet dancers have to a ballet.

The external supply chain

The transaction between the customer and the supplier is often a complex one. There may be a supply chain from original producer through to the end user. At each transaction within this supply chain, the receiving party needs to be satisfied. It is not sufficient to simply satisfy the first receiver of the product or service. All parties in the supply chain need to be satisfied before you can claim to have supplied a quality product. Admittedly, once the product leaves your premises you may lose control and therefore cannot be held accountable for any damage that may become the product, but the inherent characteristics are your responsibility.

In an increasing global market, many organizations are faced with the bulk of the cost in a product being added down or up the supply chain with less and less being added by themselves. More and more activities are being outsourced putting a greater burden on the purchasing staff to manage suppliers and commercial staff to manage customers. The integrity of the supply chain depends upon each party honouring their commitments and this depends upon each supplier having processes that have the capability to deliver quality product on time. Once products begin to flow along the supply chain any disruptions either due to poor quality or late delivery cause costs to rise further along the chain that are irrecoverable. The end customer will only pay for product that meets requirements therefore if buffer stocks have to be held and staff paid waiting time as a result of supply chain unreliability, these costs have to be born by the producers. Process capability and product and service quality along the supply chain become the most vital factors in delivering outputs that satisfy the end customer requirement.

Society

Society is a stakeholder because it can withdraw its support for an organization. It can protest or invoke legal action. While society does not put anything into an organization directly, it does sanction its existence often through local planning authorities. Society is represented by the regulators and regardless of whether or not a customer specifies applicable regulations *you* are under an obligation to comply with those that apply. The regulator is not interested in whether you satisfy your customers, your employees or your investors or in fact whether you go bankrupt! Its primary concern is the protection of society. The regulators take their authority from the law that should have been designed to protect the innocent. Regulators are certainly stakeholders because they can withdraw their approval.

> **Regulator**
>
> A legal body authorized to enforce compliance with the laws and statutes of a national government.

Employees

Employees may not be interested in the products and services, but are interested in the conditions in which they are required to work. Employees are stakeholders because they can withdraw their labour. Employees are also a resource and therefore have a dual role in the organization.

Suppliers

Suppliers are interested in the success of the organization because it may in turn lead to their success. However, suppliers are also stakeholders because they can withdraw their patronage. They can choose their customers. If you treat your suppliers badly such as delaying payment of invoices for trivial mistakes, you

Table 1.1 Criteria used by stakeholders to judge organization effectiveness or success

Stakeholder	*Success criteria*
Owner	Financial return
Employees	Job satisfaction, pay and conditions and quality of leadership
Customers	Quality of products and services
Community	Contribution to the community – jobs, support for other traders in the community – care for the local environment
Suppliers	Satisfactory mutual trading
Investors	Value of shares
Government	Compliance with legislation

may find they terminate the supply at the first opportunity possibly putting your organization into a difficult position relative to commitments made to customers.

Investors

Often the most common type of stakeholder, are investors. The owners, partners and shareholders including banks are interested in protecting their stake in the business. They will withdraw their stake if the organization fails to perform. Poorly conceived products and poorly managed processes and resources will not yield the expected return and the action of investors can directly affect the supply chain; although they are not customers, they are feeding the supply chain with much needed resources. In the event that this supply of resource is terminated, the organization ceases to have the capability to serve its customers.

The success of any organization therefore depends on understanding the needs and expectations of all the stakeholders, not just its customers and on managing the organization in a manner that leads to the continued satisfaction[4] of all parties. Table 1.1 shows the criteria used by different stakeholders. It tends to suggest that for an organization to be successful it needs to balance (not trade–off) the needs of the stakeholders such that all are satisfied. There are those who believe that a focus on customers alone will result in the other parties being satisfied. There are those who believe that a focus on shareholder value will result in all other parties being satisfied. The problem is that the interested party is motivated by self-interest and may not be willing to compromise.

Defining quality

In supplying products or services there are three fundamental parameters that determine their saleability. They are price, quality and delivery. Customers require products and services of a given quality to be delivered by or be available by a given time and to be of a price that reflects value for money. These are the requirements of customers. An organization will survive only if it creates and retains satisfied customers and this will only be achieved if it offers for sale products or services that respond to customer needs and expectations as well as requirements. While price is a function of cost, profit margin and market forces, and delivery is a function of the organization's efficiency and effectiveness. Quality is determined by the extent to which a product or service successfully serves the purposes of the user during usage (not just at the point of sale). Price and delivery are both transient features, whereas the impact of quality is sustained long after the attraction or the pain of price and delivery has subsided.

The word *quality* has many meanings:

- A degree of excellence.
- Conformance with requirements.
- The totality of characteristics of an entity that bear on its ability to satisfy stated or implied needs.
- Fitness for use.
- Fitness for purpose.
- Freedom from defects, imperfections or contamination.
- Delighting customers.

> **Quality**
>
> The degree to which a set of inherent characteristics fulfils a need or expectation that is stated, general implied or obligatory.

These are just a few meanings; however, the meaning used in the context of ISO 9000 was concerned with the totality of characteristics that satisfy needs but in the 2000 version this has changed. Quality in ISO 9000:2000 is defined as the degree to which a set of inherent characteristics fulfils the requirements. The former definition focused on an entity that was described as a product or service but with this new definition, the implication is that quality is relative to what something should be and what it is. The something may be a product, service, decision, document, piece of information or any output from a process. In describing an output, we express it in terms of its characteristics. To comment on the quality of anything we need a measure of its characteristics and a basis for comparison. By combining the definition of the terms *quality* and *requirement* in ISO 9000:2000, quality can be expressed as *the degree to which a set of inherent characteristics fulfils a need or expectation that is stated, generally implied or obligatory*.

This concept of "degree" is present in the generally accepted definition of quality in the Oxford English Dictionary and is illustrated in Figure 1.3. The diagram expresses three truths.

- Needs, requirements and expectations are constantly changing.
- Performance needs to be constantly changing to keep pace with the needs.
- Quality is the difference between the standard stated, implied or required and the standard reached.

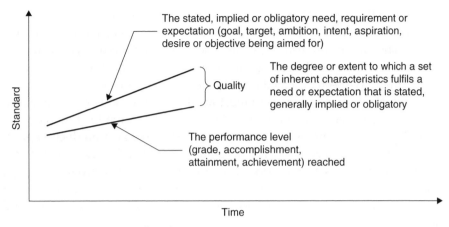

Figure 1.3 The meaning of quality

This means that when we talk of anything using the word quality it simply implies that we are referring to the extent or degree to which a requirement is met. It also means that all the principles, methodologies, tools and techniques in the field of quality management serve one purpose, that of enabling organizations to close the gap between the standard required and the standard reached. In this context, environmental, safety, security and health problems are in fact quality problems because an expectation or a requirement has not been met. If the expectation had been met there would be no problem. Having made the comparison we can still assess whether the output is "fit for use". In this sense the output may be non-conforming to specified requirements but remain fit for use.

The specification is often an imperfect definition of what a customer needs; because some needs can be difficult to express clearly. It therefore doesn't mean that by not conforming, the product or service is unfit for use. It is also possible that a product that conforms to requirements may be totally useless. It all depends on whose requirements are being met. For example, if a company sets its own standards and these do not meet customer needs, its claim to producing quality products is bogus. On the other hand, if the standards are well in excess of what the customer requires, the price tag may well be too high for what customers are prepared to pay – there probably isn't a market for a gold-plated mousetrap, for instance, except as an ornament perhaps!

The characteristics of quality

Classification of products and services

If we group products and services (entities) by type, category, class and grade we can use the subdivision to make comparisons on an equitable basis. But when we compare entities we must be careful not to claim one is of better quality than the other unless they are of the same grade. Entities of the same type have at least one attribute in common. Entities of the same grade have been designed for the same functional use and therefore comparisons are valid. Comparisons on quality between entities of different grades, classes, categories or types are invalid because they have been designed for a different use or purpose.

Let us look at some examples to illustrate the point. Food is a type of entity. Transport is another entity. Putting aside the fact that in the food industry the terms *class* and *grade* are used to denote the condition of post-production product, comparisons between *types* is like comparing fruit and trucks, i.e. there are no common attributes. Comparisons between *categories* are like comparing fruit and vegetables. Comparisons between *classes* are like comparing apples and oranges. Comparisons between *grades* are like comparing eating apples and cooking apples.

Now let us take another example. Transport is a type of entity. There are different categories of transport such as airliners, ships, automobiles and trains; they are all modes of transport but each has many different attributes. Differences between categories of transport are therefore differences in *modes* of transport. Within each category there are differences in class. For manufactured products, differences between classes imply differences in *purpose*. Luxury cars, large family cars, small family cars, vans, trucks, four-wheel drive vehicles etc. fall within the same category of transport but each was designed for a different purpose. Family cars are in a different class to luxury cars; they were not designed for the same purpose. It is therefore inappropriate to compare a Cadillac with a Chevrolet or a Rolls Royce Silver Shadow with a Ford Mondeo. Entities designed for the same purpose but having different specifications are of different grades. A Ford Mondeo GTX is a different grade to a Mondeo LX. They were both designed for the same purpose but differ in their performance and features and hence comparisons on quality are invalid.

A third example would be the service industry: accommodation. There are various categories, such as rented, leased and purchased. In the rented category there are hotels, inns, guesthouses, apartments etc. It would be inappropriate to compare hotels with guesthouses or apartments with inns. They are each in a different class. Hotels are a class of accommodation within which are grades such as 5 star, 4 star, 3 star etc., indicating the facilities offered not quality levels. It would therefore be reasonable to expect a 1 star hotel to be just as clean as a 4 start hotel.

You can legitimately compare the quality of entities if comparing entities of the same grade. If a low-grade product or service meets the needs for which it was designed, it is of the requisite quality. If a high-grade product or service fails to meet the requirements for which it was designed, it is of poor quality, regardless of it still meeting the requirements for the lower grade. There is a market for such differences in products and services but should customer's expectations change then what was once acceptable for a particular grade may no longer be acceptable and regrading may have to occur.

Where manufacturing processes are prone to uncontrollable variation it is not uncommon to grade products as a method of selection. The product that is free of imperfections would be the highest grade and would therefore command the highest price. Any product with imperfections would be downgraded and sold at a correspondingly lower price. Examples of such practice arise in the fruit and vegetables trade and the ceramics, glass and textile industries. In the electronic component industry, grading is a common practice to select devices that operate between certain temperature ranges. In ideal conditions all devices would meet the higher specification but due to variations in the raw material or in the manufacturing process only a few may actually reach full performance. The remainder of the devices has a degraded performance but still offer all the functions of the top-grade component at lower temperatures. To say that these differences are not differences in *quality* would be misleading, because the products were all designed to fulfil the higher specification. As there is a market for such products it is expedient to exploit it. There is a range over which product quality can vary and still create satisfied customers. Outside the lower end of this range the product is considered to be of poor quality.

Quality and price

Most of us are attracted to certain products and services by their price. If the price is outside our reach we don't even consider the product or service, whatever its quality, except perhaps to form an opinion about it. We also rely on price as a comparison, hoping that we can obtain the same characteristics at a lower price. In the luxury goods market, a high price is often a mark of quality but occasionally it is a confidence trick aimed at making more profit for the supplier. When certain products and services are rare, the price tends to be high and when plentiful the price is low, regardless of their quality. One can purchase the same item in different stores at different prices, some as much as 50% less, many at 10% less than the highest price. You can also receive a discount for buying in bulk, buying on customer credit card and being a trade customer rather than a retail customer. Travellers know that goods are more expensive at an airport than from a country craft shop. However, in the country craft shop, defective goods or "seconds" may well be on sale, whereas at the airport the supplier will as a rule, want to display only the best examples. Often an increase in the price of a product may indicate a better after-sales service, such as free on-site maintenance, free delivery, and free telephone support line. The discount shops may not offer such benefits.

The price label on any product or service should be for a product or service free of defects. If there are defects the label should say as much, otherwise the supplier may well be in breach of national laws and statutes. Price is therefore not an inherent feature or characteristic of the product. It is not permanent and as shown above varies without any change to the inherent characteristics of the product. Price is a feature of the service associated with the sale of the product.

Price is negotiable for the same quality of product. Some may argue that quality is expensive but in reality, the saving you make on buying low-priced goods could well be eroded by inferior service or differences in the cost of ownership.

Quality and design

In examining the terms design and quality, we need to recognize that the word design has several meanings. Here we are not concerned with design as a verb or as the name we give to a process of design or the output of the design process. In this context we are concerned with the term design as an aesthetic characteristic of a product or service rather than a quality characteristic. The quality characteristic embraces the form, fit and function attributes relative to its purpose. The attributes that appeal to the senses are very subjective and cannot be measured with any accuracy, other than by observation and comparison by human senses. So when we talk of quality and design we are not referring to whether the design reflects a product that has the correct features and functions to fulfil its purpose, we are addressing the aesthetic qualities of the product. We could use the word appearance but design goes beyond appearance. It includes all the features that we perceive by touch, smell and hearing.

If the customer requires a product that is aesthetically pleasing to the eye, or is to blend into the environment or appeal to a certain group of people, one way to measure the quality of this subjective characteristic is to present the design to the people concerned and ask them to offer their opinion.

Quality of design is a different concept and is addressed below.

Quality and cost

Philip Crosby published his book *Quality Is Free* in 1979 and caused a lot of raised eyebrows among executives because they always believed the removal of defects was an in-built cost in running any business. To get quality you had to pay for inspectors to detect the errors! What Crosby told us was that if we could eliminate all the errors and reach zero defects, we would not only reduce our costs but also increase the level of customer satisfaction by several orders of magnitude. In fact there is the cost of doing the right things right first time and the cost of *not* doing the right things right first time. The latter are often referred to as *quality costs* or the cost incurred because failure is possible. Using this definition, if failure of a product, a process or a service is not possible, there would be no *quality costs*. It is rather misleading to refer to the cost incurred because failure is possible as *quality costs* because we could classify the costs as avoidable costs and unavoidable costs. We have to pay for labour, materials, facilities, machines, transport etc. These costs are unavoidable but we are also paying in addition some cost to cover the prevention, detection and removal of errors. Should customers have to pay for the errors made by others? There is a basic cost if failure is not possible and an additional cost in preventing and detecting failures and correcting errors because our prevention and detection programmes are ineffective. However, there is variation in all processes but it is only the variation that exceeds the tolerable limits that incurs a penalty. If you reduce complexity and install failure-prevention measures you will be spending less on failure detection and correction. There is an initial investment to be paid, but in the long term you can meet your customer's requirements at a cost far less than you were spending previously. Some customers are now forcing their suppliers to reduce internal costs so that they can offer the same products at lower prices. This has the negative effect of forcing suppliers out of business. While the motive is laudable the method is damaging to industry. There are inefficiencies in industry that need to be reduced but imposing requirements will not solve the problem. Co-operation between customer and supplier would be a better solution and when neither party can identify any further savings the target has been reached. Customers do not benefit by forcing suppliers out of business. So is *quality free*?

High quality and low quality; poor quality and good quality

When a product or service satisfies our needs we are likely to say it is of good quality and likewise when we are dissatisfied we say the product or service is of poor quality. When the product or service exceeds our needs we will probably say it is of high quality and likewise if it falls well below our expectations we say it is of low quality.

These measures of quality are all subjective. What is good to one may be poor to another. In the under-developed countries, any product, no matter what the quality, is welcomed. When you have nothing, even the poorest of goods is better than none. A product may not need to possess defects for it to be regarded as poor quality which means it may not possess the features that we would expect, such as access for maintenance. These are design features that give a product its saleability. Products and services that conform to customer requirements are considered to be products of acceptable quality. However, we need to express our relative satisfaction with products and services and as a consequence use subjective terms such as high, low, good or poor quality. If a product that meets customer requirements is of acceptable quality, what do we call one that does not quite meet the requirements, or perhaps exceeds the requirements? An otherwise acceptable product has a blemish – is it now unacceptable? Perhaps not because it may still be far superior to other competing products in its acceptable features and characteristics.

While not measurable, these subjective terms enable customers to rate products and services according to the extent to which they satisfy their requirements. However, to the company supplying products and services, a more precise means of measuring quality is needed. To the supplier, a quality product is one that meets in full the perceived customer requirements.

Quality characteristics

Any feature or characteristic of a product or service that is needed to satisfy customer needs or achieve fitness for use is a *quality characteristic*. When dealing with products the characteristics are almost always technical characteristics, whereas service quality characteristics have a human dimension. Some typical quality characteristics are given below.

Product characteristics

Accessibility	Functionality	Size
Availability	Interchangeability	Susceptibility
Appearance	Maintainability	Storability
Adaptability	Odour	Strength
Cleanliness	Operability	Taste
Consumption	Portability	Testability
Durability	Producibility	Traceability
Disposability	Reliability	Toxicity
Emissivity	Reparability	Transportability
Flammability	Safety	Vulnerability
Flexibility	Security	Weight

Service quality characteristics

Accessibility	Credibility	Integrity
Accuracy	Dependability	Promptness
Courtesy	Efficiency	Responsiveness
Comfort	Effectiveness	Reliability
Competence	Flexibility	Security

These are the characteristics that need to be specified and their achievement planned, controlled, assured, improved, managed and demonstrated. These are the characteristics that form the subject matter of the product or service requirements referred to in a contract, specification or indeed ISO 9000. When the value of these characteristics is quantified or qualified they are termed *product requirements*. We used to use the term *quality requirements* but this caused a division in thinking that resulted in people regarding quality requirements as the domain of the quality personnel and technical requirements being the domain of the technical personnel. All requirements are *quality* requirements – they express needs or expectations that are intended to be fulfilled by a process output that possesses inherent characteristics. We can therefore drop the word *quality*. If a modifying word is needed in front of the word requirements it should be a word that signifies the subject of the requirements. Transportation system requirements would be requirements for a transportation system, Audio speaker design requirements would be requirements for the design of an audio speaker, component test requirements would be requirements for testing components, and management training requirements would be requirement for training managers. The requirements of ISO 9000 and its derivatives such as ISO/TS 16949, TL 9000, AS9100B and ISO 13485 are often referred to as *quality requirements* as distinct from other types of requirements but this is misleading. ISO 9000 is no more a quality requirement than is ISO 1000 on SI units, ISO 2365 for ammonium nitrate or ISO 246 for rolling bearings. The requirements of ISO 9001 are quality management system requirements – requirements for a quality management system.

Quality, reliability and safety

There is a school of thought that distinguishes between quality and reliability and quality and safety. Quality is thought to be a non-time-dependent characteristic and reliability a time-dependent characteristic. Quality is thought of as being limited to conformance to specification regardless of whether the specification actually meets the needs of the customer or society. This belief resulted in Quality Control specialists serving manufacturing and Reliability specialists serving product design. However, it is probably more to do with the assumed competence of the people involved than with definitions. Reliability engineering was perceived to require higher academic attainment than Quality Control but this was due to the limited application QC techniques at the time to manufacturing.

If we take a logical approach to the issue, when a product or service is unreliable, it is clearly unfit for use and therefore of poor quality. If a product is reliable but emits toxic fumes, is too heavy or not transportable when required to be, it is of poor quality. Similarly, if a product is unsafe it is of poor quality even though it may meet its specification in other ways. In such a case the specification is not a true reflection of customer needs. A nuclear plant may meet all the specified safety requirements but if society demands greater safety standards, the plant is not meeting the requirements of society, even though it meets the immediate customer requirements. You therefore need to identify the stakeholders in order to determine the characteristics that need to be satisfied. The needs of all these parties have to be satisfied in order for *quality* to be achieved. But, you can say, "This is a quality product as far as my customer is concerned". Figure 1.4 shows some of the characteristics of product quality – others have been identified previously.

Quality parameters

Differences in design can be denoted by grade or class but can also be the result of poor attention to customer needs. It is not enough to produce products that conform to the specifications or supply services that meet management's

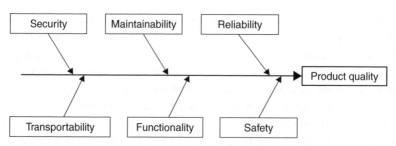

Figure 1.4 Determinants of product quality

requirements. Quality is a composite of three *parameters*: quality of design, quality of conformance and quality of use which are summarized below:

- *Quality of design* is the extent to which the design reflects a product or service that satisfies customer needs and expectations and regulatory requirements. All the necessary characteristics should be designed into the product or service at the outset.
- *Quality of conformance* is the extent to which the product or service conforms to the design standard. The design has to be faithfully reproduced in the product or service.
- *Quality of use* is the extent by which the user is able to secure continuity of use from the product or service. Products need to have a low cost of ownership, be safe and reliable, maintainable in use and easy to use.

Products or services that do not possess the right features and characteristics either by design or by construction are products of poor quality. Those that fail to give customer satisfaction by being uneconomic to use are also products of poor quality, regardless of their conformance to specifications. Often people might claim that a product is of good quality but of poor design, or that a product is of good quality but it has a high maintenance cost. These notions result from a misunderstanding because product quality is always a composite of the quality of design, conformance and use.

Dimensions of quality

In addition to quality parameters there are three *dimensions of quality* which extend the perception beyond the concepts outlined previously:

- *The business quality dimension.* This is the extent to which the business serves the needs of all stakeholders and is the outward facing view of the organization. The stakeholders are not only interested in the quality of particular products and services but judge organizations by their potential to create wealth, the continuity of operations, the sustainability of supply, care of the environment, and adherence to health, safety and legal regulations. Changes in business strategy, direction or policies might yield improvement in business quality.

- *The product quality dimension*. This is the extent to which the products and services provided meet the regulatory requirements and needs of specific customers. Enhancement to product features to satisfy more customers might yield improvement in product quality.
- *The organization quality dimension*. This is the extent to which the organization maximizes its efficiency and effectiveness and is the inward facing view of the organization. Efficiency is linked with productivity which itself is linked with the motivation of personnel and the capability or processes and utilization of resources. Effectiveness is linked with the utilization of knowledge focusing on the right things to do. Seeking best practice might yield improvement in organizational quality. This directly affects all aspects of quality. Viewing the organization as a system would redefine this dimension as, *The system quality dimension*.

Many organizations only concentrate on the product quality dimension, but the three are interrelated and interdependent. Deterioration in one leads to a deterioration in the others, perhaps not immediately but eventually.

As mentioned previously, it is quite possible for an organization to satisfy the customers for its products and services and fail to satisfy the other stakeholders. Some may argue that the producers of pornographic literature, nuclear power, non-essential drugs, weapons etc. harm society and so regardless of these products and services being of acceptable quality to their customers, they are not regarded by society as benefiting the quality of life. However, society has a way of dealing with these – through representation in government, laws are passed that regulate the activities of organizations thus imposing limits on producers of pornographic literature, nuclear power, non-essential drugs, weapons etc., so that any harm that may beset society is minimized. Within an organization, the working environment may be oppressive – there may be political infighting, the source of revenue may be so secure that no effort is made to reduce waste. In such situations organizations may produce products and services that satisfy their customers. We must separate the three concepts above to avoid confusion. When addressing quality, it is necessary to be specific about the object of our discussion. Is it the quality of products or services, or the quality of organization (or system) in which we work, or the business as a whole, about which we are talking? If we only intend that our remarks apply to the quality of products, we should say so.

Summary

In this chapter we established that individuals differ in the level of information they require to do the right things right and that this has led to the development of principles, rules and instructions. With this in mind, we approached the meaning of quality from different perspectives. We established that quality is primarily about satisfying the needs of stakeholders and proceeded to describe the stakeholders and their individual needs. We then examined various definitions of quality, identified the factors that characterise the quality of products and services and addressed several misconceptions where quality is perceived as being separate to or inclusive of price, cost, reliability etc. Finally we defined the parameters and dimensions of quality to reveal the scope of quality management and thus the basis for achieving, sustaining and improving quality that is dealt with in the next Chapter.

Chapter 2
Achieving sustaining and improving quality

Talking about goodness is easy; achieving it is difficult.

Chinese proverb

The nature of quality management

We know from the foregoing that quality is a result produced when a need, expectation, requirement or demand is met or satisfied. Something that does not satisfy the need is deemed poor quality and something that meets the need in every way is deemed excellent quality. This result (quality) is what most people try to achieve in whatever they do, in all organizations and families. Most of us want the result of our efforts to satisfy the need, expectation, requirement or demand however it is expressed. So how do we go about it?

Abraham Maslow once remarked, "If the only tool you have is a hammer, everything starts to look like a nail to you." And so it is with quality which is why over the last 50 years or so, several approaches have evolved to *achieve, sustain and improve quality*.

The ISO 9000 definition of *quality management* is *coordinated activities to direct and control an organization with regard to quality*. These activities are further identified as quality planning, quality control, quality improvement and quality assurance. In one respect these four concepts form the pillars of quality management (we address each of these later). Quality planning, quality control, quality improvement forms the Juran Trilogy[1] which Juran regards as universal. Although quality assurance is not in the Trilogy, Juran does address this concept in his Quality Control Handbook[2] but regards it quite rightly as providing confidence to all concerned that the quality function (quality planning, control and improvement and not a department with the name quality in its title) is being performed adequately.

However, specific techniques have gained the limelight sometimes pushing the basic concepts into the background or even off the stage completely and giving the impression that they are better without necessarily acknowledging that they embody all that was good in the previous approach. There have been a continual refreshment and rearrangement of the same ideas in an attempt to bring about a change in performance when the old ideas have lost their appeal or have failed to realize their potential through a lack of understanding or patience!

There are techniques that focus on a specific aspect of quality management such as Advance Product Quality Planning, quality costs, Just-in-time, quality circles, statistical process control, Design of experiments (DOE), 8D, Measurement Systems Analysis (MSA), and risk assessment techniques such as Failure Mode and Effects Analysis (FMEA) and Hazard Analysis and Critical Control Points (HACCP).

Then there are general models such as, TQC, TQM, ISO 9000, PDCA, Deming's 14 points, Crosby's Zero defects, Kaizen, PDCA, Six Sigma and Process Management that all have similar objectives but approach the achievement of these objectives slightly differently. There is so much overlap that it is not possible to illustrate in a practical way how these models and techniques align with the four pillars of quality management.

Goal management or risk management

When one examines the above approaches, what do we see? Do we see a number of models and techniques that are going to enable us to achieve our goals or do we see a number of models and techniques that are going to help us avoid failure? The first is about goal management and the second is about risk management.

If quality management was about goal management one might expect to find models and techniques covering leadership, strategy, planning, finance, marketing, selling, human resource management, engineering, education, training etc. If it were about risk management one might expect to find models and techniques covering risk assessment, probability theory, control methodologies, problem solving. In fact we do see both types but there are probably more techniques focused on risk reduction than goal achievement. What this shows is the management of quality is still developing and while many management tools and techniques exist they are not necessarily perceived as "quality" tools.

The "goal management" school is characterized by five questions:[3]

1. What are you trying to do?
2. How do you make it happen?

3. How do you know it's right?
4. How do you know it's the best way of doing it?
5. How do you know it's the right thing to do?

The "risk management" school is characterized by five different questions:

1. What could go wrong?
2. How might this affect performance?
3. How is the risk being treated?
4. How do you know the precautions are effective?
5. What action is taken to prevent a recurrence of failure or hazard?

In an ideal world, if we could design products, services and processes that could not fail to give complete satisfaction to all the stakeholders we would have achieved the ultimate goal. Success means not only that products, services and processes fulfil their function but also that the function is what customers' desire. Failure means not only that products, services and processes would fail to fulfil their function but also that their function was not what customers and other stakeholders desired. A gold-plated mousetrap that does not fail is not a success if no one needs a gold-plated mousetrap! An automobile that meets the driver's need but emits harmful gasses into the atmosphere is not a success. A typical example is the pressure being brought to bear on four-wheel drive vehicles in the UK. The belief is that four-wheel drive vehicles are gas-guzzlers and should be banned from the streets in view of their perceived effect on global warming. However, customers would not buy them if they did not satisfy their needs and expectations. Perhaps the manufacturers of such vehicles will bow to the pressure groups and slowly withdraw from the market so that they become increasingly difficult to find and those who do own them will be pilloried by society, just as smokers are in public places.

The introductory Clause of ISO 9001:1994 contained a statement that the aim of the requirements is to achieve customer satisfaction by prevention of nonconformities. (This was indicative of the failure school of thought). It was as though the elimination of nonconformity would by itself lead to satisfied customers. We know better now and this is recognized in the introductory Clause of ISO 9001:2000 which contains the following statement: "This International Standard . . . aims to enhance customer satisfaction through the effective application of the system . . . and the assurance of conformity to customer and applicable regulatory requirements." (This is indicative of the success school of thought although it is somewhat limited to customers. Perhaps a more appropriate aim might have been:

"To enhance customer satisfaction in a manner that satisfies the needs and expectations of all stakeholders through the effective application of the system"

Thus recognizing that it is customers that provide the objectives and the other stakeholders that provide the constraints on how those objectives are achieved.)

In reality you cannot be successful unless you know of the risks you are taking and plan to eliminate, reduce or control them. A unification of these approaches is what is therefore needed for organizations to achieve, sustain and improve quality. You therefore need to approach the achievement of quality from two different angles and answer two questions. What do we need to do to succeed and what do we need to do to prevent failure and harm? Of course if your answer to the first question included those things you need to do to prevent failure and harm, the second question is superfluous.

Quality does not appear by chance, or if it does it may not be repeated. One has to design quality into the products and services. It has often been said that one cannot inspect quality into a product. A product remains the same after inspection as it did before, so no amount of inspection will change the quality of the product. However, what inspection does is measure quality in a way that allows us to make decisions on whether or not to release a piece of work. Work that passes inspection should be quality work but inspection unfortunately is not 100% reliable. Most inspection relies on human judgement and this can be affected by many factors, some of which are outside our control (such as the private life, health or mood of the inspector). We may also fail to predict the effect that our decisions have on others. Sometimes we go to great lengths in preparing organization changes and find to our surprise that we neglected something or underestimated the effect of something. We therefore need other means to deliver quality products – we have to adopt practices that enable us to achieve our objectives while preventing failures from occurring and hazards from jeopardizing performance.

Quality management principles

As explained in Chapter 1, we need principles to help us determine the right things to do and understand why we do what we do. The more prescription we have the more we get immersed in the detail and lose sight of our objectives – our purpose – our reason for doing what we do. Once we have lost sight of our purpose, our actions and decisions follow the mood of the moment. They are swayed by the political climate or fear of reprisals. We can so easily forget our purpose when in heated discussion when it is not who you are, but what you say and to whom you say it that is deemed important. Those people who live by a set of principles often find themselves cast out of the club for saying what they believe. However, with presence of mind and recollection of the reasons why the principles are important for survival, they could just redeem themselves and be regarded as an important contributor.

A quality management principle is defined by ISO/TC 176 as *a comprehensive and fundamental rule or belief, for leading and operating an organization, aimed at continually improving performance over the long term by focusing on customers while*

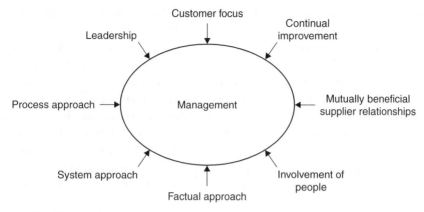

Figure 2.1   The eight quality management principles

addressing the needs of all other interested parties. Eight principles (see Figure 2.1) have emerged as fundamental to the management of quality.

All the requirements of ISO 9001:2000 are related to one or more of these principles. These principles provide the reasons for the requirements and are thus very important. Each of these is addressed below. Further guidance on the application of these principles is provided in *Quality Management Principles*.[4]

> Did you know?
> Neither the definition of a quality management principle nor the eight principles themselves contain the word QUALITY

Customer focus

This principle is expressed as follows:

Organizations depend on their customers and therefore should understand current and future customer needs, meet customer requirements and strive to exceed customer expectations.

> **The impact**
> Inward seeking focus
> to
> Outward seeking
> focus

Customers are the lifeblood of every organization. All organizations provide something to others; in fact they do not exist in isolation. We should remember that customers are not simply purchasers but any person or organization that receives a product or service from the organization. Not-for-profit organizations therefore have customers. Customer focus means putting your energy into satisfying customers and understanding that profitability or avoidance of loss comes from satisfying customers. Profit is not the reason for an organization's existence. Profit is needed in order to grow the organization so that it may satisfy more customers. A profit focus is an inward seeking focus; a customer focus is an outward seeking focus. If you focus solely on profit and take your eye off customer needs, you will lose customers and reduce your profits in the long run. Customer focus means organizing work as a process that converts customers needs into satisfied customers. It means that all processes have a customer focus.

The principle means that everyone in the organization needs to be customer-focused, not simply the top management or the sales personnel. If people were to ask themselves before making a decision, what does the customer need or expect? – the organization would begin to move its focus firmly in the direction of its customers. Customer focus is also about satisfying needs rather than wants. A customer may want ISO 9000 certification but in reality, it is business improvement that may be needed. While an ISO 9001 certificate may appear to give satisfaction initially, this may be short lived as the customer slowly realizes that possession of the ISO 9001 certificate did not result in the growth of business that was expected.

An organization applying the customer focus principle would be one in which people:

- Understood customer needs and expectations.
- Met the needs and expectations of all stakeholders.
- Communicated these needs and expectations throughout the organization.
- Have the knowledge, skills and resources required to satisfy the organization's customers.
- Measured customer satisfaction and acted on results.
- Managed customer relationships.
- Could relate their goals and targets directly to customer needs and expectations.
- Acted upon the results of customer satisfaction measurements.

Leadership

This principle is expressed as follows:

The impact
Aggravation
to
Motivation

Leaders establish unity of purpose and direction for the organization. They should create and maintain the internal environment in which people can become fully involved in achieving the organization's objectives.

Leaders exist at all levels in an organization and they are not simply the ones at the top. Within every team there needs to be a leader i.e. one who provides a role model consistent with the values of the organization. It is the behaviour of leaders (our role models) that influence our lives – not just in the business world but also in our family and leisure activities. People naturally concentrate on what they are measured. It is therefore vital that leaders measure the right things. Without a good leader an organization will go where the tide takes it, and as is so predictable with tides, they will be cast on the shoreline like the flotsam and jetsam of our society. Strong leadership will drive an organization in its chosen direction which is away from disasters but towards success. But leadership alone will not bring the right success. It needs to be in combination with all the other principles. Leadership without customer-focus will drive organizations towards profit for its own sake. Leadership without involving people will leave behind those who do not share the same vision – hence the second part of the principle. *Leaders are responsible for the internal environment.* If the workforce is unhappy, de-motivated and dissatisfied, it is the fault of the leaders. The culture, vision, values, beliefs and motivation in an organization arise from leadership. Good leadership strives to bring about a set of shared values – a shared vision so that everyone knows what the organization is trying to do and where it is going. A lack of vision and a disparate mix of values create conflict. A happy ship comes about by having good leadership. Regardless of Captain Bligh's orders, the crew's mutiny on the Bounty in 1789 was down to a failure in leadership, which was in fact a failure to create the conditions that motivated people to meet the organization's objectives.

An organization applying the leadership principle would be one in which leaders are:

- Being proactive and leading by example.
- Understanding and responding to changes in the external environment.
- Considering the needs of all interested parties.
- Establishing a clear vision of the organization's future.
- Establishing shared values and ethical role models at all levels of the organization.
- Building trust and eliminating fear.
- Providing people with the required resources and freedom to act with responsibility and accountability.
- Promoting open and honest communication.
- Educating, training and coaching people.
- Setting challenging goals and targets.
- Implementing strategy to achieve these goals and targets.

Involvement of people

This principle is expressed as follows:

People at all levels are the essence of an organization and their full involvement enables their abilities to be used for the organization's benefit.

> **The impact**
> Operate
> to
> Cooperate

It is not uncommon for those affected by decisions to be absent from the discussions with decision-makers. Decisions that stand the test of time are more likely to be made when those affected by them have been involved. Employees cannot employ a part of a person – they take the whole person or none at all. Every person has knowledge and experience beyond the job that he or she has been assigned to perform.

Some are leaders in the community; some are architects of social events, building projects and expeditions. No one is limited in knowledge and experience to the current job they do. This principle means that management should tap this source of knowledge, encourage personnel to make a contribution and utilize their personal experience. It also means that management should be open and not hide its discussions unless national or business security could be threatened. Closed-door management leads to distrust among the workforce. Managers should be seen to operate with integrity and this means involving the people.

An organization applying the involvement of people principle would be one in which people are:

- Accepting ownership and responsibility to solve problems.
- Actively seeking opportunities to make improvements.
- Actively seeking opportunities to enhance their competencies, knowledge and experience.
- Freely sharing knowledge and experience in teams and groups.
- Focusing on the creation of value for customers.
- Being innovative and creative in furthering the organization's objectives.
- Better representing the organization to customers, local communities and society at large.
- Deriving satisfaction from their work.
- Enthusiastic and proud to be part of the organization.

Process approach

This principle is expressed as follows:

> **The impact**
> Procedural approach
> to
> Process approach

A desired result is achieved more efficiently when related resources and activities are managed as a process.

All work is a process because it uses resources to perform actions that produce results. In the organizational sense, such processes add value to the input. Processes are therefore dynamic, i.e. they cause things to happen. An effective process would be one where the results were those that were required to fulfil the purpose of the organization. Every job involves people or machines equipped with resources performing a series of tasks to produce an output. No matter how simple the task, there is always an objective or a reason for doing it, the consumption of resources and expenditure of energy, a number of constraints that influence the way the work will be performed, a sequence of actions, decisions concerning their correctness, a judgement of completeness and an output which should be that which was expected. The organization exists to create and satisfy customers and other stakeholders therefore the organization's processes must serve the needs of these stakeholders.

A process is as capable of producing rubbish as a procedure is capable of wasting resources – therefore processes need to be managed effectively for the required results to be produced. The process approach to management is therefore not simply converting inputs into outputs that meet requirements but about managing processes effectively.

An organization applying the process approach principle would be one in which people are:

- Establishing what it is they want to do – what objectives they want to achieve or what outputs they want to deliver.
- Establishing measures of success – the factors that will indicate whether the objectives have been achieved or the outputs meet requirements.
- Defining the activities that are critical to achieving these objectives and delivering these outputs.
- Identifying the interfaces between the process and the functions of the organization the external customers, suppliers and other stakeholders.
- Establishing clear responsibility, authority, and accountability for managing the process.
- Defining the resources, information and competences required to deliver the required outputs.
- Identifying and measuring the inputs and outputs of the process.
- Identifying the risks and putting in place measures that eliminate, reduce or control these risks.
- Taking action to eliminate the cause of nonconforming inputs or outputs.
- Taking action to prevent use or delivery of nonconforming inputs or outputs until remedial action has been effected.
- Determining how performance will be measured against the objectives and reducing variation.
- Finding better ways of achieving the process objectives and improving process efficiency.
- Establishing whether the processes objectives remain relevant to the needs of the stakeholders and if necessary changing them.

System approach to management

This principle is expressed as follows:

Identifying, understanding and managing interrelated processes as a system contributes to the organization's effectiveness and efficiency in achieving its objectives.

A system is an ordered set of ideas, principles and theories or a chain of operations that produce specific results. To be a chain of operations, the operations need to work together in a regular relationship. Taking a systems approach to management means managing the organization as a system of processes so that all the processes fit together, the inputs and outputs are connected, resources feed the processes, performance is monitored and sensors transmit information which cause changes in performance and all parts work together to achieve the organization's objectives.

<table>
<tr><td>

The impact

Functional
approach
to
Systems approach

</td></tr>
</table>

This view of a system clearly implies a system is dynamic and not static. The system is not a random collection of elements, procedures and tasks but a set of interconnected processes. The systems approach recognizes that the behaviour of any part of a system has some effect on the behaviour of the system as a whole. Even if the individual processes are performing well, the system as a whole is not necessarily performing equally well. For example, assembling the best electronic components regardless of specification may not result in a world-class computer or even one that will run, because the components may not fit together. It is the interaction between parts and in the case of a management system, between processes, and not the actions of any single part or process that determines how well a system performs.

An organization applying the system approach principle would be one in which people are:

- Defining the system by identifying or developing the processes that affect a given objective.
- Structuring the system to achieve the objective in the most efficient way.
- Understanding the interdependencies among the processes of the system.
- Taking into account the needs of all stakeholders when making decisions or taking action.
- Understanding the impact of their actions and decision on the organization's goals and the processes that deliver outputs that are intended to satisfy these goals.
- Establishing resource constraints prior to action.

Continual improvement

This principle is expressed as follows:

<table>
<tr><td>

The impact

Error correction
to
Course correction

</td></tr>
</table>

Continual improvement of the organization's overall performance should be a permanent objective of the organization.

This means that everyone in the organization should be continually questioning its performance and seeking ways to reduce variation, continually questioning their methods and seeking better ways of doing things, continually questioning their targets and seeking new targets that enhance the organization's capability. Performance, methods and targets are the three key areas where improvement is necessary for organizations to achieve and sustain success. This results in three types of improvement, improvement by better control, improvement by better utilization of resources and improvement by better understanding of stakeholder needs. (See also under *Process management*.)

ISO 9000:2000 defines continual improvement as a recurring activity to increase the ability to fulfil requirements. Improvement is therefore relative to a timescale. If the improvement recurs once a week, once a month, once a year or once every 5 years, it can be considered as "recurring". The scale of the improvement is also relative. Improvement can be targeted at specific characteristics, specific activities, specific products, specific processes or specific organizations. When targeted at a specific characteristic it may involve reducing variation in the measured characteristic. When targeted at specific products it may involve major modification – product upgrade. When targeted at the organization it may involve major re-organization or re-engineering of processes. To appreciate the scope of meaning you need to perceive requirements as a hierarchy of needs. At the lowest level are the needs of the task, passing through to the needs of the product, the needs of the process and ultimately the needs of the organization or system. At each level continual improvement is about improving efficiency and improving effectiveness.

It has become fashionable in certain sectors to use the term "continuous improvement" rather than "continual improvement". Continuous means without breaks or interruption such as continuous stationery. "Continual" means repeated regularly and frequently.

An organization applying the continual improvement principles would be one in which people are:

- Making continual improvement of products, processes and systems an objective for every individual in the organization.
- Applying the basic improvement concepts of incremental improvement and breakthrough improvement.
- Using periodic assessments against established criteria of excellence to identify areas for potential improvement.
- Continually improving the efficiency and effectiveness of all processes.
- Promoting prevention-based activities.
- Providing every member of the organization with appropriate education and training, on the methods and tools of continual improvement.
- Establishing measures and goals to guide and track improvements.
- Recognizing improvements.

Factual approach to decision making

This principle is expressed as follows:

Effective decisions are based on the analysis of data and information.

The impact
Subjective
to
Objective

Facts are obtained from observations performed by qualified personnel using devices, the integrity of which is known. The factual approach to decision making leads us to take certain actions. To make decisions on the basis of facts we need reliable mechanisms for collecting facts such as measurement systems. We need valid methods for interpreting the facts and producing information in a form that enables sound decisions to be made. The factual approach leads us to control activities based on fact rather than opinion or emotion. It means using statistical techniques to reveal information about a process, rather than reacting to variation that is an inherent characteristic of the system. However, used in isolation this principle can be dangerous.

An obsession with numbers tends to drive managers into setting targets for things that the individual is powerless to control. A manager may count the number of designs that an engineer completes over a period. The number is a fact, but to make a decision about that person's performance on the basis of this fact is foolish, the engineer has no control over the number of designs completed and even if she did, what does it tell us about the quality of the designs? Nothing! Each design is different so the time to complete each one varies. Each customer is different so the time taken to establish customer needs varies. Setting a target for the number of designs to be completed over a period might lead to the engineer rushing them, injecting errors in order to fulfil a meaningless target. It is therefore necessary to approach the decision in a different way. Firstly decide what decision you want to make and then determine what facts you need in order to make the decision. When you know what facts you need, determine how such facts will be obtained and what methods need to be used to obtain them. Assess the risks of the information being bogus or invalid and put in place measures to ensure its integrity. Work backwards from the decision you need to make to the information you require, not forward from the information to a decision you might make with it. This gives data collection a purpose; for without purpose, data collection is a waste of resources. Don't collect data for the sake of it, just because you can on the pretext that it might come in useful.

An organization applying the factual approach principle would be one in which people are:

- Taking measurements and collecting data and information relevant to the objective.
- Ensuring the data and information are sufficiently accurate, reliable and accessible.
- Analysing the data and information using valid methods.
- Understanding the value of appropriate statistical techniques.
- Making decisions and taking action based on the results of logical analysis balanced with experience and intuition.

Mutually beneficial supplier relationships

This principle is expressed as follows:

An organization and its suppliers are interdependent and a mutually beneficial relationship enhances the ability of both to create value.

The customer-focus principle drew our attention to the fact that organizations depend on their customers. It is also valid to state that organizations depend on their suppliers. Suppliers provide the materials, resources and often many services that were once provided by internal functions. The organizations of the 21st century are more

The impact
Adversarial approach
to
Alliance approach

dependent on their suppliers than ever before. The quest for lower and lower costs with higher and higher performance has caused many organizations to consider the economics of continuing to operate their own support services. There has been a recognition that organizations were trying to be good at everything rather than being good at their core business. This has led to single-function organizations serving many customers where there is entirely mutual dependency. However, there is another reason that has led to stronger supplier relationships.

Over the last 100 years the market for goods and services has changed dramatically. Prior to the 1920s most firms focused on production in the belief that a quality product will sell itself. From the 1920s to the 1950s, many firms focused on selling what they could make regardless of whether the customer actually needed it. From the 1950s to the 1990s the market turned around from a seller's market to a buyers market as customers became more discerning and firms began to focus on identifying customer needs and producing products and services that satisfied these needs. During the last 10 years, customer orientation has been taken one step further by focusing on establishing and maintaining relationships with both the customers and the suppliers.[5] From a simple exchange between buyer and seller, there evolved strategic alliances and partnerships that cut inventory, packaging and most importantly cut the costs of acquiring new customers and suppliers. There is a net benefit to both parties. For the customer, the supplier is more inclined to keep its promises because the relationship secures future orders. There is more empathy, the customer sees the supplier's point of view and vice versa. There is more give and take that binds the two organizations closer together and ultimately there is trust that holds the partnership together. Absent will be adversarial relationships and one-off transactions when either party can walk away from the deal. The partnerships will also encourage better after-sales care and more customer focus throughout the organization (everyone knows their customers because there are fewer of them).

An organization applying the supplier relationship principle would be one in which people are:

- Identifying and selecting key suppliers on the basis of their ability to meet requirements without compromising quality.

- Establishing supplier relationships that balance short-term gains with long-term considerations for the organization and society at large.
- Creating clear and open communications.
- Initiating joint development and improvement of products and processes.
- Jointly establishing a clear understanding of customers' needs.
- Sharing information and future plans.
- Recognizing supplier improvements and achievements.

Using the principles

The principles can be used in validating the design of processes, in validating decisions, in auditing system and processes. You look at a process and ask:

- Where is the customer focus in this process?
- Where in this process is there leadership, guiding policies, measurable objectives and the environment that motivates the workforce to achieve these objectives?
- Where in this process is the involvement of people in the design of the process, the making of decisions, the monitoring and measurement of performance and the improvement of performance?
- Where is the process approach to the accomplishment of these objectives?
- Where is the systems approach to the management of these processes, the optimization of performance, the elimination of bottlenecks?
- Where in the process are decisions based on fact?
- Where is there continual improvement in performance, efficiency and effectiveness of this process?
- Where is there a mutually beneficial relationship with suppliers in this process?

Quality planning (QP)

The ISO 9000 definition states that *quality planning* is part of quality management focused on setting quality objectives and specifying necessary operational processes and related resources to fulfil the quality objectives. Juran goes further than this and defines quality planning as "The activity of establishing quality goals and developing products and processes required to meet those goals". Putting product and process development in the same definition creates an ambiguity. Although the definition is of quality planning, not product quality planning, the explanation given by Juran is clearly focused on developing product features and the processes needed to produce those product features therefore his definition is not quite as precise as it could be. Each definition is valid in a particular context.

There are two levels of planning – strategic and operational. Strategic quality planning is concerned with establishing the long-range goals of the organization, its vision, mission, values and the means to reach those goals while operational quality planning is concerned with establishing product goals and the means to reach those goals. The problem we have today with these ideas is that we tend to drop the word quality or perhaps never use it in this context so a Strategic Plan would be no different to a Strategic Quality Plan – just a different label for the same thing simply because everything we do, we do to satisfy a stakeholder and our plan to satisfy a stakeholder would be no different whether we called it a business plan, a strategic plan or a strategic quality plan. Unfortunately, when we add the word *quality* to the label we do change the perceived meaning because of what quality means to different people.

There is a universal sequence of planning activities. (This is a modified version of that appearing in the book *Juran on Quality by Design*.)

1. Establish the goals (i.e. what it is you want to achieve).
2. Identify who is impacted by these goals (i.e. the customers and other stakeholders).
3. Determine the needs of these stakeholders relative to these goals and prioritize those for action.
4. Develop products or services with features that respond to stakeholders' needs.
5. Develop processes able to produce, promote and distribute the product features.
6. Establish process controls and transfer the plans to the operating forces.

There is no single output of such planning. Planning outputs might include Business Plans, New product development plans, Process development plans and subsequent to these, product descriptions expressing all the features and characteristics that have to be achieved and process descriptions expressing all the activities to be performed, the resources needed to perform them and the controls required to maintain the desired standards.

At the highest level in the organization the planning undertaken to develop core business process might be called business system planning or business process development. At operational levels it might be called process mapping and at the tactical level perhaps the planning effort results in procedures and instructions informing staff how to perform a task.

Over the last 30 years or so, Quality Plans have been required primarily on defence contracts but these plans were not of the same type as the above. Quality Plans tend to be limited to defining the processes and procedures that will be employed on a particular project to ensure the deliverables meet contractual requirements. In some cases these plans simply refer to procedures that form part of the documented quality management system. In other cases, the plans address reliability, configuration management and other project disciplines. They often form part of a Project Plan and rarely do they include the

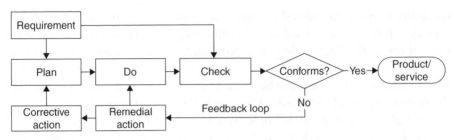

Figure 2.2   Generic control model

product development plans, indicating that quality planning is limited to control and assurance activities.

Quality planning might be a department or section in some organizations either within the quality departments or within production or operations planning. In these cases, the planning is nearly always focused on products and services rather than strategic issues.

Quality control (QC)

The ISO 9000 definition states that *quality control* (commonly abbreviated to QC) is part of quality management focused on fulfilling requirements. What the definition fails to tell us is that controls regulate performance. Control is sometimes perceived as undesirable as it removes freedom, but if everyone were free to do just as they liked there would be chaos. Controls prevent change and when applied to quality they regulate performance and prevent undesirable changes being present in the quality of the product or service being supplied. When operations are under control they are predictable and predictability is a factor that is vital for any organization to be successful. If you cannot predict what might happen when a process is initiated, you are relying on chance. The quality of products and services cannot be left to chance.

The simplest form of quality control is illustrated in Figure 2.2. Quality control can be applied to particular products, to processes that produce the products or to the output of the whole organization by measuring the overall performance of the organization.

Quality control is often regarded as a post-event activity: i.e. a means of detecting whether quality has been achieved and taking action to correct any deficiencies. However, one can control results by installing sensors before, during or after the results are created. It all depends on what you want to control.

The progressive development of controls from having no control of quality to installing controls at all key stages from the beginning to the end of the product cycle is illustrated in Figure 2.3. As can be seen, if you have no controls, quality products are produced by chance and not by design. The more controls you install the more certain you are of producing products of consistent quality but

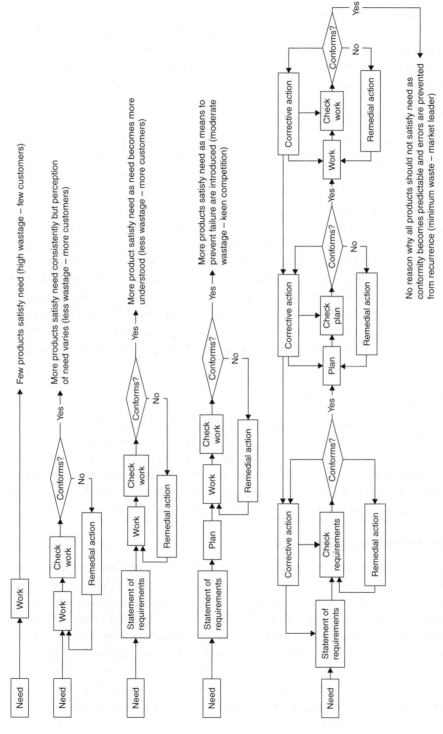

Figure 2.3 Development of controls

more control does not mean more inspection neither does it mean that the checking of work has to be performed by personnel different from those who carried out the work. In Figure 2.3, the work, checks, remedial action and corrective action could well be performed by the same individual. In some cases each task may be performed by different organizations. It rather depends on what the most effective and efficient solution might be for particular organizations.

Control before the event

Some failures cannot be allowed to occur and so must be prevented from happening through rigorous planning and design. One example is the use of reliability prediction performed before the design is complete to predict whether product reliability will meet the specification. Another is the use of competence-based assessment techniques where personnel are under close supervision until they demonstrate competences following which supervisory controls are removed. This allows you to remove output checks because you know that if you were to inspect the work you would find it to be correct. Instead of checking every product produced, you check competency periodically and assign responsibility to personnel for checking their own work. Another method is the use of prevention-based error-proofing mechanisms that sense an abnormality that is about to happen, and then signal the occurrence or halt processing, depending on the severity, frequency or downstream consequences. (This has been referred to as "autonomation", see Appendix A.)

Control during the event

Some failures must be corrected immediately using automatic controls or error proofing. By continuous monitoring of parameters in a processing plant the temperature, pressure, quantities etc., are adjusted to maintain output within specified limits. Electronic components are designed so that they can only be inserted in the correct orientation. Computer programs are designed so that routines will not run unless the correct type of data is entered in every field.

Control after the event

Where the consequences of failure are less severe or where other types of sensors are not practical or possible, output verification can be used as a means of detecting failure early in the process and preventing the subject product passing through subsequent stages and increasing the cost of rectification. Although errors have occurred, measures taken to contain them or remove the defective products from the production stream automatically are another form of error-proofing methods. These are also referred to as leading measures. Product inspection and test is *control after the event* because it occurs after the product is produced but before the product is released out of the organization's control. These are leading measures.

Where failure cannot be measured without observing trends over longer periods, you can use information controls or lagging measures. Many managers receive reports weeks or months after the week in which the deeds were done. Reports produced on long-range frequencies are often only of use to long-range decisions such as setting objectives, policy making etc. They do not stop immediate operations but may well be used to stop further operations when limits are exceeded. The danger in control after the fact is not only the slowness of reporting but also the oscillating effect of any action that is taken. If data on utilization does not reach the manager until weeks after the effort was spent, it is highly likely that when he or she takes action, the demand will have changed and staff will be working overtime to catch up. Observing the overtime the manager recruits more staff but by the time they are operational the demand has reduced once again.

It is often deemed that quality assurance serves prevention and quality control detection, but a control installed to detect failure before it occurs serves prevention, such as reducing the tolerance band to well within the specification limits. So quality control can prevent failure. Assurance is the result of an examination whereas control produces a result. *Quality assurance* does not change the product, whereas *quality control* does.

Quality control as a label

"Quality control" is also the term used as the name of a department. In most cases Quality Control Departments perform inspection and test activities and the name derives from the authority that such departments have been given. They sort good products from bad products and authorize the release of the good products. It is also common to find that Quality Control Departments perform supplier control activities, which are called Supplier Quality Assurance or Vendor Control. In this respect they are authorized to release products from suppliers into the organization either from the supplier's premises or on receipt in the organization.

To control anything requires the ability to effect change, therefore the title Quality Control Department is a misuse of the term, because such departments do not in fact change the quality of the product they inspect. They do act as a regulator if given the authority to stop release of product, but this is control of supply and not of control of quality. Authority to change product usually remains in the hands of the producing departments. It is interesting to note that similar activities within a Design Department are not called "quality control" but "design assurance" or some similar term. "Quality control" has for decades been a term applied primarily in the manufacturing areas of an organization and it is therefore difficult to change people's perceptions after so many years of the term's incorrect use.

In manufacturing, inspection and test activities have been transferred into the production departments of organizations, sometimes retaining the labels and sometimes reverting to the inspection and test labels. However, the term quality control is used less frequently in the west probably because of the decline of manufacturing. It has not been widely used in the service sector. A reason for this could be that it is considered more of a concept than a function.

Universal sequence of steps

The following steps can accomplish control of quality, or anything else for that matter (Juan J M 1995):

1. Determine the subject of control i.e., what is to be regulated.
2. Define a unit of measure – express the control subject in measurable terms such as quantities, ratios, indices, rating etc.
3. Establish a standard level of performance – a target to aim for.
4. Select a sensor to sense variance from specification.
5. Install the sensor at the stage in the process appropriate to whether you need to control before, during or after results are produced.
6. Collect and transmit data to a place for analysis.
7. Verify the results and establish whether the variance is within the range expected for a stable process (the status quo).
8. Diagnose the cause of any variance beyond the expected range.
9. Propose remedies and decide on the action needed to restore the status quo.
10. Take the agreed action and check that process stability has been restored.

Standards

Without a standard there is no logical basis for making a decision.[6] Within trade and commerce, standards have existed for thousands of years. People needed an equitable basis on which to judge if the fish was fresh, the fruit was ripe, the gold was pure. Standards were needed not only for material things but also for behaviour, for communication, for government. It was necessary to establish a basis for making a comparison between correct and incorrect, right and wrong, good and bad, success and failure. In primitive societies, knowledge of fitness for use was communicated easily and quickly. A trader selling bad meat was soon kicked out of the market. In the modern world such knowledge cannot be communicated as quickly or as reliably or as dependably so it has to be conveyed through documented specifications. The Internet is quick but not necessarily secure or dependable. The written specification becomes a substitute for knowledge of quality and the standard of acceptability. Standards should therefore define the criteria that will indicate whether our performance is acceptable.

In simple terms, standards are the way things ought to be. They are the accepted norms in a society, the acceptance criteria in engineering and the success criteria in process management. We can see evidence of this in our societies. It is what differentiates one country from another. If there were no standards, no norms, nothing would remain the same – not even human body temperature. Imagine if every time you boarded a bus to take you into the city the fare was different, the driver spoke a different language, the route was different and when you finally arrived and went shopping, you found a size 12 was now a size 21, coffee came in square cups and it tasted more like tea. It would drive you mad. We need stability and standards serve this purpose in our society.

Standards have evolved to enable biological and material things to function and societies to exist in relative harmony.

In the field of quality management standards play a significant role. Standards are what we should be doing. Standards are used to judge whether an output is of good or poor quality. Without any standards we simply have an output of indeterminate quality.

For any quantitative or qualitative parameter there should be a standard value that has been agreed so that a decision can be made following measurement. Taking some examples to illustrate the concept:

- How much should we sell? – The quota is the standard.
- How wide should this shelf be? – The specification is the standard.
- How much can I spend? – The budget is the standard.
- How much time have I got to do this job? – The schedule is the standard.
- How fast can I travel on this road? The traffic signs are the standard.
- What price should we charge? – The market is the standard.
- How should this be performed? The procedure is the standard.
- What error rate is acceptable? The process capability index is the standard.
- How will we make this happen? The plan is the standard.
- Is air travel safe? The latest air accident statistics is the standard.

The way standards are expressed is very important. If standards are expressed poorly we will not be able to confirm conformity therefore standards should be:[6]

- *Attainable* by ordinary people applying themselves with reasonable effort under normal conditions.
- *Economic* to set and administer relative to the activity being addressed.
- *Applicable* to the conditions under which they are to be used.
- *Consistent* in meaning so as to unify communication and consistent in time so as to reflect current knowledge.
- *All-inclusive* by covering all interrelated activities thereby avoiding conflict with activities for which standards have not been set.
- *Understandable* by being expressed in clear, unambiguous and simple terms with no possibility of misinterpretation.
- *Stable* for long enough to provide predictability and amortize the effort in preparing them.
- *Maintainable* so that elements can be added, changed and updated without a complete redesign.
- *Legitimate* by being officially approved by the sponsoring body.
- *Equitable* by being a fair basis for comparison by the people who have the responsibility for meeting them.

Standards are targets to aim for but are also targets to change. If an organization had not managed to lower its product defect rate below 2% for many years, 2% defective becomes the norm and is built into budgets and estimates. Quality improvement takes place when the standard is challenged and a new level of performance achieved.

If standards are to be set and imposed on those responsible for attaining the standard, they need to have the consent of the users. This creates a need for user groups to be formed with participation by representatives of the group of users in the company, sector, region, nation or group of nations. As a result we get company standards, sector standards, national standards etc.

When seeking a standard for a particular quantity, material, product, process or system you can turn to the vast array of national and international standards with confidence that your interests have been represented in the making of these standards and that through periodic review they are maintained current.

Measurement

If the standard defines what we should be doing, measurement tells us what we are doing. Therefore without measurement we really know very little about our performance or the quantity or quality of an output. The control of quality depends on an ability to measure quality be it the quality of products, services, processes, systems, organizations or simply the quality of actions and decisions. Without measurement we won't even know whether we are getting better, getting worse or staying the same. The size of the performance gap shown in Figure 1.3 will not be known.

Measurement is the act of measuring. It is a process of associating numbers with physical quantities and phenomena. Where abstract characteristics such as quality, safety, reliability, courtesy etc. are to be measured, they have to be translated into quantities that can be measured. So for instance if we want to know whether food is safe to eat, rather than get people to sample it, we might count the bugs in it and if the bug count is below a certain level (the standard) we deem it to be safe for human consumption. Therefore, providing the standards are expressed in measurable terms we can measure conformity.

To measure something we need a:

1. Sensor (a detecting device that can be human with or without measuring instruments).
2. Converter if the sensor is not human (a device for converting the signal from the sensor into a form that the human senses can detect).
3. Transmitter where the measurement is done remotely (a device for transmitting the signal to a receiver for analysis).

Sensors need to be accurate, precise, reliable and economic. Sensors that tell lies are of use only to those who wish to deceive. It is too easy to look at a clock, a speedometer, a thermometer or any other instrument and take it for granted

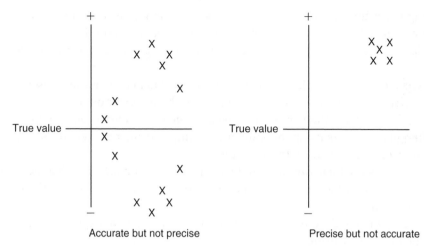

Figure 2.4   Accuracy and precision

that it is telling you the truth. We often put more credence into the readings we get from instruments than we do from our own sensors but both can be equally inaccurate.

Accuracy and precision are often perceived as synonyms but they are quite different concepts. Accuracy is the difference between the average of a series of measurements and the true value. Precision is the amount of variation around the average. So you can have a measuring device that gives a large variation around the true value with repeated measurements but whose average is the true value (see Figure 2.4).

Alternatively you could have a device which gives small variation with repeated measurements around a value which is wide of the true value. The aim is to obtain both accuracy and precision. The difference in accuracy and precision can cause expensive errors. You should not assume that the result you have obtained is both accurate and precise unless the device has been calibrated immediately prior to use and the results of its accuracy and precision provided.

There are two systems used for maintaining the accuracy and integrity of measuring devices – a calibration system and a verification system. The calibration system determines the accuracy of measurement and the verification system determines the integrity of the device. If accuracy is important then the device should be included in the calibration system. If accuracy is not an issue but the device's form, properties or function is important then it should be included in the verification system.

Measurement processes must be in statistical control so that all variation is due to common cause and not special cause. It is often assumed that the measurements taken with a calibrated device are accurate and indeed they are if we take account of the variation that is present in every measuring system and bring the system under statistical control. Variation in measurement processes arises due to bias, repeatability, reproducibility, stability and linearity.

Bias is the difference between the observed average of the measurements and the reference value.

Repeatability is the variation in measurements obtained by one appraiser using one measuring device to measure an identical characteristic on the same part.

Reproducibility is the variation in the average of the measurements made by different appraisers using the same measuring instrument when measuring an identical characteristic on the same part.

Stability is the total variation in the measurements obtained with a measurement system on the same part when measuring a single characteristic over a period of time.

Linearity is the difference in the bias values through the expected operating range of the measuring device.

It is only possible to supply parts with identical characteristics if the measurement processes as well as the production processes are under statistical control.

In an environment in which daily production quantities are in the range of 1,000 to 10,000 units, inaccuracies in the measurement processes that go undetected can have a disastrous impact on customer satisfaction and consequently profits.

Calibration is a process that has evolved to enable us to establish the accuracy and precision of our measuring devices. It ensures the integrity of measurement but is not limited to physical devices although much of what is written about calibration is concerned with such things. The characteristics of bias, repeatability, reproducibility, stability and linearity in a measuring system are just as relevant when the measuring device is a school examination, a training assessment, a driving test or any other device for assessing the knowledge, skill or competence of personnel to achieve prescribed standards. What value are the results of an examination if a written answer to a question receives widely different marks from different examiners? What value is a college degree if not all recipients are graded using the same measuring process of known integrity?

Variation

Variation is present in all systems. Nothing is absolutely stable. If you monitor the difference between the measured value and the required value of a characteristic and plot it on a horizontal timescale in the order the products were produced, you would notice that there is variation over time. There does not have to be a required value to spot variation. If you monitor any parameter over time (duration, resource consumption, strength, weight etc.) you will see a pattern of variation that with an appropriate scale will show up significant deviations from the average. If you plot the values as a histogram you will observe that there is a distribution of results around the average. As you repeat the plot for a new set of measurements of the same characteristic, you will notice that there is variation between this second set and the first. In studying the results you will observe variation in:

- The location of the average for each plot.
- The spread of the values.
- The shape of the distribution.

The factors causing these variations are referred to as "assignable" or "special causes".

Special cause

The cause of variations in the location, spread and shape of a distribution are considered special or assignable because the cause can be assigned to a specific or special condition that does not apply to other events. They are causes that are not always present. Wrong material, inaccurate measuring device, worn out tool, sick employee, weather conditions, accident, stage omitted are all one-off events that cannot be predicted. When they occur they make the shape, spread or location of the average change. The process is not predictable while special cause variation is present. Eliminating the special causes is part of quality control – see steps 9–11 above.

Once all the special causes of variation have been eliminated the shape and spread of the distribution and the location of the average become stable, the process is under control – the results are predictable. However, it may not be producing conforming product. You may be able to predict that the process could produce one defective product in every 10 produced. There may still be considerable variation but it is random. A stable process is one with no indication of a special cause of variation and can be said to be in *statistical control*. Special cause variation is not random – it is unpredictable. It occurs because something has happened that should not have happened so you should search for the cause immediately and eliminate it. The person running the process should be responsible for removing special causes unless these causes originate in another area when the source should be isolated and eliminated.

Common cause

Once the special cause of variation has been removed, the variation present is left to chance, it is random or what is referred to as common causes. This does not mean that no action should be taken but to treat each deviation from the average as a special cause will only lead to more problems. The random variation is caused by factors that are inherent in the system. The operator has done all she can to remove the special causes, the rest are down to management. This variation could be caused by poor design, working environment, equipment maintenance or inadequacy of information. Some of these events may be common to all processes, all machines, all materials of a particular type, all work

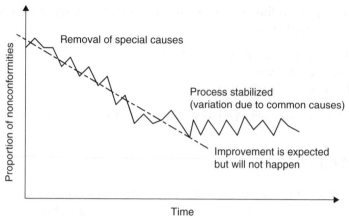

Figure 2.5 Stabilizing processes

performed in a particular location or environment, or all work performed using a particular method. This chain of events is illustrated in Figure 2.5.

This shows that by removing special causes, the process settles down and although nonconformities remain, performance becomes more predictable. Further improvement will not happen until the common causes are reduced and this requires action by management. However, the action management takes should not be to look for a scapegoat – the person whom they believe caused the error, but to look for the root cause – the inherent weakness in the system that causes this variation.

Common cause variation is random and therefore adjusting a process on detection of a common cause will destabilize the process. The cause has to be removed, not the process adjusted. When dealing with either common cause or special cause problems the search for the root cause will indicate whether the cause is random and likely to occur again or a one-off event. If it is random, only action on the system will eliminate it. If it is a one-off event, no action on the system will prevent its recurrence, it just has to be fixed. Imposing rules will not prevent a nonconformity caused by a worn out tool that someone forgot to replace. A good treatment of common cause and special cause variation is given in Out of the Crisis.[7]

With a stable process the spread of common cause variation will be within certain limits. These limits are not the specification limits but are limits of natural variability of the process. These limits can be calculated and are referred to as the Upper and Lower Control Limits (UCL and LCL respectively). The control limits may be outside the upper and lower specification limits to start with but as common causes are eliminated, they close in and eventually the spread of variation is all within the specification limits. Any variation outside the control limits will be rare and will signal the need for corrective action. This is illustrated in Figure 2.6.

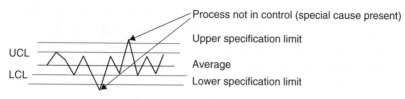

Figure 2.6   Control limits and specification limits

Table 2.1   10 Step process yield

Stage	Yield/stage	Total % yield	Initial population 1 million
1	0.80	80	800,000
2	0.80	64	640,000
3	0.80	51.2	512,000
4	0.80	41	409,600
5	0.80	32.8	327,680
6	0.80	26.2	262,144
7	0.80	21	209,715
8	0.80	16.8	167,772
9	0.80	13.4	134,218
10	0.80	10.7	107,374

Keeping the process under control is process control. Keeping the process within the limits of the customer specification is quality control. The action needed to make the transition from process control to quality control is an improvement action and this is dealt with under Quality improvement.

Six sigma as a statistical concept

In a perfect world, we would like the range of variation to be well within the upper and lower specification limits for the characteristics being measured but invariably we produce defectives. If there were an 80% yield from each stage in a 10-stage process, the resultant output would be less than 11% and as indicated in Table 2.1 we would obtain only 107,374 good products from an initial batch of 1 million.

Even if the process stage yield were 99% we would still obtain 95,617 less products than we started with. It is therefore essential that multiple stage processes have a process stage yield well in excess of 99.99% and it is from this perspective that the concept of six sigma emerges.

The small Greek letter s is σ and is called sigma. It is the symbol used to represent the standard deviation in a population. We use s for standard deviation as measured by a sample of finite magnitude. Standard deviation is the square root of the variance in a population. In plain English, standard deviation tells us how tightly a set of values is clustered around the average of those same values. In statistical speak, standard deviation is a measure of dispersion (spread or variability) about a mean value (or average) of a population that exhibits a normal distribution and is expressed by the formula:

$$\sigma = \sqrt{\frac{\sum (x - \mu)^2}{n}}$$

where x is a value such as mass, length, time, money, μ is the mean of all values, Σ is capital sigma and is the mathematical shorthand for summation and n is the number in the population.

When the variance is computed in a sample, the formula is:

$$s = \sqrt{\frac{\sum (x - \bar{x})^2}{n}}$$

where $\bar{x}$ is the mean of the sample and n the sample size.

However, small samples tend to underestimate the variance of the parent population and a better estimate of the population variance is obtained by dividing the sum of the squares by the number of degrees of freedom. Variance in a population thus becomes:

$$s = \sqrt{\frac{\sum (x - \bar{x})^2}{n - 1}}$$

When the population of a variable is concentrated about the mean the standard deviation is small indicating stability and when the population of a variable is spread out from the mean the standard deviation is large indicating volatility.

When the frequency distribution of a set of values of a variable is symmetrical about a mean it may approximate to a normal distribution represented by the equation:

$$y = \frac{1}{\sqrt[\sigma]{2\pi}} e^{\frac{-(x - \bar{x})^2}{2\sigma^2}}$$

where y is the height of the curve at any point along the scale of x and e is the base of the Napierian logarithms (2.7183) and π the well known ratio of the circumference of a circle to its diameter which to 3 decimal places is = 3.142.

The shape of the normal distribution embraces:

68.26% of the population within ± 1 standard deviation around the mean
95.46% of the population within ± 2 standard deviations around the mean
99.74% of the population within ± 3 standard deviations around the mean and

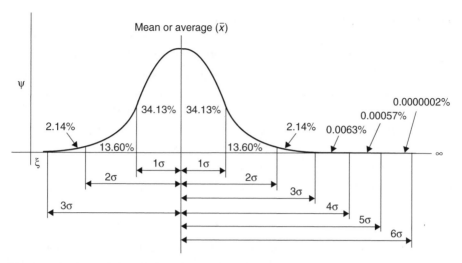

Figure 2.7   Normal distribution and standard deviation

99.9937 of the population within ±4 standard deviations around the mean, which is 100% for most applications. In industries producing millions of products even greater performance is deemed necessary especially when all output is being shipped to one customer. This represented diagrammatically and extended to 6 standard deviations in Figure 2.7.

Assuming a normal distribution of results at the six sigma level you would expect 0.002 parts per million or ppm but when expressing performance in ppm, it is common practice to assume that the process mean can drift 1.5 sigma in either direction. The area of a normal distribution beyond 4.5 sigma from the mean is 3.4 ppm. As control charts will detect any process shift of this magnitude in a single sample, the 3.4 ppm represents a very conservative upper boundary on the non-conformance rate.[8]

Although the concept of six sigma can be applied to non-manufacturing processes you cannot assume as was done in Table 2.1 that the nonconformities in a stage output are rejected as unusable by the following stages. A person may pass through 10 stages in a hospital but you cannot aggregate the errors to produce a process yield based on stage errors. Patients don't drop out of the process simply because they were kept waiting longer than the specified maximum. You have to take the whole process and count the number of errors per 1 million opportunities.

Table 2.2 shows the number of products meeting requirements and the equivalent defects per million products for a range of standard deviations. In Table 2.2, six sigma (6σ) translates into 2 errors per billion opportunities but what Motorola found was that processes drift over time, what they call the Long-Term Dynamic Mean Variation. Motorola judged this variation as typically falling between 1.4 and 1.6 sigma, and will therefore account for special cause variation causing drift over the long term (years not months). Views do appear to differ on why

Table 2.2 Process yield at various sigma values

Sigma	Product meeting requirements %	Number of errors per million products	
		Assuming normal distribution	Assuming 1.5 sigma drift
1	68.26	317400.000	697672.15
2	95.45	45,500.000	308770.21
3	99.73	2,700.000	66810.63
4	99.9937	63.000	6209.70
5	99.999943	0.570	232.67
6	99.9999998	0.002	3.40

the 1.5 sigma drift is applied but in any event in most situations whether six sigma is 2 errors per billion or 3.4 errors per million opportunities matters not to most people – it is only a target.

However, every measurement process, however complicated, has certain underlying assumptions that mean the results are valid only when certain conditions apply.

There are four assumptions that typically underlie all measurement processes; namely, that the data from the process at hand "behave like":

1. Random samples.
2. From a fixed distribution.
3. With the distribution having fixed location; and
4. With the distribution having fixed variation.

If the four underlying assumptions hold, then we have achieved probabilistic predictability – the ability to make probability statements not only about the process in the past, but also about the process in the future. In short, such processes are said to be "in statistical control". Thus attempts at reaching six sigma levels in a process that is not in statistical control will be futile.

Six sigma as a strategic concept

In addition to being a statistical concept, the term Six Sigma is also used to describe a rigorous and disciplined methodology that uses data and statistical analysis to measure and improve a company's operational performance by identifying and eliminating process "defects". In this sense it is a project-based initiative that identifies actual problems and eliminates their cause. A project would be any endeavour to reach six sigma levels in an aspect of performance. These projects are not limited to manufacturing and the techniques can be applied to any process in any organization. The aim is simply to reduce variation so that the number of errors falls to less than 3.4 per million opportunities for each product or service transaction. An "opportunity" is defined as a chance for non-conformance.

When one considers the number of things than go right in an organization it probably runs into millions. If one considers the number of ways a product or service might fail it might run into double digits. If you produce 12,000 units per year and each unit has 500 components that could fail you would have 6 million opportunities for failure.

The Six Sigma methodology is not a revolutionary way of thinking, and it does not provide a radically new set of quality tools. It is more of an evolutionary development in the science of continuous improvement that combines the best elements from many earlier quality initiatives some of which date back more than 50 years.

The label "six sigma" was first given to these improvement techniques in Motorola in about 1987 when they married the concept of process capability and product specifications and began to express process capability in terms of defects per million opportunities (DPMO). As a result of winning the Baldrige Award in 1988, Motorola was compelled to share its quality practices with others. When in 1995 Jack Welsh, the CEO of General Electric (GE) adopted Six Sigma, many organizations took notice and this was followed by an explosion in literature and training on Six Sigma. Like many new initiatives, there is much misunderstanding and of course there is an economic limit to any improvement – absolute zero defects is only free if you put the specification limits well outside the process capability and the process remains capable which of course cannot be guaranteed.

It is interesting to note that Toyota does not have a six sigma programme.[9] They prefer instead to use a seven-step problem solving process.

Six Sigma projects range from tackling a particular problem with the surface finish on a shaft to redesigning both products and business processes.

The steps in a typical Six Sigma programme would be:

- Identify the organization's biggest problems.
- Assign the best people to fix these problems.
- Providing the necessary resources and management support.
- Grant uninterrupted time to work on the problems.
- Undertake the necessary changes that will eliminate the problems.

At its core, Six Sigma revolves around a few key concepts.[10]

Concept	Description
Critical to Quality:	Attributes most important to the customer
Defect:	Failing to deliver what the customer wants
Process Capability:	What your process can deliver
Variation:	What the customer sees and feels
Stable Operations:	Ensuring consistent, predictable processes to improve what the customer sees and feels
Design for Six Sigma:	Designing to meet customer needs and process capability

The objective of the Six Sigma methodology is reduction in variation and this is achieved through a prescribed problem solving process called DMAIC (define, measure, analyse, improve, control). By induction and training, staff begin to use this problem solving technique to identify and resolve problems that are preventing the organization from achieving defined targets. Largely because most processes are not designed to be capable, (i.e. not designed to deliver conforming outputs every time), the Six Sigma projects bring about performance improvement by better control. In other words, they bring the process under control so that it delivers conforming output in the manner it should have done when the process was designed. Although manufacturing processes are often designed, non-manufacturing processes are not – they evolve and successive re-organizations only tend to deal with the symptoms not the root causes so using the Six Sigma methodology for non-manufacturing processes can bring about much needed improvement. However, it is no replacement for good process design.

The DMAIC problem solving technique is explained in the panel.

DMAIC Problem Solving Technique (As expressed by GE)

DEFINE

- Define the Customer, their Critical to Quality (CTQ) issues, and the Core Business Process involved.
- Define who customers are, what their requirements are for products and services, and what their expectations are.
- Define project boundaries – the stop and start of the process.
- Define the process to be improved by mapping the process flow.

MEASURE

- Measure the performance of the Core Business Process involved.
- Develop a data collection plan for the process.
- Collect data from many sources to determine types of defects and metrics.
- Compare to customer survey results to determine shortfall.

ANALYSE

- Analyse the data collected and process map to determine root causes of defects and opportunities for improvement.
- Identify gaps between current performance and goal performance.
- Prioritize opportunities to improve.
- Identify sources of variation.

IMPROVE

- Improve the target process by designing creative solutions to fix and prevent problems.
- Create innovate solutions using technology and discipline.
- Develop and deploy implementation plan.

CONTROL

- Control the improvements to keep the process on the new course.
- Prevent reverting back to the "old way".
- Require the development, documentation and implementation of an ongoing monitoring plan.
- Institutionalize the improvements through the modification of systems and structures (staffing, training, incentives).

Restoring the status quo

Corrective action restores the status quo i.e. it brings performance back to where it should have been before the incident of unacceptable variation. Corrective action is the pattern of activities that traces the symptoms of a problem to its cause, produces solutions for preventing recurrence of the problem, implements the change and monitors that the change has been successful. Corrective action provides a feedback loop in the control cycle. Whilst the notion of *correction* implies that it could be as concerned with the nonconforming item as with the cause of nonconformity, correcting the nonconforming item is a remedial action. It doesn't stop it recurring. ISO 9000 does not use the term remedial action except in the context of a repair. Preventing the recurrence of nonconformity is a corrective action. A problem has to exist for you to take corrective action. When actual problems don't exist but there is a possibility of failure, the action of preventing the occurrence of nonconformity (or any problem for that matter) is a *preventive action*. So we have Remedial Action, Corrective Action and Preventive Action, each with a different meaning.

> **Putting terms in the right order**
>
> ***Preventive action*** serves to prevent the nonconformity from **occurring**
>
> ***Inspection*** detects nonconformity
>
> ***Nonconformity control*** identifies, segregates and rectifies the nonconforming item
>
> ***Corrective action*** serves to prevent the nonconformity from **recurring**.

Nonconformities are caused by factors that should not be present in a process. There will always be variation but variation is not nonconformity. Nonconformity arises when the variation exceeds the permitted limits. The factors that cause nonconformity on one occasion will (unless removed) cause nonconformity again and again. As the objective of any process must be to produce conforming output, it follows therefore that it is necessary to eliminate the causes of non-conformity. This does not simply apply to products of the production process but to products of all processes – mission management, demand creation and demand fulfilment.

It is important to distinguish between four separate actions when dealing with nonconformity:

- Action to remove the specific nonconformity in the nonconforming item. This may take the form of return for completion of operations, rework, repair, scrap or temporary change to specification (i.e. a concession).
- Action to discover other occurrences of the nonconformity. The variation may have been discovered in a sample therefore there may be other nonconforming items elsewhere.
- Action to prevent recurrence in the short term (this is the local action taken on the immediate cause and often referred to as "containment action").
- Action to prevent recurrence in the long term (this is the action taken on the root cause and is the only true corrective action).

Quality improvement (QI)

Firstly we need to put *quality improvement* in context because it is a minefield of terms and concepts that overlap one another. There are three things that are certain in this life, death, taxes and change! We cannot improve anything unless we know its present condition and this requires measurement and analysis to tell us whether improvement is both desirable and feasible. Improvement is always relative. Change is improvement if it is beneficial and a retrograde step if it is undesirable but there is a middle ground where change is neither desirable (beneficial) nor undesirable, it is inevitable and there is nothing we could or should do about it. Change is a constant. It exists in everything and is caused by physical, social or economic forces. Its effects can be desirable, tolerable or undesirable. Desirable change is change that brings positive benefits to the organization. Tolerable change is change that is inevitable and yields no benefit or may have undesirable effects when improperly controlled. The challenge is to cause desirable change and to eliminate, reduce or control undesirable change so that it becomes tolerable change. Juran writes on improvement thus "Putting out fires is not improvement of the process – Neither is discovery and removal of a special cause detected by a point out of control. This only puts the process back to where it should have been in the first place".[11] This we call *restoring the status quo*. If eliminating special causes is not improvement but maintaining the status quo, that leaves two areas where the improvement is desirable – the reduction of common cause variation and the raising of standards.

Figure 2.8 illustrates the continuing cycle of events between periods of maintaining performance and periods of change. The transition from one target to another may be gradual on one scale but considered a breakthrough on another

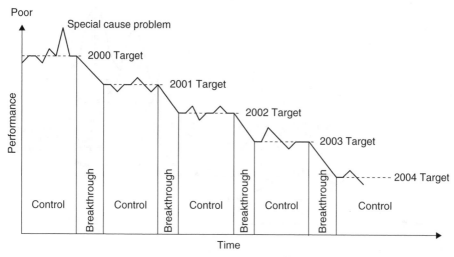

Figure 2.8   Continual improvement

scale. The variation around the target value is due to common causes that are inherent in the system. This represents the expected performance of the process. The spike outside the average variation is due to a special cause, a one-off event that can be eliminated. These can be regarded as fires and is commonly called *fire fighting*. Once removed the process continues with the average variation due to common causes.

When considering improvement by raising standards, there are two types of standards: one for results achieved and another for the manner in which the results are achieved. We could improve on the standards we aim for, the level of performance, the target or the goal but use the same methods. There may come a point when the existing methods won't allow us to achieve the standard, when we need to devise a new method, a more efficient or effective method or due to the constraints on us, we may choose to improve our methods simply to meet existing standards.

This leads us to ask four key questions:

1. Are we doing it right?
2. Can we keep on doing it right?
3. Are we doing it in the best way?
4. Is it the right thing to do?

The ISO 9000 definition of *quality improvement* states that it is that part of quality management focused on increasing the ability to fulfil quality requirements. If we want to reduce the common cause variation we have to act on the system. If we want to improve efficiency and effectiveness we also have to act on the system and both are not concerned with correcting errors but concerned with doing things better and doing different things.

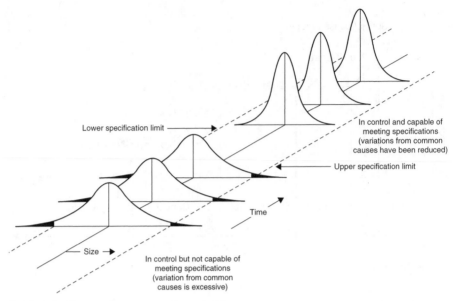

Figure 2.9   From process control to capable process

There is a second dimension to improvement – it is the rate of change. We could improve "gradually" or by a "step change". Gradual change is also referred to as incremental improvement, continual improvement or *kaizen*. "Step change" is also referred to as "breakthrough" or a "quantum leap". Gradual change arises out of refining the existing methods, modifying processes to yield more and more by consuming less and less. Breakthroughs often require innovation, new methods, techniques, technologies and new processes.

Are we doing it right?

Would the answer be this?   No we are not because sometimes we do it we get it wrong and have to do it again.

Or would it be this?   Yes we are because every time we do it we get it right and we never have to do it over again.

Quality improvement in this context is for better control and is about improving the rate at which an agreed standard is achieved. It is therefore a process for reducing the spread of common cause variation so that all products meet agreed standards. This is illustrated in Figure 2.9. It is not about removing special cause variation, i.e. this requires the corrective action process.

This type of improvement is only about reducing variation about a mean value or closing the gap between actual performance and the target. This is improvement by better control and in some sectors is not regarded as improvement at all. In the automotive sector, continual improvement is implemented once manufacturing processes are capable and stable or product characteristics are predictable and meet customer requirements.[12] The target remains static and the organization gets better and better until all output meets the target or falls between the acceptance limits.

When a process is stable the variation present is only due to random causes. There may still be unpredictable excursions beyond the target due to a change in the process but this is special cause variation. Investigating the symptoms of failure, determining the root cause and taking action to prevent recurrence can eliminate the special cause and reduce random causes. A typical quality improvement of this type might be to reduce the spread of variation in a parameter so that the average value coincides with the nominal value. Another example might be to reduce the defect rate from three sigma to six sigma. The changes that are needed to meet this objective might be simply changes in working practices or perhaps complex changes that demand a redesign of the process or a change in working conditions. These might be achieved using existing methods or technology but it may require innovation in management or technology to accomplish.

Can we keep on doing it right?

Would the answer be this?　No we can't because the supply of resource is unpredictable, the equipment is wearing out and we can't afford to replace it.

Or would it be this?　Yes we can because we have secured a continual supply of resources and have in place measures that will provide early warning of impending changes.

This question is about continuity or sustainability. It is not enough to do it right first time once, i.e. you have to keep on doing it right and this is where a further question helps to clarify the issue.

What affects our ability to maintain this performance?

It could be resources as in the example, but to maintain the status quo might mean innovative marketing in order to keep the flow of customer orders of the type that the process can handle. Regulations change, staff leave, emergencies do happen: Can you keep on doing it right under these conditions?

Are we doing it in the best way?

Would the answer be this?　We have always done it this way and if it isn't broke why fix it?

Or would it be this?　Yes we think so because we have compared our performance with the best in class and we are as good as they are.

One might argue that any target can be met providing we remove the constraints and throw lots of money at it. Although the targets may be achieved, the achievement may consume too much resource; time and materials may be wasted – there may be a better way of doing it. By finding a better way you release resources to be used more productively and therefore bring about improvement through better utilization of resources.

Over 19 years since the introduction of ISO 9000, it is strange that more organizations did not question if there was a better way than writing all those procedures, filling in all those forms, insisting on all those signatures. However, ISO 9000 did not require these things – but there was more than one way of interpreting the requirement.

The search for a better way is often more effective when in the hands of those doing the job and you must therefore embrace the "leadership" and "involvement of people" principles in conjunction with continual improvement.

Is it the right thing to do?

Would the answer be this?	I don't know – we always measure customer satisfaction by the number of complaints.
Or would it be this?	Yes I believe it is because these targets relate very well to the organization's objectives.

Quality improvement in this context is accomplished by raising standards and is about setting a new level of performance, a new target that brings additional benefits for the stakeholders. These targets are performance targets for products, processes and the system. They are not targets established for the level of errors, such as nonconformities, scrap, and customer complaints. Such targets are not in fact targets at all, they are simply historical standards of performance.

One needs to question whether the targets are still valid so we ask, "How do we know this is the right thing to do?" These new targets have to be planned targets as exceeding targets sporadically is a symptom of out-of-control situations. Targets need to be derived from the organization's goals but as these change the targets may become disconnected. Targets that were once suitable are now obsolete – they are not the right things to do any longer. We need to ask, "Are these targets still relevant to the stakeholder needs?"

Functions are often measured by their performance against budget. We need to ask whether this is the right thing to do – does it lead to optimizing organizational performance? You may have been desensitized to the level of nonconformities or customer complaints – they have become the norm – is this the right level of performance to maintain or should there be an improvement programme to reach a much lower level of rejects.

New standards are created through a process that starts with an analysis of stakeholder needs and expectations followed by the identification of opportunities for change, then a feasibility stage, progressing through research and development to result in a new standard, proven for repeatable applications. Such standards result from innovations in technology, marketing and management. This is improvement by better understanding of stakeholder needs. A typical

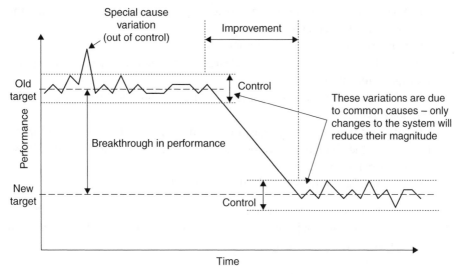

Figure 2.10   Breakthrough and control

quality improvement of this type might be to redesign a range of products to increase the achieved reliability from 1 failure every 5,000 hours to 1 failure every 100,000 hours. Another example might be to improve the efficiency of the service organization so as to reduce the guaranteed call-out time from the specified 36 to 12 hours or improve the throughput of a process from 1,000 to 10,000 components per week. Once again, the changes needed may be simple or complex and might be achieved using existing technology but it may require innovation in technology to accomplish.

The transition between where quality improvement stops and quality control begins is where the level has been set and the mechanisms are in place to keep quality on or above the set level. In simple terms, if quality improvement reduces quality costs from 25% of turnover to 10% of turnover, the objective of quality control is to prevent the quality costs rising above 10% of turnover. This is illustrated in Figure 2.10.

Improving quality by better control or raising standards can be accomplished by the following steps.

1. Determine the objective to be achieved, e.g. new markets, products or technologies, or new levels of organizational efficiency or managerial effectiveness, new national standards or government legislation. These provide the reasons for needing change.
2. Determine the policies needed for improvement, i.e. the broad guidelines to enable management to cause or stimulate the improvement.
3. Conduct a feasibility study. This should discover whether accomplishment of the objective is feasible and propose several strategies or conceptual solutions for consideration. If feasible, approval to proceed should be secured.

4. Produce plans for the improvement that specifies the means by which the objective will be achieved.
5. Organize the resources to implement the plan.
6. Carry out research, analysis and design to define a possible solution and credible alternatives.
7. Model and develop the best solution and carry out tests to prove it fulfils the objective.
8. Identify and overcome any resistance to the planned change in standards.
9. Implement the change, i.e. put new products into production and new services into operation.
10. Put in place the controls to hold the new level of performance.

This improvement process will require controls to keep improvement projects on course towards their objectives. The controls applied should be designed in the manner described previously.

Quality assurance (QA)

The ISO 9000 definition states that *quality assurance* (commonly abbreviated to QA) is part of quality management focused on providing confidence that quality requirements will be fulfilled. Both the customers and the managers have a need for quality assurance because they are not in a position to oversee operations for themselves. They need to place trust in the producing operations, thus avoiding constant intervention.

Customers and managers need:

1. Knowledge of what is to be supplied. (This may be gained from the sales literature, contract or agreement.)
2. Knowledge of how the product or service is intended to be supplied. (This may be gained from the supplier's proposal or offer.)
3. Knowledge that the declared intentions will satisfy customer requirements if met. (This may be gained from personal assessment or reliance on independent certifications.)
4. Knowledge that the declared intentions are actually being followed. (This may be gained by personal assessment or reliance on independent audits.)
5. Knowledge that the products and services meet the specified requirements. (This may be gained by personal assessment or reliance on independent audits.)

You may wonder why one needs to do (4) if you are doing (5) anyway! You can gain an assurance of quality by testing the product or service against prescribed standards to establish its capability to meet them. However, this only gives confidence in the specific product or service purchased and not in its continuity or consistency during subsequent supply. Another way is to assess the organization that supplies the products or services against prescribed standards to establish its capability to produce products of a certain standard. This approach may provide assurance of continuity and consistency of supply.

Quality assurance activities do not control quality, they establish the extent to which quality will be, is being or has been controlled. All quality assurance activities are post-event activities and off-line and serve to build confidence in results, in claims, in predictions, etc. If a person tells you they will do a certain job for a certain price in a certain time, can you trust them or will they be late, overspent and over limits? The only way to find out is to gain confidence in their capability and that is what quality assurance activities are designed to do. Quite often, the means to provide the assurance need to be built into the process, such as creating records, documenting plans, documenting specifications, reporting reviews etc. Such documents and activities also serve to control quality as well as assure it. ISO 9001 provides a basis for obtaining an assurance of quality, if you are the customer, and a basis for controlling quality, if you are the supplier.

Quality assurance is often perceived as the means to prevent problems but this is not consistent with the definition in ISO 9000. In one case the misconception arises due to people limiting their perception of quality control to control after the event; not appreciating that you can control an outcome before the event by installing mechanisms to prevent failure, such as automation, error-proofing and failure prediction.

In another case, the misconception arises due to the label attached to the ISO 9000 series of standards. They are sometimes known as the quality assurance standards when in fact, as a family of standards, they are quality management system standards. The requirements within the standards do aim to prevent problems, and consequently the standard is associated with the term *quality assurance*. ISO 9001 is designed for use in assuring customers that suppliers have the capability of meeting their requirements. It is true that by installing a quality management system, you will gain an assurance of quality, but assurance comes about through knowledge of what will be, is being or has been done, rather than by doing something. Assurance is not an action but a result. It results from obtaining reliable information that testifies to the accuracy or validity of some event or product.

Labelling the prevention activities as quality assurance activities may have a negative effect, particularly if you have a Quality Assurance Department. It could send out signals that the aim of the Quality Assurance Department is to prevent things from happening! Such a label could unintentionally give the department an image of a law enforcement role.

Quality Assurance Departments are often formed to provide both customer and management with confidence that quality will be, is being and has been achieved. However, another way of looking on Quality Assurance Departments is as Corporate Quality Control. Instead of measuring the quality of products, they are measuring the quality of the business and by doing so are able to assure management and customers of the quality of products and services. The following steps can obtain an assurance of quality:

1. Acquire the documents that declare the organization's plans for achieving quality.
2. Produce a plan that defines how an assurance of quality will be obtained, i.e. a quality assurance plan.
3. Organize the resources to implement the plans for quality assurance.
4. Establish whether the organization's proposed product or service possesses characteristics that will satisfy customer needs.
5. Assess operations, products and services of the organization and determine where and what the quality risks are.
6. Establish whether the organization's plans make adequate provision for the control, elimination or reduction of the identified risks.
7. Determine the extent to which the organization's plans are being implemented and risks contained.
8. Establish whether the product or service being supplied has the prescribed characteristics.

In judging the adequacy of provisions you will need to apply the relevant standards, legislation, codes of practice and other agreed measures for the type of operation, application and business. These activities are quality assurance activities and may be subdivided into design assurance, procurement assurance, manufacturing assurance, etc. Auditing, planning, analysis, inspection and test are some of the techniques that may be used.

Level of attention to quality

In the first section of the Introduction to ISO 9001 is a statement that might appear progressive but depending on how it is interpreted could be regressive. The statement is: "The adoption of a quality management system should be a strategic decision of an organization". What would top management be doing if they did this? Would they be:

a) Agreeing to implement the requirements of ISO 9001 and subject the organization to periodic third party audit as evidence of commitment to quality?
b) Agreeing to document the approach they take to the management of product quality and to subsequently do what they have documented?
c) Agreeing to manage the organization as a system of interconnected processes as a method of delivering stakeholder satisfaction?

It all comes down to their understanding of the word *quality* and this is what will determine the level of attention to quality.

Whilst the decision to make the *management of quality* a strategic issue will be an executive decision, the attention it is given at each level in the organization

Table 2.3 Attention levels

Organizational level	Principle process focus	Basic team structure	Performance issue focus	Typical quality system focus	Ideal quality system focus
Enterprise	Strategic	Cross-Business	Ownership	Market	Strategic
Business	Business	Cross-Functional	Customer	Administrative	Business Process
Operations	Work	Departmental	Process	Task Process	Work Process

will have a bearing on the degree of success attained. There are three primary organization levels: the *enterprise level*, the *business level* and the *operations level*.[13] Between each level there are barriers.

At the enterprise level, the executive management responds to the "voice" of ownership and is primarily concerned with profit, return on capital employed, market share etc. At the business level, the managers are concerned with products and services and so respond to the "voice" of the customer. At the operational level, the middle managers, supervisors, operators, etc. focus on processes that produce products and services and so respond to the "voice" of the processes carried out within their own function.

In reality, these levels overlap, particularly in small organizations. The Chief Executive Officer (CEO) of a small company will be involved at all three levels whereas in the large multinational, the CEO spends all of the time at the enterprise level, barely touching the business level, except when major deals with potential customers are being negotiated. Once the contract is won, the CEO of the multinational may confine his or her involvement to monitoring performance through metrics and goals.

Quality should be a strategic issue that involves the owners because it delivers fiscal performance. Low quality will cause fiscal performance ultimately to decline.

The typical focus for a quality management system is at the operations level. ISO 9000 is seen as an initiative for work process improvement. The documentation is often developed at the work process level and focused on functions. Much of the effort is focused on the processes within the functions rather than across the functions and only involves the business level at the customer interface, as illustrated in Table 2.3. For the application of quality management principles to be successful, quality has to be a strategic issue with every function of the organization embraced by the management system that is focused on satisfying the needs of all stakeholders.

Summary

In this chapter we have examined basic concepts and principles that underpin the body of knowledge of quality management. We have examined a plethora of terms, discarded the misconceptions and extracted the key messages in order to arrive at some universal principles that will help us discover the right things to do in achieving, sustaining and improving quality. In examining terms like quality control and quality assurance we have shown that these terms are not simply names for departments within an organization or processes but much broader concepts that apply to the management of any activity. We have paid particular attention to quality control because it is this more than any other topic that has been misunderstood. We have examined the concepts of standards, measurement and variation in some depth as these are at the heart of quality management. Finally we have shown that the achievement of quality is a strategic issue that requires a systems approach and this will be dealt with next.

Chapter 3
A systems approach

The people may be made to follow a path of action, but they may not be
made to understand it.

Confucius (551 479 BCE) Chinese philosopher

Systems thinking

A system is an ordered set of ideas, principles and theories or a chain of operations that produce specific results and to be a chain of operations, they need to
work together in a regular relationship. Shannon defined a system as a group or
set of objects united by some form or regular interaction or interdependence to
perform a specified function.[1] Deming defines a system as a series of functions or
activities within an organization that work together for the aim of the organization. These three definitions appear to be consistent although worded differently.

A quality management system is not a random collection of procedures, tasks
or documents (which many quality systems are). Quality management systems
are like air conditioning systems – they need to be designed. All the components
need to fit together, the inputs and outputs need to be connected, sensors need to
feed information to processes which cause changes in performance and all parts
need to work together to achieve a common purpose.

ISO 9000 defines a quality management system as a set of interrelated or interacting elements that achieve the quality policy and quality objective. But the
word elements is not defined and the word quality gets in the way of our thinking. It makes us think that quality management systems operate alongside environmental management systems, safety management systems, and financial
management systems. In Clause 3.11 of ISO 9000 it is stated that the quality management system is "that part of the organization's management system that
focuses on the achievement of outputs in relation to the quality objectives", therefore the quality management system must exist to achieve the organization's
quality objectives. It would appear therefore that other parts of the management

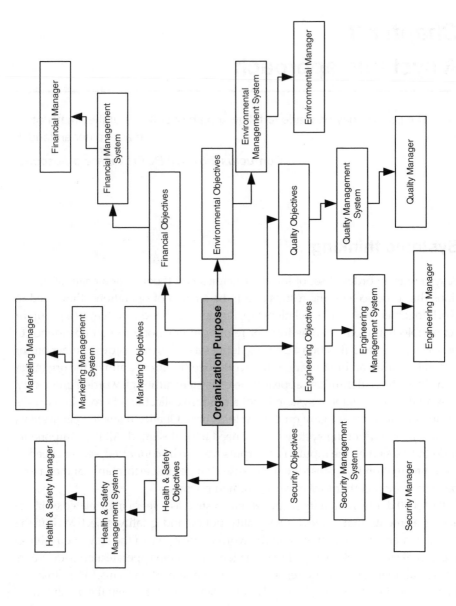

Figure 3.1 Multiple management systems

system are intended to serve the achievement of specific objectives. For example we could establish:

- Safety systems to serve safety objectives.
- Environmental systems to serve environmental objectives.
- Security systems to serve security objectives.
- Human resource systems to serve human resource objectives.
- Marketing systems to serve marketing objectives.
- Innovation systems to serve innovation objectives.
- Financial systems to serve financial objectives.

Many organizations have appointed specific managers to achieve each of these objectives so that we have for instance, an Environmental Manager, fulfilling Environmental Objectives through an Environmental Management System and a Quality Manager fulfilling Quality Objectives through a Quality System. Do the same for the others and you would have multiple management systems as illustrated in Figure 3.1. This is what functional management produces and as a result puts the managers in potential conflict with each other as each tries to achieve their objectives independently of the others. Many of these objectives are in reality not objectives at all but constraints that exist only by virtue of the organization's necessity to satisfy customers as is discussed below.

However, several questions arise; "Are quality objectives, objectives of the same kind as the other objectives or are these other objectives a subset of quality objectives?" and "Is the quality management system just one of a series of systems or is it the parent system of which the others are a part?"

> **Food for thought**
>
> The QMS is not part of the management system – IT IS the management system.

To find the answer it is necessary to go back a step and ask: Which comes first an objective or a need? We don't set financial objectives because we think its a good idea, there is a need that has its origins in the organization's mission statement. The mission statement tells us what our goal is and where are we going. Without customers there is no business therefore the basic purpose of a business is to satisfy a particular want in society and so create a customer. Its mission is related to these wants and is expressed in specific terms. To be effective, a mission statement should always look outside the business not inside.[2] For example a mission that is focused on increasing market share is an inwardly seeking mission whereas a mission that is focused on bringing cheap digital communication to the people is an outwardly seeking mission statement. From the mission statement we can ask, "What affects our ability to accomplish our goal?" The answers we get become our critical success factors and it is these factors that shape our objectives.

- If our success depends on the safety of our products, we need safety objectives.
- If our success depends on securing the integrity of information entrusted to us by our customers, then we need security objectives.

Figure 3.2 The business management cycle (a specialist's view)

- If our success depends on the impact our operations have on the environment, we need environmental objectives.
- If our success depends on capital investment in modern plant and machinery, we need financial objectives.

This list is incomplete, but if we were to continue, would we find a reason for having quality objectives? Business will only create customers if it satisfies their needs therefore success in all businesses depends on fulfilling customer needs and expectations.

Quality is defined in ISO 9000 as the degree to which a set of inherent characteristics fulfils requirements. Note that the definition is not limited to customer requirements and the inherent characteristics are not limited to products. It could apply to any set of requirements – internal or external, technical or non-technical including health, safety and environmental requirements. It could also apply to any process outcome: products, services, decisions, information, impacts, etc. It extends to all those with an interest in the business. Quality is therefore a term that describes the condition of business outcomes. Everything a business does must directly or indirectly affect the condition of its outcomes and therefore all business objectives are quality objectives. Consequently, we do not need quality objectives in addition to all the other objectives because all objectives are quality objectives and the quality management system is not part of the management system – it *is* the management system. We can therefore describe the relationship between the management system and the organization diagrammatically as shown in Figure 3.2.

All the objectives only arise as a result of the organization seeking to create and satisfy customers. There is no environmental objective, impact or anything else if the organization does not have customers. Objectives for the environment, safety, security, finance, human resources etc. only have meaning when taken in the context of what the business is trying to do – which is to create and satisfy customers. While many might argue that *the purpose of business* is to make money for the shareholders or owners this is different from *the purpose of a business,* which is to create and retain customers and do this in a manner that satisfies the needs and expectations of all stakeholders. Without a customer there is no business at all therefore customer needs must come first. Satisfying customers becomes the only true objective – all others are *constraints* that affect the manner in which the organization satisfies its customers. It may help therefore if we view any objective that serves a stakeholder other than the customer as a *constraint* or a *requirement* that impacts the manner in which customer objectives are achieved.

The management system is the way the organization operates, the way it carries out its business, the way thing are. Its purpose is to enable the organization to accomplish its mission, its purpose, its goals and its objectives. All organizations possess a management system. Some are formal – some are informal. Even in a one-person business, that person will have a way of working – a way of achieving his or her objectives. That way is the system and it comprises the behaviours, processes and resources employed to achieve those objectives. The system comprises everything that affects the results. It only has to be formalized when the relationships grow too large for one person to manage by relying on memory.

It is unlikely that you will be able to produce and sustain the required quality unless you organize yourselves to do so. Quality does not happen by chance – it has to be managed. No human endeavour has ever been successful without having been planned, organized and controlled in some way.

Scope of the system

As the quality management system is the means by which the organization achieves its objectives, it follows that the scope of the system (what it covers) is every function and activity of the organization that contributes to these objectives. This should leave no function or activity outside the system. The system must also include suppliers because the organization depends on its suppliers to achieve its objectives. The chain of processes from the customer interface and back again includes the suppliers.

Including every function and activity within the system should not be interpreted as compelling every function and activity to certification to ISO 9001 – far from it. The scope of the system does not need to be the same as the scope of certification, a point addressed further in Chapter 5.

Design of the system

Imagine you are designing an air-conditioning system. You would commence by establishing the system requirements, then design a system that meets the requirements, document the design and build a prototype. You would then test it and when satisfied it functions under the anticipated operating conditions, launch into production. If problems are detected during production, solutions would be developed and the design documentation changed before recommencing production. If problems were experienced during maintenance, the design documentation would be consulted to aid in the search for the fault. If improvements are to be made, once again the design documentation would be consulted and design changes made and the documentation revised before implementation in production. This traditional cycle for products therefore has some redeeming features:

- Design does not commence without a specification of requirements – if it does, the wrong product is likely to be designed.
- Designs are documented before product is manufactured – if they are not, it is likely that the product cannot be manufactured or will not fit together or function as intended.
- Designs are proven before launching into production – if they are not, the product will probably fail on test or in service.
- Design documentation is changed before changes are implemented in production – if it is not, the product will be different each time it is made; solved problems will recur and no two installations will be alike.

If we apply the same logic to the design and implementation of a management system, we would

- Define the requirements before commencing management system design i.e. we would establish the objectives the system is required to achieve (the vision, mission, corporate goals etc.).
- Document the management system design before implementation i.e. define and document the business processes to a level of detail necessary to ensure objectives can be achieved.
- Verify that the management system meets the requirements before commitment to full operation.
- Document changes to the management system before implementation in practice.

But what often happens is:

- Management system development commences without a specification of requirements or a clear idea of the objectives it needs to achieve; often the system exists only to meet ISO 9000, or some other standard.

- The management system is documented before it has been designed.
- The management system is made fully operational before being verified it meets the requirements.
- Changes are made to practices before they are documented.
- Improvements are made to the management system without consulting the documentation because it is often out of date.

As the management system is the means by which the organization achieves its objectives, the management system delivers the organization's products. (This includes hardware, software, services and processed material including information products.) If we consult ISO 9000:2000 again we will find that a product is defined as a result of a process and so it would appear that it is the organization's processes that produce its products. Therefore the management system must comprise the processes by which the organization achieves its objectives. Perhaps these are the *elements* that are addressed in the ISO 9000 definition of a system.

If we analyse the factors on which the quality of these products depend we would deduce they include:

- The style of management – (autocratic, democratic, participative, directive etc.).
- The attitude and behaviour of the people (positive, negative etc.).
- The capability of the available resources – (capacity, responsiveness, technology).
- The quantity and quality of the available resources – (materials, equipment, finance, people).
- The condition and capability of the facilities, plant and machinery.
- The physical environment in which people work – (heat, noise, cleanliness etc.).
- The human environment in which people work – (freedom, empowerment, health and safety).

It follows therefore that a management system consists of the processes required to deliver the organization's products and services as well as the resources, behaviours and environment on which they depend. It is therefore not advisable to even contemplate a management system simply as a set of documents or a set of processes that simply converts inputs into outputs. Three out of the seven factors above relate to the human element – we therefore cannot afford to ignore it.

Following the argument above, if the management system is a collection of processes, we can think of the organization as a system of interconnected processes and therefore change Figure 3.2 so that it reflects reality as shown in Figure 3.3.

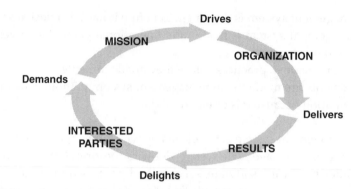

Figure 3.3   The business management cycle (a pragmatic view)

Integrated management

Increasingly, customers, regulatory bodies and the community pressure groups are demanding that organizations demonstrate responsible environmental performance, provide a safe working environment, provide quality products and services and demonstrate Corporate Social Responsibility (CSR). ISO 9000 has been around since 1987 but with the publication of several other management system standards addressing the natural environment, occupational health and safety and information there has been a growing desire to bring together these management systems into one integrated system.

With each new standard a new specialism is born and so there is confusion as to what is being integrated.

Quite literally, to integrate means to combine parts into a whole, bringing parts together or amalgamating parts to make complete, to desegregate or to incorporate into a larger unit.[3]

In the context of management, integration might be putting all the internal management practices into one system or bringing together separate disciplines to work on a problem, or joining together the processes that serve a particular objective. Many organizations have chosen an approach that they regard as integrated but as there is no universally agreed approach to integrated management they all differ relative to the principles upon which they are based.

If we divide management into general management, quality management, environmental management, security management etc., integrated management might be the bringing together of all these parts into a whole. But dividing management like this is not breaking it into parts. It is simply a way of looking at management. In reality the effectiveness and efficiency of operations is not affected by this unless we start segregating work and responsibilities according to these labels which of course does not happen in practice. The staff responsibilities might be separated so as to focus attention on specific aspects with product quality, personnel safety, information security etc., planned by different teams but with the implementation carried out simultaneously by line personnel. There is no practical way a job could be passed to one person to satisfy quality requirements and to another to satisfy environmental requirement etc. The nature of work is such that every action has to be an integrated action but it is often the case that the quality, safety and environmental aspects of a job are not managed effectively.

If we assume organizations have several management systems we could formalize and document each one separately. This would result in a set of documents addressing quality management, another set addressing environmental management, another set addressing health and safety management and so on. This approach is illustrated in Figure 3.1. Here we see the result of developing a separate system for each series of business objectives. Quality objectives are made the responsibility of the Quality Manager who achieves them through a Quality Management System. Likewise, Environmental objectives are made the responsibility of an Environmental Manager who achieves them through an Environmental Management System and so on. It is a neat solution but the outputs of the organization cannot be put into these convenient compartments.

An integrated management system therefore might be the bringing together of all these sets of documents into one set thereby eliminating duplication.

This approach opens up a few questions that need to be answered.

- Was the system we are integrating disintegrated beforehand or was it simply not completely documented?
- Did we really have separate management systems or were we deceived by documenting certain aspects of the way we work simply to satisfy external standards?
- While there will be a reduction in documentation how do we gain a significant change in performance by doing this?

A set of documents is not a system in the context of management as explained previously. The definitions of a system given above clearly indicate that its components function together to achieve an objective therefore these components cannot be simply documents – they are dynamic processes.

Even if we were to conceive of separate dynamic systems it is still difficult to imagine a system in which a job could be passed to one person to satisfy quality requirements and to another to satisfy environmental requirement etc. This is not to say that all systems are dynamic. The metric system for example is a system of units for the purpose of measuring physical quantities. A system of government tends to be the principles and laws by which a nation is governed. However, the principles and laws would not be a full description of the system if we said nothing about their effect on society and the mechanism that brings about this effect. In both cases we tend to separate the system from the means by which it is implemented but perhaps this is not healthy as it leads to the wrong conclusions about systems. *Ryszard Kapuscinski (b. 1932), a Polish journalist* wrote:

"Although a system may cease to exist in the legal sense or as a structure of power, its values (or anti-values), its philosophy, its teachings remain in us. They rule our thinking, our conduct, our attitude to others. The situation is a demonic paradox: we have toppled the system but we still carry its genes".

The word *system* in the term 'management system', as used in ISO 9000 and other management system standards, has become to be understood as a system that functions to achieve objectives thus demonstrating that a system is more than a set of documents. From a study of ISO 9000, the management system is clearly one that is established to achieve quality objectives. Likewise, from a study of ISO 14000, one draws the conclusion that the system is established to achieve environmental objectives. It is therefore more than simply the description or the policies, standards, guides and procedures. It also supports the view that if we were to integrate all these systems we would have just one system, the purpose of which is to achieve all the organizations objectives – in other words a business management system.

The term Integrated Management System or IMS, implies that the word *integrated* is being used as an adjective – it's a term describing a characteristic of a management system or organization and therefore when describing an integrated management system only the words management and system should have initial capital letters. To do otherwise would be like abbreviating an effective management system as EMS or an ineffective management system as IMS! It is clear that the use of the term Integrated Management System (IMS) only has meaning in the context where specific structures have been established solely for the purpose of satisfying separate and individual external standards such as ISO 9001 and ISO 14001 and there is a need to combine these structures together. Hence the term IMS is a misnomer.

If we view the organization as a system (as recommended by Deming), there is only one system in the organization and this exists (as does the organization) to fulfil the mission. This mission should have been derived from an analysis of stakeholder needs and expectations and as we already know, processes bring together activities, resources and behaviours to achieve results. Therefore *"the set of interconnected and managed processes that function together to achieve goals that have been derived from an analysis of stakeholder needs and expectations"* we can legitimately refer to as the business management system. We don't need to use the word *integrated* because a management system that functions in this way will be integrated. However, a management system that enables the organization to fulfil a mission that has not been derived from an analysis of stakeholder needs we will have to call an ineffective management system (IMS)!

Summary

In this chapter we have examined the nature of systems and in particular management systems and shown that they all serve to achieve goals. We have shown that the name we give to the system derives from the goals we wish to achieve.

We have exposed the gulf between the customer and management perceptions of quality and the importance of bringing these closer together and concluded that organizations have goals and these goals are achieved through a system of managed processes. We have also exposed the myth that organizations have multiple management systems and in reality have only one system – a system that enables the organization to satisfy all its stakeholders and accomplish its mission. We have also explored the idea of integrated management systems and drawn the conclusion that these too are a myth, created by the proliferation of management system standards rather than a business need. We will now move onto look at two very different ways at establishing a management system.

Chapter 4
Managing quality using ISO 9000

ISO 9000 is a tool to help you achieve an objective. It must not, itself, become the objective.

Matt Seaver ISO/TC 176

Introduction

A historical perspective

ISO 9000 is a symptom of practices that were around centuries before anyone coined the term quality management. It is in some respects a natural progression that will continue to evolve. One cannot be certain when the concepts that underpin ISO 9000 were first derived. The principles of inspection against standards have been around since the Egyptians built the Pyramids. There is some evidence to suggest that associations of traders and craftsmen called *collegia* existed in ancient Rome as a means of monopolizing trade and establishing trading practices. The *collegia* did survive in the Byzantine Empire and particularly in what is now Istanbul. The *Book of the Prefect*, a manual of government probably drawn up around the year 900, describes an elaborate guild organization whose primary function was the imposition of rigid controls, especially for financial and tax raising purposes on every craft and trade in the city.[1] As communities grew in size and formed towns, craftsmen or merchants formed guilds for mutual aid and protection and for the furtherance of their professional interests. By the 11th century in Europe, guilds performed a variety of important functions in the local economy among which were their monopoly of trade, the setting of standards for the quality of goods and the integrity of trading practices. So what we find from a historical perspective is that

- Standards are an ancient concept that have survived several millennia.
- A means of verifying compliance often follows the setting of standards.

- The formalizing of working practices is centuries old and seen as a means to consistently meet standards.
- Market regulation (relative to the standard of goods and services) has been around for centuries for the protection of both craftsmen and traders.

Formal quality systems did not appear until the early 1950s. Quality Control, as an element of quality management emerged as a function in industry after WWII and the principles were codified by J M Juran in his Quality Control Handbook of 1951. In 1959 the first national standard, Mil Std 9858 on quality program requirements was issued by the US Department of Defense. This standard formed the foundation of all quality system standards that followed. This progression is illustrated in Figure 4.1.

The general philosophy of ISO 9000

Since the dawn of civilization the survival of communities has depended on trade. As communities grow they become more dependent on others providing goods and services they are unable to provide from their own resources. Trade continues to this day on the strength of the customer-supplier relationship. The relationship survives through trust and confidence. A reputation for delivering a product or a service to an agreed specification, at an agreed price on an agreed date is hard to win and organizations will protect their reputation against external threat at all costs. But reputations are often damaged not by those outside but by those inside the organization. Broken promises, whatever the cause, harm reputation and promises are broken when an organization does not do what it committed itself to do. This can arise either because the organization accepted a commitment it did not have the capability to meet or it had the capability but failed to manage it effectively.

This is what the ISO 9000 family of standards is all about. It is a set of criteria that when applied correctly, will help organizations develop the capability to create and retain satisfied customers. It is not a product standard – there are no requirements for specific products or services – only criteria that apply to the

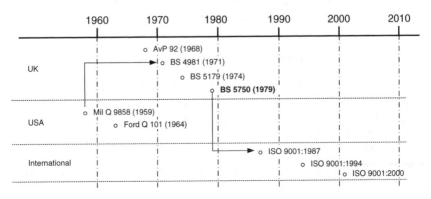

Figure 4.1   Evolution of ISO 9000

management of an organization when determining customer needs and expectations and supplying products and services that are intended to satisfy those needs and expectations.

Unfortunately, one cannot pick up one standard in the ISO 9000 family and get a clear understanding of what ISO 9000 is all about. Each standard was produced by a different committee and although ISO 9001 and ISO 9004 are supposed to be a consistent pair there are concepts within ISO 9000 that are not carried through clearly to the other standards and there are ambiguities that none of the standards resolve so one has to read between the lines, make connections and draw conclusions for it to make any sense. There follows an overview that aims to bridge this gap.

The *organization's purpose* is its reason for existing and can be expressed through vision and mission statements. The relationship between purpose, policy and objectives are blurred in the standard because from an assurance viewpoint *corporate values* seem to be irrelevant although with such revelations like Enron, Worldcom and Shell, it may not be long before values or corporate responsibility will be recognized by these standards.

The *quality policy* exists to shape behaviour and establishes the core values in an organization and therefore equates with the corporate policy – no benefits are gained from specifically expressing a quality policy and ignoring other policies because all policies influence the behaviours that are key to satisfying the needs of stakeholders.

Quality is a strategic objective that is established to fulfil the needs and expectations of all stakeholders and therefore equates with the corporate objectives – no benefits are gained from ranking quality equally with other objectives.

The *quality management system* is *the* management system that enables the organization to fulfil its purpose and mission. Organizations have only one system – no benefits are gained from formalizing part of a system that focuses on quality.

The *adequacy, suitability and effectiveness* of the management system is judged by how well the system enables the organization to achieve its objectives, operate efficiently and fulfil its purpose and mission – no benefits are gained from simply focusing on one aspect of performance when it is a combination of factors that deliver organizational performance.

A quest for confidence

In a nutshell

The ISO 9000 family of standards will stop you making promises you can't fulfil and help you keep those you can.

Customers need confidence that their suppliers can meet their quality, cost and delivery requirements and have a choice as to how they acquire this confidence. They can select their suppliers in one of several ways:

a) Purely on the basis of past performance, reputation or recommendation.

b) By assessing the capability of potential suppliers themselves.

c) On the basis of an assessment of capability performed by a third party.

Most customers select their suppliers using option (a) or (b) but there will be cases where these options are not appropriate either because there is no evidence for using option (a) or resources are not available to use option (b) or it is not economic. It is for these situations that a certification scheme was developed. Organizations submit to a third party audit that is performed by an accredited certification body independent of both customer and supplier. An audit is performed against the requirements of ISO 9001 and if no nonconformities are found, a certificate is awarded. This certificate provides evidence that the organization has the capability to meet customer and regulatory requirements relating to the supply of certain specified goods and services. Customers are now able to acquire the confidence they require simply by establishing whether a supplier holds an ISO 9001 certificate covering the type of products and services they are seeking. However, the credibility of the certificate rests on the competence of the auditor and the integrity of the certification body neither of which are guaranteed. (This is addressed further in Chapter 5.)

A quest for capability

Trading organizations need to create and retain satisfied customers to survive. This depends on their capability to:

a) Identify customer needs and expectations.

b) Convert customer needs and expectations into products and services that will satisfy them.

c) Attract customers to the organization.

d) Supply the products and services that meet customer requirements.

Many organizations develop their own ways of working and strive to satisfy their customers in the best way they know how. Increased global competition has led to more stringent customer expectations with regard to quality. To be competitive and to maintain good economic performance, organizations need to employ increasingly effective and efficient ways of managing the organization. In choosing the best way for them, they can either go through a process of trial and error, select from the vast body of knowledge on management, or utilize one or more management models available that combine proven principles and concepts. ISO 9000 represents one of these models. Others are Business Excellence Model, Six Sigma, Capability Maturity Model and Process Management.

Having given the organization the capability to do (a) to (d) above, customer confidence can be built up by reputation, customer assessments or third party assessment. If a customer requires confidence to be demonstrated through an ISO 9001 assessment, the organization has no option but to seek ISO 9001 certification if it wishes to retain business from that particular customer or market

> In B2B relationships where confidence in capability is developed by reputation there might be no need for certification.

sector. In the UK alone there are about 2.5 million trading organizations and less than 2.5% have been registered to ISO 9001. It is therefore reasonable to assume that over 95% of organizations in the UK are able to give their customers confidence in their capability without becoming registered to ISO 9001 but this should not be assumed to mean that the concepts embodied in the ISO 9000 family of standards are flawed. It simply means that in the majority of organizations many of these concepts are employed but they have yet to find a need to pursue formal certification to ISO 9001. Nevertheless in the particular business-to-business relationship, confidence is developed by reputation rather than certification.

However, it is important to recognize that there is no requirement in ISO 9000 for certification. The family of standards can be used in helping an organization discover the right things to do as well as assess for itself the extent to which its goals and processes meet international standards. Only where customers are imposing ISO 9001 in purchase orders and contracts would it be necessary to obtain ISO 9001 certification.

Anatomy of the standards

There are three standards in the ISO 9000 family

ISO 9000 Quality management systems – Fundamentals and vocabulary

ISO 9001 Quality management systems – Requirements

ISO 9004 Quality management systems – Guidelines for performance improvements.

Each of the standards has a different purpose, intent, scope and applicability as indicated in Table 4.1.

These standards provide a vehicle for consolidating and communicating concepts in the field of quality management that have been approved by an international committee of representatives from national standards bodies. It is not their purpose to fuel the certification, consulting, training and publishing industries. The primary users of the standards are intended to be organizations acting as either customers or suppliers. But we should not forget that their primary purpose is to improve the capability of organizations to satisfy their customers and other stakeholders. Broken promises create massive problems for society thus making quality key to survival.

Basic approach

The most important clause in ISO 9000 is clause 2.3. There is a clause 2.3 in ISO 9000 but not in ISO 9001 and just because it is not in ISO 9001 doesn't mean you

Table 4.1 Overview of the ISO 9000 family of standards

Attribute	ISO 9000 Family	ISO 9000	ISO 9001	ISO 9004
Purpose	To assist organizations operate effective quality management systems	To facilitate common understanding of the concepts and language used in the family of standards	To provide an equitable basis for assessing the capability of organizations to meet customer and applicable regulatory requirements	To assist organizations satisfy the needs and expectations of all stakeholders
Intent	To facilitate mutual understanding in national and international trade and help organizations achieve sustained success	To be used in conjunction with ISO 9001 and ISO 9004	To be used for contractual and certification purposes	To assist organizations purpose continual improvement. It is not intended as a guide to meeting the requirements of ISO 9001
Scope	The management of quality	Defines the principles and fundamental concepts and terms used in the ISO 9000 family	Defines the requirements of a quality management system, the purpose of which is to enable organization to continually satisfy their customers	Provides guidelines for improving the performance of organizations and them to satisfy enabling all stakeholders
Applicability	Applies to all organizations regardless of size or complexity	Applies to all terms used in the ISO 9000 family	Applies where an organization needs to demonstrate its ability to provide products and services that meet customer and regulatory requirements and aims to enhance customer satisfaction	Applies to organizations seeking guidance on developing quality management systems and improving their performance
Facts and figures	3 Standards	81 Definitions	8 Sections 51 Clauses 250+ Requirements	8 Sections 64 Clauses No requirements

should ignore it. All three standards are equally important because they depend on each other. The principles, concepts and terminology that underpin ISO 9001 are addressed by ISO 9000 and those aspects that apply beyond product conformity are addressed by ISO 9004.

ISO 9000 clause 2.3 identifies the following basic steps to developing and implementing a quality management system: as a means to satisfying the needs and expectations of customers and other interested parties

1. Determine the needs and expectations of customers and other interested parties.
2. Establish the quality policy and quality objectives of the organization (these would be derived from 1 above).
3. Determine the processes and responsibilities necessary to attain the quality objectives.
4. Determine and provide the resources necessary to attain the quality objectives.
5. Establish methods to measure the effectiveness and efficiency of each process.
6. Apply these measures to determine the effectiveness and efficiency of each process.
7. Determine means of preventing nonconformities and eliminating their causes.
8. Establish and apply a process for continual improvement of the quality management system.

The four sections of ISO 9001 contain requirements that embody this approach but also prescribe requirements derived from the quality management principles that were addressed in Chapter 2. The requirements are not presented in any specific order or as a process and in some respects they follow no particular prescription except that they arise from failures that experience had shown led to poor product quality. The sections of ISO 9001 and ISO 9004 are as follows:

Introduction.
1. Scope.
2. Normative references.
3. Terms and definitions.
4. Quality management system.
5. Management responsibility.
6. Resource management.
7. Product realization.
8. Measurement, analysis and improvement.

Quality management system (development)

Section 4 of ISO 9001 contains the basic requirements for establishing a management system rather than any particular component of the system. In some instances they are duplicated in other Clauses of the standard but this is no bad thing because it emphasizes the principle actions necessary to develop, implement, maintain and improve such a system. Unlike previous versions, the focus has moved away from documentation towards processes and therefore these general requirements capture some of the key activities that are required to develop an effective system.

Quality management system
4.1   General requirements
4.2   General documentation requirements
4.2.1 System documentation
4.2.2 Quality manual
4.2.3 Control of documents
4.2.4 Control of quality records

Although the Clauses in Section 4 are not intended as a sequence there is a relationship that can be represented as a cycle, but first we have to lift some Clauses from Section 5 to commence the cycle. The words in bold indicate the topics covered by the Clauses within Sections 4 and 5 of the standard. The cycle commences with the *Organization's purpose* (Clause 5.3 requires the quality policy has to be appropriate to the organization's purpose) through which are passed *customer requirements* (Clause 5.2 requires customer requirements to be determined) from which are developed *objectives* (Clause 5.4.1 requires objectives to be consistent with the quality policy). In planning to meet these objectives the *processes are identified* and their *sequence and interaction* determined. Once the relationship between processes is known, the *criteria and methods* for effective operation and control can be developed and *documented*. The processes are described in terms that enable their effective communication and a suitable way of doing this would be to compile the process descriptions into a *quality manual* that not only references the associated *procedures* and *records* but also shows how the processes interact. Before implementation the processes need to be *resourced* and the *information* necessary to operate and control them deployed and brought under *document control*. Once operational the processes need to be *monitored* to ensure they are functioning as planned. *Measurements* taken to verify that the processes are delivering the required output and actions taken to *achieve the planned results*. The data obtained from monitoring and measurement that is captured on *controlled records* needs to be *analysed* and opportunities for *continual improvement* identified and the agreed actions *implemented*. Here we have the elements of the process development process that would normally be part of mission management but that process is largely addressed in the standard through Management Responsibility.

If every quality management system reflected the above linkages the organization's products and services would consistently satisfy customer requirements.

Management responsibility

While the implementation of *all* requirements in ISO 9001 is strictly management's responsibility, those in Section 5 of the standard are indeed the responsibility

Management responsibility
5.1 Management commitment
5.2 Customer focus
5.3 Quality policy
5.4 Planning
5.4.1 Quality objectives
5.4.2 Quality management system planning
5.5 Responsibility, authority and communication
5.5.1 Responsibility and authority
5.5.2 Management representative
5.5.3 Internal communication
5.6 Management review
5.6.1 General
5.6.2 Review input
5.6.3 Review output

of top management. All clauses in this section commence with the phrase "Top management shall. . ." The first four clauses clearly apply to the strategic planning processes of the organization rather than to specific products. However, it is the board of directors that should take note of these requirements when establishing their vision, values, mission and objectives. These requirements are amongst the most important in the standard. There is a clear linkage between customer's needs, policy, objectives and processes. One leads to the other in a continuous cycle. Although the clauses in Section 5 are not intended as a sequence, each represents a part of a process that establishes direction and keeps the organization on course. If we link the requirements together in a cycle (indicating the headings from ISO 9001 in bold italic type) the cycle commences with a *Vision* – a statement of what we want to be or do, and then a *Focus on customers* for it is the customer that will decide whether or not the organization survives. It is only when you know what your market is, who your customers will be and where they will be that you can define the *Purpose* or *Mission* of the organization. From the purpose or mission you can devise the *Policies or Values* that will guide you on your journey. These policies help frame the *Objectives*, the milestones en route towards your destination. The policies won't work unless there is *Commitment* so that everyone pulls in the same direction. *Plans* have to be made to achieve the objectives and these plans need to identify and layout the *Processes* that will be employed to deliver the results – for all work is a process and without work nothing will be achieved. The plans also need to identify the *Responsibilities and Authority* of those who will be engaged in the endeavour. As a consequence it is essential that effective channels of *Internal Communication* be established to ensure that everyone understands what they are required to achieve and how they are performing. No journey should be undertaken without a means of knowing where you are, how far you have to go, what obstacles are likely to lie in the path ahead or what forces will influence your success. It is therefore necessary to collate the facts on current performance and predictions of what lies ahead so that a *Management Review* can take place to determine what action is required to keep the organization on course or whether any changes are necessary to the course or the capability of the organization for it to fulfil its purpose and mission – and so we come full circle. What the requirements of Section 5 therefore address is the mission management process with the exception of process development, which happens to be addressed in Section 4 of the standard.

Resource management

Section 6 of ISO 9001 draws together all the resources-related requirements that were somewhat scattered in previous versions. Resource management is a key business process in all organizations. In practice, resource management is a collection of related processes that are often departmentally oriented.

Resource management
6.1 Provision of resources
6.2 Human resources
6.2.1 General
6.2.2 Training, awareness and competency
6.3 Infrastructure
6.4 Work environment

- Financial resources are controlled by the Finance Department.
- Purchased materials, equipment and supplies are controlled by the Purchasing Department.
- Measuring equipment maintenance is controlled by the Calibration Department.
- Plant maintenance is controlled by the Maintenance Department.
- Staff development is controlled by the Human Resources Department.
- Building maintenance is controlled by the Facilities Management Department.

These departments control the resources in as much that they might plan, acquire, maintain and dispose of them but do not manage them totally because they are not the sole users or customers of the resource. They therefore only perform a few of the tasks necessary to manage resources. Collectively they control the human, physical and financial resources of the organization.

Whatever the resource, firstly it has to be planned, then acquired, deployed, maintained and eventually disposed of. The detail of each process will differ depending on the type of resource being managed. Human resources are not "disposed off" but their employment or contract terminated. Although ISO 9001 does not address disposal of any resources because it only focuses on intended product, resource disposal impacts the environment and other stakeholders and if an automotive company discharges waste into the ground water, it could lead to prosecutions that displease their customer.

The standard does not address financial resources specifically but clearly they are required to implement and maintain the management system and hence run the organization. Purchasing is not addressed under resource management but under product realization. However, the location of Clauses should not be a barrier to the imagination because their location is not governed by the process approach but by user expectations. Regretably, we cannot link the clauses of this section of the standard into a cycle as we have with the other sections.

Product realization

Product Realization as expressed in Section 7 of ISO 9001 is the Demand Fulfilment Process (see Chapter 6) that has interfaces with Resource Management and Demand Creation processes. It is also the Order to Cash process implying that the inputs are orders and the output is cash, therefore it would include the invoicing and banking activities. However the Product Realization requirements include requirements for purchasing, a process that could fit as comfortably under resource management because it is not limited to the acquisition of components but is a process that is used for acquiring all physical resources including services. Section 7 also includes requirements for control of measuring devices which would fit more comfortably into Section 8 but it omits the control of nonconforming product which is more to do with handling product than measurement. Product realization does not address demand creation or marketing. The demand has already been created when the customer approaches the organization with either an order or invitation to tender. Note that Demand Creation is addressed by the standard only through Clause 5.2 and that product design is located in Section 7 simply because it refers to the design of customer specific products. If the products were designed in order to create a demand this work process would be part of Demand Creation.

If we link the requirements together in a cycle (indicating the headings from ISO 9001 in bold type), having marketed the organization's capability and attracted a customer, the cycle commences by the need to *communicate with customers* and *determine the requirements* of customers, of regulators and of the organization relative to the product or service to be supplied. This will undoubtedly involve more *customer communication* and once requirements have been determined we need to *review the requirements* to ensure they are understood and confirm we have the capability to achieve them. If we have identified a need for new products and services, we would then need to *plan product realization* and in doing so use *preventive action* methods to ensure the success of the project and take care of any *customer property* on loan to us. We would undertake product *design and development* and in doing so we would probably need to *identify product*, *purchase* materials, components and services, build prototypes using the process of *production provision* and *validate* new *processes*. After *design validation* we would release product information into the market to attract customers and undertake more *customer-communication*. As customers enquire about our offerings we would once more *determine the requirements* in order to match customer needs with product offerings and our ability to supply.

Now faced with real customers demanding our products, we would *review the requirements* and confirm we had the capability to supply the product in the quantities and to the delivery schedule required before entering into a commitment to supply. We would then proceed to *plan product realization* once again and undertake *production or service provision*. During production or service delivery we would maintain *traceability* of the product if applicable, perform *measurement and monitoring* and *control the measuring and monitoring devices*. We would *monitor and measure processes* and *monitor and measure products* at each stage of the process. If we found unacceptable variations in the product we would undertake the *control of nonconforming product* and *analyse data* to facilitate *corrective action*. Throughout production or service delivery we would seek the *preservation of product* and take care of *customer property*. Once we had undertaken all the *product verification* and *preserved* the product for delivery, we would ship the product to the customer or complete the service transaction. To complete the cycle *customer communication* would be initiated once more to obtain feedback on our performance.

Here we have linked together all the Clauses in Section 7 and many in Section 8 of the standard because the two cannot be separated.

Measurement, analysis and improvement

Measurement, analysis and improvement processes are vital to the achievement of quality. Until we measure using devices of known integrity, we know little about a process or its outcomes. But if we measure using instruments that are unfit for purpose, we will be misled by the results. With the results of valid measurement we can make a judgement on the basis of facts. The facts will tell us whether we have met the target. Analysis of the facts will tell us whether the target can be met using the same methods or better methods or whether the target is the right target to aim for. Measurements without a target value to compare results of measurement are measurements without a purpose. The target value is therefore vital but arbitrary values demotivate personnel. Targets should always be focused on purpose so that through the chain of measures from corporate objectives to component dimensions there is a soundly based relationship between targets, measures, objectives and the purpose of the organization, process or product.

Measurement tells us whether there has been a change in performance. Change is a constant. It exists in everything and is caused by physical, social or economic forces. When we measure the same parameter on different items we expect slight variation. However, if we measure the same parameter using the same device we might not expect there to be a change, but the inaccuracies inherent in the measuring system will lead to a variation in readings. To understand change we need to understand its cause. Some change is represented by variation about a norm and is predictable – it is a natural phenomenon of a process and when it is within acceptable limits it is tolerable. Other change is represented by erratic behaviour and is not predictable but its cause can be determined and eliminated through measurement, analysis and improvement.

Measurement, analysis and improvement are strictly sub-processes within each business process. However parent processes will often capture data from monitoring and measurements within sub-processes. This may happen when assessing a variety of data from individual processes to determine customer satisfaction or for discovering common cause problems and subsequently devising company wide improvement programmes.

There is a sort of logic in the structure of the requirements in this section but there are some gaps. It would have assisted understanding if the same terms as used in Clause 8.1 had been used in the headings of Clauses 8.2 to 8.5. In that way the relationships would have been more obvious. The general requirements of Clause 8.1 are amplified by Clauses 8.2 to 8.5 so the requirements in Clause 8.1 are not separate to those in Clauses 8.2 to 8.5 with the exception of Clause 8.3 on the control of nonconforming product and those on statistical techniques. This later requirement is stated once because it applies to all monitoring, measurement and analysis processes. Clause 8.3 on nonconforming product appears in Section 8 not because it has anything to do with measurement, analysis and improvement but because its inclusion in Section 7 would imply that it could be excluded from the management system (see ISO 9001 Clause 1.2).

It should not be assumed that Section 8 includes all requirements on measurement, analysis and improvement.

Measurement and monitoring is also addressed by:

- Management representative (5.5.2) – in the context of reporting on system performance.
- Management review (5.6) – in the context of reviewing system adequacy.
- Control of monitoring and measurement devices (7.6).
- Design and development verification (7.3.5).
- Design and development validation (7.3.6).
- Verification of purchased product (7.4.3).

Analysis is also addressed by:

- Management review (5.6) – in the context of changes that could affect the management system.
- Control of design and development changes (7.3.7) – in the context of evaluation of the effects of change.
- Control of monitoring and measuring devices (7.6) – in the context of measurement systems.

Improvement is also addressed by:

- Management review (5.6) – in the context of changes to quality policy.
- Control of design and development changes (7.3.7).
- Internal communication (5.5.3) – in the context of communicating the effectiveness of the management system.
- Provision of resources (6.1) in the context of resources needed for continual improvement.

We can link the requirements of Section 8 together in a number of separate cycles (indicating the headings from ISO 9001 in bold italic type).

During the design and development of the business and work processes we would undertake a review of the established practices to identify potential problems and undertake *preventive action* to prevent occurrence of such problems. Before implementing the management system processes or any changes thereto, we would perform *internal audits* (or undertake *process validation*) to determine whether these processes met the relevant requirements of the standard, enabled the organization to fulfil its *policies* and *objectives* and produce the required products and services. Any potential problems discovered would be subject to *preventive action* to prevent occurrence of such problems. At appropriate stages in the production process we would *monitor and measure product* for compliance with specified requirements, periodically undertake *product audits* to establish the effectiveness of the process controls, initiate *control of nonconforming product* on detecting nonconformity and undertake *corrective action* when process targets had not been met. After introducing new or changed practices and periodically thereafter, we would perform *internal audits* to determine whether the planned arrangements were being implemented as intended and undertake *corrective action* to bring about *improvement* by better control. Periodically we would *monitor and measure processes* for their ability to achieve planned results and undertake *process audits* to establish whether the achieved results arose from implementing the planned arrangements and if necessary, undertake corrective action to reduce variation and bring about *improvement* by better control. We would also *analyse data* resulting from these reviews and bring about *improvements* by better utilization of resources. Some time after establishing the *organization's purpose,* setting *policies* and *objectives* that were *customer focused* and installed the enabling *processes* we would collect and *analyse data* in order to monitor *customer satisfaction* and undertake *corrective action* to bring about *improvement* by better control.

One observes from this consolidation that the order in which the Clauses are mentioned is not remotely the same as the order they are addressed in the standard, that some Clauses in the standard appear several times and others are drawn from other sections thus demonstrating that you cannot treat the Clauses in isolation or in any particular sequence.

Performance improvement

ISO 9001 contains a set of requirements, which if met, will enable organizations to supply products, and services that satisfy customer requirements. Depending on how these requirements are interpreted it may enable organizations to go much further but organizations are not compelled to do so to gain certification. ISO 9004 covers a wider range of objectives than ISO 9001 and addresses the continual improvement of an organization's overall performance and therefore goes beyond customers and addresses the needs and expectations of all stakeholders.

The strategy underpinning this consistent pair of standards is that you can develop your management system so that it meets ISO 9001 and hence give you the capability of satisfying customer requirements, and subsequently implement the recommendations of ISO 9004 to extend the scope of your management system so that it enables you to satisfy all stakeholders.

You could of course start with ISO 9004 and then simply apply for ISO 9001 certification. The self assessment questionnaire in ISO 9004 is useful but the assessment criteria for the Excellence Model is far better and wider ranging.

Summary

In this Chapter we have examined the roots of ISO 9000 and shown that the principles on which it is based were born many centuries ago. We have shown how ISO 9000 certification came out of a quest for confidence by customers and how organizations were motivated to establish management systems as a way of increasing their capability so as to create and retail satisfied customers. We have examined the relationship between the standards in the ISO 9000 family and shown how each of the primary requirements in ISO 9001 are linked together to form a coherent set of elements. After analysing each section of ISO 9001 requirements in plane English a picture emerges that enables us to see how we can manage the achievement of quality using ISO 9000. Going further to embrace the recommendations of ISO 9004 will get you closer to the Excellence Model.

ISO 9000 is a useful family of standards and has had more success that any other initiative primarily because ISO 9001 certification has been used as a pre-requisite for trade. As a result neither of the other standards in the family (ISO 9000 and ISO 9004) have penetrated as deep as ISO 9001 so the concepts and principles upon which ISO 9000 is based are not widely understood. There has been a rather narrow interpretation of the requirements which regrettably has prevented ISO 9000 from becoming a model of excellence that Chief Executive Officers would use in the running of their business.

The many misconceptions that have surrounded the standard are addressed in the next chapter.

Chapter 5
How ISO 9000 made us think about quality

A system, whether physical or metaphysical, commonly owes its success to
its novelty; and is no sooner canvassed with impartiality than its weakness
is discovered.

David Hume (1711–1776), Scottish philosopher

Introduction

Although it is now six years since the publication of ISO 9000:2000, there is still
a lot to be learnt from the way this standard has been used over the past 20 years.
The lessons are not only applicable to ISO 9000. Whether you are contemplating using six sigma, balanced score card, TQM or any other approach to change,
you may find that any new fad can generate the same perceptions and misconceptions as ISO 9000.

Also, for many organizations outside the engineering, food and medicines
industries, ISO 9000 was their first encounter with quality management.
Whereas quality control had been a feature of these industries since before
1960, for many it was not until they were exposed to ISO 9000 that they became
aware that the principles, tools and techniques of quality management could be
applied in any enterprise – but unfortunately ISO 9000 was not the ideal vehicle
to do this.

Since the publication of the ISO 9000 family of standards in 1987 a new
industry has grown in its shadow. The industry is characterized by Standards
Bodies, Accreditation Bodies, Certification Bodies, Consulting Practices, Training
Providers, Software Providers and a whole raft of publications, magazines, web
sites and schemes – all in the name of quality! But has ISO 9000 and its derivates
such as ISO/TS 16949 fulfilled its promise? There are those with vested interests that would argue that it has improved the efficiency and effectiveness of

organizations. Equally others would argue that it has done tremendous damage to industry. One of the problems in assessing the validity of the pros and cons of the debate is the very term ISO 9000 because it means different things to different people.

Perceptions that have been confirmed time and again by consultants, other organizations and frequent audits from the certification bodies over the last 20 years makes these perceptions extremely difficult to change. If ISO 9000 is perceived rightly or wrongly, as a badge on the wall or a set of documents, then that is what it is. If this was not the intent of ISO 9000 then clearly we have to do something about it. But why should these perceptions be changed? After all, can over 500,000 organizations have got it wrong? Some organizations in fact did use ISO 9000 wisely but they are likely to be in the minority. Many organizations also chose not to pursue ISO 9000 certification and focused on TQM but that too led to dissatisfaction with the results. It may be useful to take a look at these perceptions – look at how we have come to think about ISO 9000, quality, quality systems, certification and inspection. It is interesting to note that even those responsible for the standard recognized the weaknesses of the 1994 version.

Pierre F. Caillibot (Canada) Chairman of the ISO technical committee responsible for the ISO 9000 family of standards (TC 176) wrote in 2001[1] that "one of the main problems with the 1994 version was that it left the door open to confusion between ends and means, and could therefore lead to an unwanted degree of variability in understanding the minimum requirement threshold. Between the rationale for the standard and a minimalist interpretation of its contents, there was an embarrassing margin which was liable to damage its credibility."

A realization of these perceptions will hopefully enable us to approach the subject of quality management with a different perspective or at least provide food for thought.

How we think about ISO 9000

To the advocate, ISO 9000 is a standard and all the negative comments have nothing to do with the standard but the way it has been interpreted by organizations, consultants and auditors. To the critics, ISO 9000 is what it is perceived to be and this tends to be the standard and its support infrastructure. This makes any discussion on the subject difficult and inevitably leads to disagreement.

Some people often think about ISO 9000 as a system. As a group of documents, ISO 9000 is in fact a set of interrelated ideas, principles and rules and could therefore be considered a system in the same way that we refer to the metric system or the imperial system of measurement. ISO 9000 is both an international standard and until December 2000, was a family of some 20 international standards. As a standard, ISO 9000 was divided into four parts with Part 1 providing guidelines on the selection and use of the other standards in the family. The family of standards included requirements for quality assurance and guidelines on quality management. Some might argue that none of these are in fact standards in the sense of being quantifiable. The critics argue that the standards are too open to interpretation to be standards – anything that produces such a wide variation is surely an incapable process with one of its primary causes being a series of objectives that are not measurable. Only ISO 8402 of the ISO 9000 family was invoked but this has changed with the 2000 version. However, if we take a broader view of standards, any set of rules, rituals, requirements, quantities, targets or behaviours that have been agreed by a group of people could be deemed to be a standard. Therefore, by this definition, ISO 9000 is a standard.

ISO 9000 is also perceived as a label given to the family of standards and the associated certification scheme. However, certification was never a requirement of any of the standards in the ISO 9000 family – this came from customers. Such notions as "We are going for ISO 9000" imply ISO 9000 is a goal like a university degree and like that there are those who pass who are educated and those who merely pass the exam. You can purchase degrees from unaccredited universities just as you can purchase ISO 9000 certificates from unaccredited certification bodies. The acceptance criteria is the same, it is the means of measurement and therefore the legitimacy of the certificates that differ.

As many organizations did not perceive they had a quality management system before they embarked on the quest for ISO 9000 certification, the programme, the system and the people were labelled "ISO 9000" as a kind of shorthand. Before long, these labels became firmly attached and difficult to shed and consequently why people refer to ISO 9000 as a "system".

How we think about quality management systems

All organizations have a way of doing things. For some it rests in the mind of the leaders, for others it is translated onto paper and for most it is a mixture of both. Before ISO 9000 came along, organizations had found ways of doing things that worked for them. We seem to forget that before ISO 9000, we had built the pyramids, created the mass production of consumer goods, broken the sound barrier, put a man on the moon and brought him safely back to earth. It was organizational systems that made these achievements possible. Systems, with all their inadequacies and inefficiencies, enabled mankind to achieve objectives that until 1987 had completely revolutionized society. The next logical step was to improve these systems and make them more predictable, more efficient and more effective – optimizing performance across the whole organization – not focusing on particular parts at the expense of the others. What ISO 9000 did was to encourage the formalization of those parts of the system that served the achievement of product quality – often diverting resources away from the other parts of the system.

ISO 9000 did require organizations to establish a quality system as a means of ensuring product met specified requirements. What many organizations failed to appreciate was that they all have a management system – a way of doing things and because the language used in ISO 9000 was not consistent with the language of their business, many people did not see the connection between what they did already and what the standard required. People may think of the organization as a system, but what they don't do is manage the organization as a system. They fail to make linkages between actions and effects and will change one function without considering the effects on another. (Neither ISO 9000 nor its derivatives has brought about an improvement in this situation. However, the connectivity is emphasized in other approaches such as Process Management and Six Sigma.)

New activities were therefore bolted onto the organization such as management review, internal audit, document control, records control, corrective and preventive action without putting in place the necessary linkages to maintain system integrity. What emerged was an organization with warts as illustrated in Figure 5.1. This was typical of those organizations that merely pursued the "badge on the wall". Such was the hype, the pressure and the razzmatazz, that the part that was formalized using ISO 9000 became labelled as the ISO 9000 quality system. It isolated parts of the organization and made them less efficient. Other organizations recognized that quality was an important issue and formalized part of their informal management system. When ISO 14001 came along this resulted in the formalization of another part of their management system to create an Environmental Management System (EMS). In the UK at least, with the advent of BS 8800 on Occupational Health and Safety Management Systems (OHSMS), a third part of the organization's management system was formalized. The effect of this piecemeal formalization is illustrated in Figure 5.2. This perception of ISO 9000, ISO 14000 and any other management system standard is also flawed – but it is understandable.

The 1994 edition of the ISO 9000 family of standards was characterized by its focus on procedures. In almost every element of ISO 9001 there was a requirement for the supplier to establish and maintain documented procedures to control some aspect of an organization's operations. So much did this requirement

Figure 5.1   Bolt-on systems

Figure 5.2   Separate systems

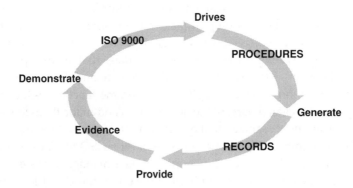

Figure 5.3   The conformity cycle

pervade the standard that it generated the belief that ISO 9000 was simply a matter of documenting what you do and doing what you document. This led to the perception that ISO 9000 built a bureaucracy of procedures, records and forms with very little effect on quality. What emerged was a cycle of conformity. Organizations started by reading the standard, producing procedures to comply with the standard and then generating records that were used as evidence to demonstrate compliance with ISO 9000 to external auditors. This is illustrated in Figure 5.3.

The 1994 version also created a perception that quality systems only exist to assure customers that product meets requirements. ISO 9001 was often referred to as a Quality Assurance standard because customers used it for obtaining an assurance of the quality of products being supplied. This perception is illustrated in Figure 5.4, in which the organization is represented as a circle containing islands that serve the assurance of quality and with the remainder of the organization running the business. This is one reason why Toyota terminated its ISO 9000 certification programme – it did not cover important aspects of the business such as cost management.

Assurance equates with provision of objective evidence and this equates with the generation and maintenance of documentation i.e. procedures and

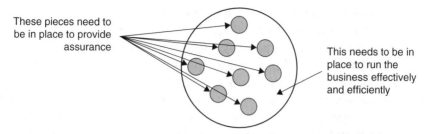

These pieces need to be in place to provide assurance

This needs to be in place to run the business effectively and efficiently

Figure 5.4   Separating assurance activities from management activities

records. With the pressure from auditors to show evidence, organizations were persuaded to believe that if it wasn't documented it didn't exist and this ultimately led to the belief that quality systems were a set of documents. These systems tended to be sets of documents that were structured around the elements of a standard. None of the standards required this, but this is how it was implemented by those who lacked understanding. However, ISO 9001 Clause 4.2.1 required suppliers to establish a quality system to ensure (not assure) that product met specified requirements. In other words, it required the system to cause conformity with requirements. A set of documents alone cannot cause product to conform to requirements. When people change the system they invariably mean that they update or revise the system documentation. When the system is audited invariably it is the documentation that is checked and compliance with the standard verified. There is often little consideration given to processes, resources, behaviours or results. As few people seem to have read ISO 8402, it is not surprising that the documents are perceived as a system. (Note: In talking with over 600 representatives of UK companies in 1999 and 2000 the author discovered that less than 10% had read ISO 8402.) But ISO 8402 defined a system rather differently. A quality system was defined as *the organization structure, procedures, processes and resources needed to implement quality management* – clearly not a set of documents. The 1994 version required a system to be established and documented. If the system was a set of documents, why then require it to be established as well as documented? (We have no evidence to show that the authors understood the difference so it is rather patronizing to speculate that they did!)

The persistence of the auditors to require documentation led to situations where documentation only existed in case something went wrong – in case someone was knocked down by a bus. While the unexpected can result in disaster for an organization it needs to be based on a risk assessment. There was often no assessment of the risks or the consequences. This could have been avoided simply by asking the question "so what?" So there are no written instructions for someone to take over the job but even if there were, would it guarantee there were no hiccups? Would it *ensure* product quality? Often the new person sees improvements that the previous person missed or deliberately chose not to make – often the written instructions are of no use without training and often the written instructions are of no value whatsoever.

There has also been a perception in the service industries that ISO 9000 quality systems only deal with the procedural aspects of a service and not the professional aspects. For instance in a medical practice, the ISO 9000 quality system is often used only for processing patients and not for the medical treatment. In legal practices, the quality system again has been focused only on the administrative aspects and not on the legal issues. The argument for this is that there are professional bodies that deal with the professional side of the business. In other words, the quality system only addresses the non-technical issues, leaving the profession to address the technical issues. This is not *quality management*. The quality of the service depends on both the technical and non-technical aspects of the service. Patients who are given the wrong advice would remain dissatisfied even if their papers were in order or even if they were given courteous attention and advised promptly. To achieve quality one has to consider both the product and the service. A faulty product delivered on time, within budget and with a smile remains a faulty product!

How we think about certification

Pressure for certification

When an organization chooses not to pursue ISO 9000 certification or not to retain the ISO 9000 certificate, it should make no difference to the way the organization is managed. It's similar to the man who chooses not to take the course examination. He still has the knowledge he has acquired whether or not he takes the examination and gets a certificate. What he cannot do is demonstrate to others that he has reached a certain level of education without having to prove it every time. People who know him don't care that he didn't take the examination. It is only those who don't know him that he will have difficulty convincing.

> **A historical perspective**
>
> ISO 9000 came out of the defence industry where there was a long tradition of command and control. It followed the same pattern of imposing requirements to prevent failures that experience had shown led to poor product quality.

Many organizations were driven to seek ISO 9000 certification by pressure from customers rather than as an incentive to improve business performance and therefore sought the quickest route to certification. The critics called this coercion and like most command and control strategies, believed it resulted in managers cheating just to get the badge. What was out of character was that suppliers that were well known to customers were made to jump through this hoop in order to get a tick in a box in a list of approved suppliers. It became a "necessary evil" to do business. Certainly when perceived as a means to get a badge, the standard was no more than a marketing tool. It could have been used as a framework for improvement but the way it was imposed on organizations generated fear brought about by ignorant customers who mistakenly believed that imposing ISO 9000 would improve quality. To achieve anything in our society we inevitably have to impose rules and regulations – what the critics regard as *command and control* – but unfortunately, any progress we make masks the disadvantages of this strategy and because we only do what we are required to do, few people learn. When people make errors more rules are imposed until we are put in a straightjacket and productivity plummets.

ISO 9001 Certification is not a requirement of any of the standards in ISO 9000 family, nor is it encouraged by the standard. It is however encouraged by governments and this is where the misunderstanding arises. Governments encouraged organizations to use ISO 9000 alongside product standards in their purchasing strategy so as to raise the standard of quality in national and international trade.[2] Certification became a requirement of customers – they mandated it through contracts. ISO 9000 was a convenient standard to use in order for customers to gain an assurance of quality. ISO 9000 was launched at a time when customers in the western world took an adversarial approach to their suppliers. ISO 9000 did not require purchasers to impose ISO 9000 on their suppliers. What it *did* require was for purchasers to determine the controls necessary to ensure whether purchased product met their requirements. But the easy way of meeting this requirement was to impose ISO 9000. (Unfortunately this approach is being used in the automotive industry where 2nd, 3rd, or 4th tier suppliers are being coerced into getting ISO/TS 16949 certification.) It saved the purchaser from having to assess for themselves the capability of suppliers. Unfortunately the assessment process was ineffective because it led to suppliers getting the badge that were not capable of meeting their customer's requirements. ISO 9001:1994 required suppliers to establish a quality system to ensure that product met specified requirements but it allowed organizations to specify their *own requirements* – provided they did what they said they did, they could receive the certificate. As there were no specific requirements in the standard that caused the auditors to verify that these requirements were those needed to meet the needs and expectations of customers, organizations could produce rubbish and still receive the badge. What was being checked was *consistency* – not *quality*.

Before ISO 9000, organizations were faced with meeting all manner of rules and regulations. Government inspectors and financial auditors frequently examined the books and practices for evidence of wrong-doing but none of these resulted in organizations creating something that was not integrated within the routines they applied to manage the business. When ISO 9000 came along, many organizations embarked on a course of action that was perceived to have no value except to keep the badge – the ISO 9000 certificate. Activities were only documented and performed because the standard required it. Take away the certification and there was no longer a business need for many of these procedures and activities.

ISO 9000-1:1994 in fact suggested that there were two approaches to using ISO 9000: "management-motivated" and "stakeholder-motivated". It suggested that the supplier should consult ISO 9000-1 to understand the basic concepts but few organizations did this. It also suggested that with the management-motivated approach organizations should firstly design their systems to ISO 9004-1 and then choose an appropriate assessment standard. In addition it suggested that with the stakeholder-motivated approach an organization should initially implement a quality system in response to the demands of customers and then select ISO 9001, ISO 9002 or ISO 9003 as appropriate for assessment. It suggested that having found significant improvements in product quality, costs and internal operating results from this approach, the organization would initiate a management-motivated approach based on ISO 9004. Those suppliers that actually obtained such benefits no doubt did initiate a management-motivated approach but many only focused on getting a certificate and therefore did not gain any benefits apart from the marketing advantage that ISO 9000 certification brought.

This eminently sensible approach has been changed in the ISO 9000:2000 family of standards. It is now suggested that, "beginning with ISO 9000:2000, you adopt ISO 9001:2000 to achieve a first level of performance. The practices described in ISO 9004:2000 may then be implemented to make your quality management system increasingly effective in achieving your own business goals."[3] It must be said that it is a retrograde step to place ISO 9004 in the role of being a tool for system improvement rather than system development and improvement, although when one examines the text of ISO 9004 it clearly contains guidance on both system development and improvement.

The approach to certification

Believing that ISO 9000 was only about "documenting what you do", organizations set to work on responding to the requirements of the standard as a list of activities to be carried out. Again, this belief became so widespread that ISO co-ordinators or ISO 9000 project managers were appointed to establish and maintain the quality system. In some organizations, managers were assigned responsibility for meeting the requirements of a particular element of the standard even though there was not only no requirement to do so, but also no business benefit from doing so. Consultants were engaged to write the documents and apart from some new procedures governing internal audits, management review and document control, very little changed. There was a lot of money thrown at these projects in the quest to gain certification. However, none of the surveys conducted since 1987 have shown any significant improvement in an organization's overall performance – quite simply because nothing changed, not the processes, not the people nor the culture. The "system" existed just to keep the badge on the wall. The ninth ISO survey[4] indicated that 9,862 certificates had been withdrawn at the end of 1999 and of these 473 were for reasons of either insufficient return on investment or no business advantage. However some 7,186 organizations discontinued certification for reasons unknown, indicating that certification was probably perceived as not adding value.

The approach to auditing

To make matters worse, the certification scheme established to assess the capability of organizations perpetuated this belief. These third party auditors would reinforce the message by commencing their interviews with the question "Have you got a procedure for . . . ?" Audits would focus on seeking evidence that the organization was implementing its procedures. This technique was not limited to ISO 9001 assessments, it also pervaded assessments against ISO 9000 derivatives. Desperate to put the "badge on the wall" organizations responded to the auditor's expectations and produced quality manuals that mirrored the structure of the standard – manuals containing nothing more than the requirements of Section 4 of ISO 9001 or ISO 9002, reworded as policy statements. The auditor would therefore establish an organization's readiness for the audit by the closeness with which the quality manual addressed the requirements of the standard rather than by examining performance. A more sensible approach might have been to ask for the last 3 months data for the key processes to establish if the processes were stable.

Instead of using the whole family of standards as a framework, the standards became a stick with which to beat people. Managers would ask, where does it say that in the standard and if the auditor or consultant could not show them, the manager did nothing. The astute manager would ask, "Why would I want to do that?" and if the auditor or consultant could not give a sound business case for doing it, the manager did nothing.

Auditor training

Customers of auditor training courses behaved as though all they wanted was a training certificate. This led to lower standards. The auditors were poorly trained and the trainers became a victim of the system. Rules forced training bodies to cover certain topics in a certain time. Commercial pressure resulted in training bodies cutting costs to keep the courses running. Customers would not pay for more than they thought they needed but they did not know what they needed. Tell them what is required to convert a novice into a competent auditor and they wince! When there are providers only too willing to relieve them of their cash, customers opt for the cheaper solution. Had customers of training course been purchasing a product that failed to function there would have been an outcry, but the results of training were less likely to be measured. The training auditors received focused on auditing for conformity and led to auditors learning to catch people out. It did not lead to imparting the skills necessary for them to conduct audits that added value for organizations.

The effect of competition

Certification bodies were also in competition and this led to auditors spending less time conducting the audit that was *really* needed. They focused on the easy things to spot and not on whether the system was effective. Had the provision of certification services not been commercialized, there would not have been pressure to compromise quality. Organizations stayed with their certification body because they gave them an easy ride. What certification body would deliberately do things to lose customers? They will do everything they can to keep customers – even if it means turning a blind eye. Certification bodies were also barred from making suggestions on improvement because it was considered to be consulting. They therefore stuck to familiar ground. The accreditation bodies were supposed to be supervising the certification bodies but they also needed revenue to be able to deploy assessors in sufficient numbers to maintain the integrity of the certification scheme. It had to be commercially viable at the outset otherwise the whole certification scheme would not have got off the ground because governments would not have been prepared to sponsor it. It is interesting that in the UK, there has been considerable protest against privatising the National Air Traffic Service for fear that profits will compromise air space safety. There was no outcry against commercially operated quality system certification but equally unsafe products could emerge out of an ineffective quality system and enter the market. Certification in the automotive sector is somewhat different where an industry led accreditation and witness audit scheme operates that might just make third party audits less prone to abuse.

Misplaced objectives

The certification scheme also added another dimension – that of scope. The scope of certification was determined by the organization so that only those parts of the quality system that were in the scope of certification were assessed. The quality system may have extended beyond the scope of certification and the scope of the standard but been far less than the scope of the business. This is illustrated in Figure 5.5.

> **Food for thought**
>
> Is our goal to survive the audit or to improve our performance?

Quality managers scurried around before and after the assessor and in doing so led everyone else to believe that all that was important to the assessor was documentation. This led others in the organization to focus on the things the auditor looked for not on the things that mattered – they became so focused on satisfying the auditor that

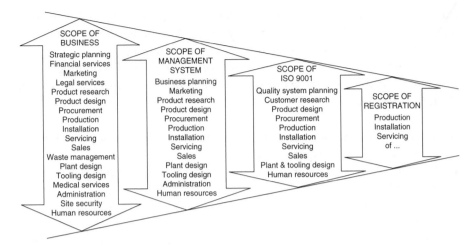

Figure 5.5 The scoping effect

they lost sight of their objectives. They focused on surviving the audit and not on improving the performance. It has the same effect as the student who crams for an examination. The certificate may be won but an education is lost. What would the organization rather have – a certificate or an effective management system? Organizations had it in their power to terminate the contract with their Certification Body if they did not like the way they handled the assessment. They had it in their power to complain to the Accreditation Body if they were not satisfied with the service rendered by the Certification Body but on both counts they failed to take any action. Certification Bodies are suppliers, not regulators. What went wrong with ISO 9000 assessments is that the auditors lost sight of the objective to improve the quality of products and services. They failed to ask themselves whether the discrepancies they found had any bearing on the quality of the product. Many of the nonconformities were only classified as such because the organization had chosen to document what it did regardless of its impact on quality. Auditors often held the view that if an organization took the trouble to document *it*, *it* must be essential to product quality and therefore by not doing *it*, product quality must be affected!

How ISO 9000 made us move our eye off the ball

ISO 9000 was conceived to bring about an improvement in product quality. It was believed that if organizations were able to demonstrate that they were operating a quality system that met international standards, customers would gain greater confidence in the quality of products they purchased. It was also believed that by operating in accordance with documented procedures, errors would be reduced and consistency of output ensured. If you find the best way of achieving a result, put in place measures to prevent variation, document it and train others to apply it, it follows that the results produced should be consistently good. But it didn't work that way, primarily because organizations did not understand that processes are different from procedures.

The requirements of the standard were perceived to be a list of things to do to achieve quality. The ISO co-ordinator would often draw up a plan based on the following logic:

- We have to identify resource requirements so I will write a procedure on identifying resource requirements.
- We have to produce quality plans so I will write a procedure on producing quality plans.
- We have to record contract reviews so I will write a procedure on recording contract reviews.
- We have to identify design changes so I will write a procedure on identifying design changes.

The requirements in the standard were often not expressed as results to be achieved. Requirements for a documented procedure to be established resulted in just that. Invariably the objectives of the procedure were to *define something* rather than to *achieve something*. This led to documentation without any clear purpose that related to the achievement of quality. Those producing the documentation were focusing on meeting the standard not on achieving quality. Those producing the product were focusing on meeting the customer requirement but the two were often out of sync. As quality assurance became synonymous with procedures, so people perceived that they could achieve quality by following procedures. The dominance of procedures to the exclusion of performance is a misunderstanding of the implementers. The standard required a documented system *that ensured product met specified requirements* thereby indicating a clear purpose. Once again the implementers lost sight of the objective. Or was it that they knew the objective but in order to meet it, the culture would have to change and if they could get the badge without doing so, why shouldn't they?

Issuing a procedure was considered to equate to the task being completed. Unfortunately, for those on the receiving end, the procedures were filed and forgotten. When the auditor came around, the individual was found to be totally unaware of the "procedure" and consequently found noncompliant with it. However, the auditor would discover that the individual was doing the right things so the corrective action was inevitably to change the procedure. The process of issuing procedures was not questioned, the individual concerned was blamed for not knowing the procedure and the whole episode failed to make any positive contribution to the achievement of quality. But it left the impression on the individual that quality was all about following procedures. It also left the impression that quality was about consistency and providing you did what you said you would do regardless of it being in the interests of satisfying customers, it was OK. One is left wondering whether anyone consulted the dictionary in which quality is defined as *a degree of excellence*?

Another problem was that those who were to implement requirements were often excluded from the process. Instead of enquiring as to the best way of meeting this requirement, those in charge of ISO 9000 implementation assumed that issuing procedures would in fact cause compliance with requirements. It requires a study of the way work gets done to appreciate how best to meet a requirement. Procedures were required to be documented and the range and detail was intended to be appropriate to the complexity of the work, the methods used and the skills and training needed. The standard also only required work instructions where their absence would adversely affect quality. It is as though the people concerned did not read the requirement properly or had no curiosity to find out for themselves what ISO had to say about procedures – they were all too ready to be told what to do without questioning why they should be doing it.

More often than not, the topics covered by the standard were only a sample of all the things that need to be done to achieve the organization's objectives. The way the standard classified the topics was also often not appropriate to the way work was performed. As a consequence, procedures failed to be implemented because they mirrored the standard and not the work. ISO 9000 may have required documented procedures but it did not insist that they should be produced in separate documents, with titles or an identification convention that was traceable to the requirements. Unfortunately this insistence of documented procedures has not subsided entirely. There are still six mandatory documented procedures required by ISO 9001:2000 indicating a complete lack of imagination. They could have eliminated all requirements for documented procedures had they required a risk assessment be carried out.

Critics argue[5] that ISO 9000 did not enable organizations to reduce variation as a result of following the procedures. It is true that ISO 9000 did not explain the theory of variation – it could have done, but perhaps it was felt that this was better handled by the wealth of literature available at the time. However, ISO 9000 did require organizations to identify where the use of statistical techniques was necessary for establishing, controlling and verifying process capability but this was often misunderstood. Clause 4.14 of ISO 9001 required corrective action procedures – i.e. procedures to identify variation and eliminate the cause so this should have resulted in a reduction in variation. The procedures did not always focus on results – they tended to focus on transactions – sending information or product from A to B. The concept of corrective action was often misunderstood. It was believed to be about fixing the problem and preventive action was believed to be about preventing recurrence. Had users read ISO 8402 they should have been enlightened. Had they read Deming they would have been enlightened but in many cases the language of ISO 9000 was a deterrent to learning. Had the auditors understood variation, they could have assisted in clarifying these issues but they too seemed ignorant – willing to regard Clause 4.20 as not applicable in many cases. But in the automotive industry, things were different. SPC and process capability studies had been part of the quality programmes for many years, although these techniques were often only applied to the production line.

Clause 4.6 of the undervalued and forgotten standard ISO 9000-1 dated 1994, starts with "The International Standards in the ISO 9000 family are founded upon the understanding that all work is accomplished by a process". In Clause 4.7 it starts with "Every organization exists to accomplish value-adding work. The work is accomplished through a network of processes". In Clause 4.8 it starts with "It is conventional to speak of quality systems as consisting of a number of elements. The quality system is carried out by means of processes which exist both within and across functions". Alas, few people read ISO 9000-1 and as a result the baggage that had amassed was difficult to shed especially because there were few if any certification bodies suggesting that the guidance contained in ISO 9000-1 should be applied. Unfortunately, this message from ISO 9000-1 was not conveyed through the requirements of ISO 9001 and also ISO 9001 was not intended as a design tool. It was produced for contractual and assessment purposes but was used as a design tool instead of ISO 9000-1 and ISO 9004-1.

How we think about reviews, inspections and audits

Audits of the quality system were supposed to determine its effectiveness but effectiveness seemed to be judged by the extent to which procedures were being followed. ISO 9001 Clause 4.1.3 did state that *the system should be reviewed for its continuing suitability and effectiveness in satisfying the requirements of the standard and the supplier's quality policy and objectives.* The words underlined were added in the 1994 revision. Clause 4.17 did require internal audits to *verify whether quality activities and related results comply with planned arrangements and to determine the effectiveness of the quality system.* Again the words underlined were added in the 1994 revision. But the original and modified wording seemed to have had no effect. Quality systems continued to be judged on product nonconformities, audit findings and customer complaints.

The management review was supposed to question the validity of these procedures, the validity of the standards and the performance of the system. It was supposed to determine whether the system was effective – i.e. whether the system enabled people to do the right things right. But effectiveness was not interpreted as doing the right things; it was interpreted as conforming to the standard. It led to quality being thought of as conformity with procedures. The reviews and audits therefore focused on deficiencies against the requirements of the standard and deviations from procedure rather than the results the system was achieving. But as the system was not considered to be the way the organization achieved its results, it was not surprising that these totally inadequate management reviews continued in the name of keeping the badge on the wall. Audits did not establish that people were doing the right things – had they done so the system would have been changed to one that *caused people to do the right things right without having to be told*.

It was often thought that the standard required review, approval, inspection and audit activities to be performed by personnel independent of the work. Critics argue that as a consequence both worker and inspector assumed the other would find the errors. ISO 9000 does not require independent inspection. There is no requirement that prohibits a worker from inspecting his or her own work or approving his or her own documents. It is the management that chooses a policy of not delegating authority for accepting results to those who produce them. There will be circumstances when independent inspection is necessary either as a blind check or when safety, cost, reputation or national security could be compromised by errors. What organizations could have done, and this would have met ISO 9000 requirements, is to let the worker decide on the need for independent inspection except in special cases. Alternatively they could have carried out a risk assessment and imposed independent inspection where the risks warranted it. However, inspection is no substitute for getting it right first time and it is well known that you cannot inspect quality into an output if it was not there to begin with.

Is ISO 9000:2000 any different?

There are those who want to believe that the standard has not changed very much (if at all) and do not believe it has changed in its intent and as a consequence do not have to change their approach. The sad thing is that if the standard is perceived as not having significantly changed, it will continue to wreak havoc by being interpreted and used in the same inappropriate way that it has been for the last 20 years. But there is another way. By looking at ISO 9000 as a framework on which can be built a successful organization (rather than as a narrow set of minimum requirements) significant benefits can be gained. There are real benefits from managing organizations as a set of interconnected processes focused on achieving objectives that have been derived from an understanding of the needs of customers and other stakeholders.

While the requirements of ISO 9001 are expressed in a way that takes the reader through a cycle starting with the organization's purpose, leading onto quality policy and quality objectives and ending with performance being reviewed against objectives, there remain many inconsistencies and distractions that could lead to confusion. Many of the linkages between purpose, policy, objectives, processes and results are inferred – they are not expressed unambiguously. It is only by searching for understanding that a clear logic emerges. The use of the word *quality* creates an anomaly and tends to represent the standard as simply a tool to meet customer product or service quality requirements and no others. This is not to say that the standard is flawed. It is only saying that the concepts could be presented more clearly.

Misconceptions about the ISO 9000 family

Various misconceptions exist about the ISO 9000 family of standards. All of the following are untrue:

1. Products can be certified against ISO 9001. (Only organizations can be certified as compliant with ISO 9001.)
2. ISO 9001 is a management system. (Although the title of clause 0.3 of ISO 9001 is "Compatibility with other management systems" it is not intended to imply that ISO 9001 is a management system – ISO 9001 is a document not a system.)
3. The standard requires that you say what you do, do what you say and prove it. (A system needs to be established that enables the organization to satisfy the requirements of its customer and other stakeholders.)
4. The quality management system is the quality manual, procedures, instruction and records. (The quality manual, procedures, instruction and records is simply a description of the system – the system is that which generates the results, that which produces the outputs, that satisfy the stakeholders.)
5. Only 6 documented procedures are required. (The number of procedures required are those that are deemed necessary for the effective control and operation of the organization's processes.)
6. Process mapping is required for all processes. (The documentation can be in any form or medium. Processes need to be defined and documented to the extent necessary for effective operation and control.)
7. You have to appoint a Quality Manager. (A person needs to be appointed to ensure the system is established, implemented and maintained – what the job title is, is for the organization to decide.)
8. Job descriptions are required. (The responsibilities, authority and competences need to be defined – what the document is titled is for the organization to decide.)
9. All out of date documents have to be removed. (Obsolete documents may be retained if clearly identified as such.)
10. All purchases have to be from approved suppliers. (Suppliers need to be capable of meeting the organization's requirements.)
11. Purchase orders must be signed. (Orders need to be passed through a process that will ensure their adequacy prior to release.)

12. Documents have to carry an approval signature. (Documents need to be passed through a process that will ensure their adequacy prior to release.)
13. All measurements have to be made with calibrated instruments. (Measurement methods need to produce results of an accuracy and precision consistent with the measurement requirements.)

Summary

In this chapter we have examined the various perceptions about ISO 9000 and its infrastructure. These have arisen from personal observation, discussion with clients and colleagues and studying John Seddon's contribution in – *The Case Against ISO 9000*.

Wherever appropriate the perceptions are challenged from a basis of what the standard actually requires. This is no excuse for the resultant confusion. The standard could have been better written but it is unfair to put all the blame on the standard. The standards bodies, certification bodies, accreditation bodies, training providers, consultants, software providers and many others have contributed to this confusion. Commercial interests have as usual compromised quality. We have followed like sheep, pursued goals without challenging whether they were the right goals but most of all we have forgotten why we were doing this. It was to improve quality, but clearly it has not.

ISO 9000 merely brings together concepts that have been applied in organizations for many years – not some unique concepts of management that only exist to put a "badge on the wall", but it appears that the use of international standards to consolidate and communicate these concepts has not been as effective as we believed it would be. The BNFL problems with fake quality control records, the Firestone problem with unqualified materials, the SA 80 rifle that jams in cold weather, laser guided bombs that miss the target and the spate of problems with the railways in the UK all send the signal that we have not solved the problem of effectively managing quality. This is despite ISO 9000 and the teachings of Juran, Deming, Feigenbaum, Ishikawa, Crosby and the latest fad Six Sigma. ISO 9000:2000 is unlikely to change this situation because all these problems are caused by people who for one reason or another chose not to do the right things. All we can hope for is that people will learn from the mistakes of the past, use the family of standards more intelligently and raise the bar enough to enable more organizations to satisfy more customers and do less harm to society.

ISO 9000 has been influenced by disparate interests and thus is watered down, disjointed and tainted. An approach to the management of quality that has escaped this kind of treatment is process management and is presented in the next chapter. It is not yet the subject of national or international standards but many of the principles were adopted in the revision of ISO 9000. It is an approach that has yet to reach maturity.

Chapter 6

Managing quality using the process approach

> I must create a system or be enslaved by another man's;
> I will not reason and compare: my business is to create.
>
> **William Blake** *(1757–1827), English poet*

A general philosophy of process management

Function approach versus process approach

Most organizations are structured into functions that are collections of specialists performing tasks. The functions are like silos into which work is passed and executed under the direction of a function manager before being passed into another silo. In the next silo the work waits its turn because the people in that silo have different priorities and were not lucky enough to receive the resources they requested. Each function competes for scarce resources and completes a part of what is needed to deliver product to customers. This approach to work came out of the industrial revolution influenced firstly by Adam Smith and later by Frederick Taylor, Henry Fayol and others. When Smith and Taylor made their observations and formulated their theories, workers were not as educated as they are today. Technology was not as available and machines not as portable. Transportation of goods and information in the 18th and 19th centuries was totally different from today. As a means to transform a domestic economy to an industrial economy the theory was right for the time. Mass production would not have been possible under the domestic systems used at that time.

Drucker, defined a function as a collection of activities that make a common and unique contribution to the purpose and mission of the business.[1] Functional structures often include marketing, finance, research & development and production that are divided into departmental structures that include design, manufacturing, tooling, maintenance, purchasing, quality, personnel and accounting etc. In some cases the function is carried out by a single department and in other cases it is split among several departments. However, the combined expertise of all these departments are needed to fulfil a customer's requirement. It is rare to find one department or function that fulfils an organizational objective without the support of other departments or functions and yet, the functional structure has proved to be very successful primarily because it develops core competences and hence attracts individuals who want to have a career in a particular discipline. This is the strength of the functional structure but because work is always executed as a process it passes through a variety of functions before the desired results are achieved. This causes bottlenecks, conflicts and sub-optimization. A functional approach tends to create gaps between functions and does not optimize overall performance. One department will optimize its activities around its objectives at the expense of other departments. For example, the Purchasing function may have as its objective the minimization of costs and select suppliers on lowest price not realizing or even ignoring the fact that product quality is lower and as a consequence the Production function cannot meet its objectives for product quality. Similarly, a Finance function may have as its objective the optimization of cash flow and hold back payment of supplier invoices. Once again the production function feels the impact as suppliers refuse to deliver goods until outstanding invoices have been paid. One approach that aims to avoid these conflicts is what is referred to as "balancing objectives". On face value this might appear to be a solution but balancing implies that there is some give and take, a compromise or reduction in targets so that all objectives can be met. The result is often arrived at by negotiation implying that quality is negotiable when in reality it is not. Customers require products that meet their requirements not products that more or less meet their requirements.

When objectives are derived from stakeholder needs, internal negotiation is not a viable approach. The only negotiation is with the customer. If the customer requires X and the organization agrees to supply X, it is under an obligation to do so in a manner that satisfies the other stakeholders. If the organization cannot satisfy the other stakeholders by supplying X, it should negotiate with the customer and reach an agreement whereby the specification of X is modified to allow all stakeholders to be satisfied. If such an agreement cannot be reached the organization has to decline to supply under those conditions.

Some of the other differences are indicated in Table 6.1.

Functional outputs are indeed different from process outputs and obviously make an important contribution, but it is the outputs from business processes that are purchased by customers not the functional outputs.

When we organize work functionally the hierarchy can be represented by the waterfall diagram of Figure 6.1. In this diagram we observe that the top-level description of the way work is managed is contained in a Quality Manual with supporting Department Manuals. A common mistake when converting to a

Table 6.1 Function versus process

Attribute	Functional approach	Process approach
Objectives focus	Satisfying departmental ambitions	Satisfying stakeholder needs
Inputs	From other functions	From other processes
Outputs	To other functions	To other processes
Work	Task focused	Result focused
Teams	Departmental	Cross functional
Resources	Territorial	Shared
Ownership	Departmental manager	Shared
Procedures	Departmental based	Task based
Performance review	Departmental	Process

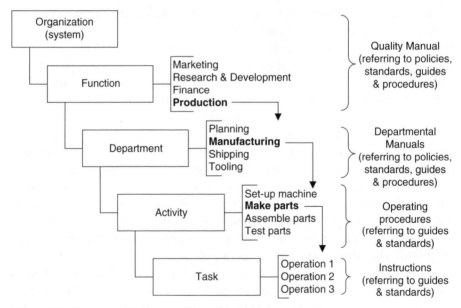

Figure 6.1 Functional decomposition of work

process approach is to simply group activities together and call them processes but retaining the Function/Department division. This perpetuates the practice of separating organization objectives into Departmental objectives and then into process objectives. This is not strictly managing work as a process at an organizational level. A more effective approach ignores functional and departmental boundaries as represented by Figure 6.2.

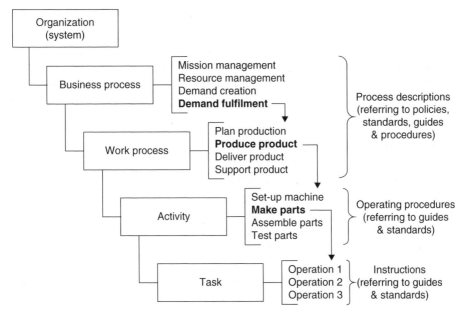

Figure 6.2 Process decomposition of work

Superficially it may appear as though all we have done is to change some words but it is more profound than that. By positioning the Business process at the top level we are changing the way work is managed. Instead of managing results by the contributions made by separate functions and departments, we manage the process which delivers the results regardless of which function or department does the work. This does not mean we disband the functions/departments; they still have a role in the organization or work. Work can be organized in three ways.[2] By stages in a process, by moving work to where the skill or tool is located or assembling a multi-skilled team and moving it to where the work is. In all of these cases we can still manage the work as a process or as a function. It comes down to what we declare as the objectives, how these were derived and how we intend to measure performance. If we ask three questions, "What are we trying to do, how will we make it happen and how will we know it's right?" we can either decide to make it happen through a process or through a number of functions/departments and measure performance accordingly. By "making it happen" through a process we overcome the disadvantages of the functional approach.

Business process re-engineering

Re-engineering is the fundamental rethinking and radical redesign of business processes to achieve dramatic improvements in critical contemporary measures of performance such as costs, quality, service and speed.[3] Business process re-engineering is about turning the organization on its head. Abandoning the old traditional way of organizing work as a set of tasks to organizing it as a process. According to Hammer, re-engineering means scrapping the organization charts and starting again. But this does not need to happen. Process Management is principally about managing processes that involve people. A functional organization structure might well reflect the best way to develop the talents, skills and competence of the people but not the best way of managing stakeholder needs and expectations.

Managing processes as well as functions

It ought to be possible to manage people one way and manage the work that they do in another way. It works with Project Management where the functional authority is retained by the line departments and project authority rests with a Project Manager. In project management, staff are seconded to a project and are responsible to a Project Manager for their contribution to the project, but their line manager retains responsibility for their performance. If we adopt the same approach with process management, functional authority would be retained by the line manager and process authority would rest with a Process Manager. All it does is give people two sets of objectives, one set based on the objectives of the process and the other set based upon the objectives of the function. The function will now focus on developing knowledge, techniques, skills and competences rather than producing business outputs.

Processes in the Excellence Model

The notion of Process Management has been evolving over a number of decades but has gained real momentum during the 1990s through a number of fashions and trends including "business re-engineering", "the business as a system" and "process mapping". The introduction of national quality awards such as the Malcolm Baldrige Award in the US (MBNQA), European Quality Award, UK Business Excellence Award and many others across the world has also brought in the notion of Process Management.

All of the "excellence" models are based upon a number of common, underlying principles, namely Leadership including organizational culture; Planning including strategy, policies, stakeholder expectation, resources; Process and Knowledge Management including innovation and problem solving, and finally Performance Results covering all stakeholder expectations. Pivotal to organizational success is effective and efficient process management. The EFQM Excellence Model® in Figure 6.3 clearly illustrates these principles and the importance of processes as an enabler of results.

However, on first encounter, the EFQM Excellence Model® appears to suggest that processes are separate from Leadership, People, Policy and Strategy, Partnerships and Resources because Processes are placed in a box with these factors shown as "inputs". This also suggests that the processes are more concerned with the "engine room" than the "boardroom". In reality, there are

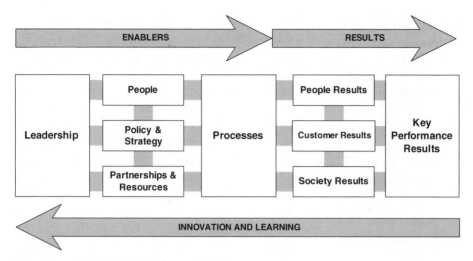

Figure 6.3 The EFQM Excellence Model

processes in the boardroom as well as the engine room. Clearly there must be strategic planning processes, policy-making processes, resource management processes, processes for building and maintaining partnerships and above all processes for leading the organization towards its goals. However, we must not forget that fundamentally the EFQM Excellence Model® is an assessment tool. It was not intended to be a design tool. It is used in assessing an organization's commitment to the excellence principles and to allow comparison of such commitment and performance between organizations.

Finding a definition

There are different schools of thought on what constitutes a process.

A process is defined in ISO 9000 as *a set of interrelated or interacting activities which transforms inputs into outputs* and goes on to state *that processes in an organization are generally planned and carried out under controlled conditions to add value*. The inclusion of the word *generally* tends to suggest that organizations may have processes that are not planned, not carried out under controlled conditions and do not add value and indeed they do!

Juran defines a process[4] as a systematic series of actions directed to the achievement of a goal. In Juran's model the inputs are the goals and required product features and the outputs are products possessing the features required to meet customer needs. The ISO 9000 definition does not refer to goals or objectives.

Hammer defines a process[5] as a collection of activities that takes one or more kinds of inputs and creates an output that is of value to the customer. Hammer places customer value as a criterion for a process unlike the ISO 9000 definition.

Davenport defines a process[6] as a structured measured set of activities designed to produce a specified output for a particular customer or market.

> **Procedures versus Processes**
>
> *The procedural approach is* about doing a task, conforming to the rules, doing what we are told to do.
>
> *The process approach* is about understanding needs, finding the best way of fulfilling these needs, checking whether the needs are being satisfied and in the best way and checking whether our understanding of these needs remains valid.

The concept of adding value and the party receiving the added value is seen as important in these definitions. This distinguishes processes from procedures.

It is easy to see how these definitions can be misinterpreted but it doesn't explain why for many it results in flowcharts they call processes. They may describe the process flow but they are not in themselves processes because they simply define transactions. A series of transactions can represent a chain from input to output but it does not cause things to happen. Add the resources, the behaviours, the constraints and make the necessary connections and you might have a process that will cause things to happen. Therefore any process description that does not connect the activities and resources with the objectives and results is invalid. In fact any attempt to justify the charted activities with causing the outputs becomes futile. The process approach would therefore be more accurately expressed as an approach to managing work in which the activities, resources and behaviours function together in such a relationship as to produce results consistent with the process objectives.

Process models

In the context of organizational analysis, a simple model of a process is shown in Figure 6.4. This appeared in ISO 9000–1:1994 but clearly assumes everything other than inputs and outputs are contained in the process. The process transforms the inputs into outputs but the diagram does not in itself indicate whether these outputs are of added value.

Figure 6.5 reminds us that processes can produce outputs that are not wanted therefore if we want to model an effective process we should modify the information displayed.

Another model (Figure 6.6) taken from BS 7850:1992[7] shows resources and controls to be external to the process implying that they are drawn into the process when needed and yet without either a process cannot function. So can a process be a process without them? If it can't, the label on the box should either be "activities" or these inputs should be removed. Some controls might be an output of another process as are resources but controls would be built-in to the process during process design and resources would be acquired when building a process other than any output specific resources. Therefore in this respect the diagram is misleading but it has been around for many years.

The process model adopted by ISO/TC 176 did show procedures as an external input to a process[8] but the updated version in 2003[9] (Figure 6.7) shows resources as inputs and qualifies the outputs as being "Requirements Satisfied" which is a far cry from simply outputs. The central box is also different. The

Figure 6.4   Simple process model

Figure 6.5   Unwanted process outputs

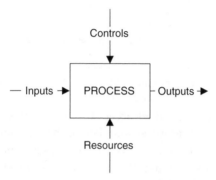

Figure 6.6   BS 7850 process model

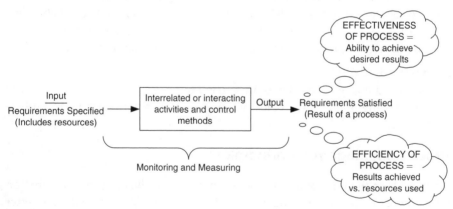

Figure 6.7   ISO 9000 process model

process label has now changed to activities which is more accurate. However, the diagram implies that as the resources are inputs they are all transformed into outputs or consumed by the process which clearly cannot be the case. People and facilities are resources and are not transformed or consumed by the process (assuming the process is functioning correctly!).

Therefore there would appear to be a difference between a process that transforms inputs into outputs and one that takes a requirement and produces a result

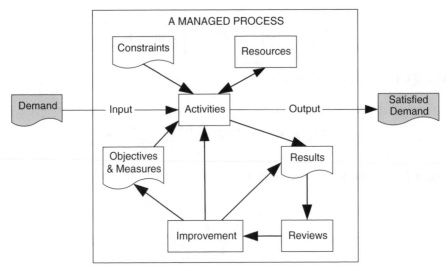

Figure 6.8 Advanced process model

that satisfies this requirement. If we accept that a process is a series of interrelated activities, behaviours and resources that delivers a result and an effective process as being one that achieves an objective, a more useful model might be that of Figure 6.8. This model shows that the process is resourced to receive a demand and when a demand is placed upon the process a number of predetermined activities are carried out using the available resources and constrained in a manner that will produce an output that satisfies the demand as well as the other stakeholders. These activities have been deemed as those necessary to achieve a defined objective and the results are reviewed and action taken where appropriate to

a) Improve the results.
b) Improve the way the activities are carried out.
c) Improve alignment of the objectives and measures with current and future demands.

Process management principles

As a result of the foregoing a set of seven principles has begun to emerge on which effective process management is based. They all begin with the letter "C" but that was not intentional until five of the seven turned out that way and then it seemed possible that "7C"s were within reach.

Consistency of purpose

Processes will deliver the required outputs when there is consistency between the process purpose and the external stakeholders. When this principle is applied the process objectives, measures, targets, activities, resources and reviews will have been derived from the needs and expectations of the stakeholders.

Clarity of purpose

Clear measurable objectives with defined targets establish a clear focus for all actions and decisions and enable the degree of achievement to be measured relative to stakeholder satisfaction. When this principle is applied people know what they are trying to do and how their performance will be measured.

Connectivity with objectives

The actions and decisions that are undertaken in any process will be those necessary to achieve the objectives and hence there will be demonstrable connectivity between the two. When this principle is applied the actions and decisions that people take will be those necessary to deliver the outputs needed to achieve the process objectives and no others.

Competence and capability

The quality of process outputs is directly proportional to the competence of the people, including their behaviour, and is also directly proportional to the capability of the equipment used by these people. When this principle is applied personnel will be assigned on the basis of their competence to deliver the required outputs and equipment will be selected on the basis of its capability to produce the required results.

Certainty of results

Desired results are more certain when they are measured frequently using soundly based methods and the results reviewed against the agreed targets. When this principle is applied people will know how the process is performing.

Conformity to best practice

Process performance reaches an optimum when actions and decisions conform to best practice. When this principle is applied work is performed in the manner intended and there is confidence that it is being performed in the most efficiency and effective way.

Clear line of sight

The process outputs are more likely to satisfy stakeholder expectations when periodic reviews verify whether there is a clear line of site between objectives, measures and targets and the needs and expectations of stakeholders. When this principle is applied, the process objectives, measures and targets will periodically, change causing realignment of activities and resources, thus ensuring continual improvement.

Using the principles

Whether you design, manage, operate, or evaluate a process you can apply these principles to verify whether the process is being managed effectively and is robust. You simply take one of the principles and look for evidence that it is being properly applied.

You will note that each principle has two parts. There is the principle and a statement of its application. So if we wanted to know whether there was consistency of purpose in a particular process, we review the principle, note what it says about its application and then examine in this case the process objectives, measures, targets, activities, resources and reviews to find evidence that they have been derived from the needs and expectations of the stakeholders. Clearly we would need to discover what the process designers established as the needs and expectations of the stakeholders. It would not be sensible for us to define stakeholder needs and expectations as this would more than likely yield different results. We are more interested in what data the process designers used. It is therefore more effective if questioning is used as the investigatory technique rather than a desk study.

Processes in context

If we regard Figure 3.2 as a realistic portrayal of the business cycle and we view the organization as a collection of interconnected processes we can derive a clear context for business processes. From this diagram we can conclude that

- The mission arises out of an analysis of stakeholder needs (there would certainly be little point in having a mission that conflicted with these needs).
- The mission is accomplished by the organization which as we have stated is a set of interconnected processes therefore the business processes exist to fulfil that mission.
- The results the stakeholders are looking for to satisfy their needs must equate to the business outputs.
- Business outputs are generated by business processes therefore the objectives for these processes are the business objectives (deliverable results).
- The business processes should therefore be designed to produce outputs that satisfy stakeholder needs.
- Within business processes we will find all the lower level processes because there should be no process or activity which exists outside this envelope.
- There is therefore only one system – a system of interconnected processes.
- Over time stakeholder needs and expectations change which in turn will modify the demands upon the business and its mission, and consequently the business processes and so the cycle continues.

Process classification

There are two classes of organizational processes – macro-processes and micro-processes. Macro-processes are multi-functional in nature consisting of numerous micro-processes. Macro-processes deliver business outputs and have been referred to as *Business Processes* for nearly a decade or more. For processes to be

Table 6.2 Relationship of business process to work processes

Scope	Business process	Work process
Relationship to organization hierarchy	Unrelated	Closely related
Ownership of process	No natural owner	Departmental head or supervisor
Level of attention	Executive level	Supervisory or operator level
Relationship to business goals	Directly related	Indirectly related and sometimes (incorrectly) unrelated
Responsibility	Multi-functional	Invariably single function (but not exclusively)
Customers	Generally external or other business processes	Other departments or personnel in same department
Suppliers	Generally external or other business processes	Other departments or personnel in same department
Measures	Quality, cost delivery	Errors, quantities, response time
Units of measure	Customer satisfaction, shareholder value, cycle time	% Defective, % Sales cancelled, % Throughput

classed as business processes they need to be in a chain of processes having the same stakeholder at each end of the chain. The input is an input to the business and the output is an output from the business. This is so that the outputs can be measured in terms of the inputs. If the outputs were a translation of the inputs they could not be measured against the inputs.

Micro-processes deliver departmental outputs and are task oriented. In this book these are referred to as *Work Processes*. A management system is not just a collection of work processes, but also the interconnection of business processes. The relationship between these two types of processes is addressed in Table 6.2.[10]

The American Quality and Productivity Centre published a Process Classification framework in 1995 to encourage organizations to see their activities from a cross-industry process viewpoint instead of from a narrow functional viewpoint. The main classifications were as follows:

1. Understand markets and customers.
2. Develop vision and strategy.
3. Design products and services.
4. Market and sell.
5. Produce and deliver for manufacturing.
6. Produce and deliver for service organizations.
7. Invoice and service customers.
8. Develop and manage human resource.
9. Manage information resources.

10. Manage financial and physical resources.
11. Execute environmental management program.
12. Manage external relationships.
13. Manage improvement and change.

This classification was conceived out of a need for organizations to make comparisons when benchmarking their processes. It was not intended as a basis for designing management systems. We can see from this list that several processes have similar outputs, e.g. there are a group of processes with resources as the output. Also, some of these processes are not core processes but themes running through core processes, e.g. the process for executing an environmental management program has a process design element but its implementation will be embodied in other result producing processes as it does not on its own form part of a chain of processes. Similarly with managing external relations, there will be many processes that have external interfaces so rather than one process there should be objectives for external relationships that are achieved by all processes with external interfaces.

There is a view that product design is not a business process because the stakeholders are different at each end. On the input end could be sales and the output end could be produce and deliver. Under this logic, produce and deliver would not be a business process because on the input could be product design and the output could be the customer. Therefore the business process flow is: customer to sales; sales to product design, product design to produce and deliver; produce and deliver to customer and customer to bank. Using this logic we could combine another group of these processes so that the business process is "order to cash". The important point here is that the measure of success is not whether a design is completed on time, or a product meets its specification but whether the products designed, produced and delivered satisfy customer requirements to the extent that the invoice is paid in full.

With this approach, there would be one process that creates a demand for the organization's products and services. This is often referred to as marketing but this is also the label given to a department, therefore we need a different term to avoid confusion. A suitable name might be Demand creation process.

Having created a demand, there must be a process that fulfils this demand. This might be production but if the customer requirement is detailed in performance terms rather than in terms of a solution, it might also include product design. There are many other ways of satisfying a demand and once again to avoid using labels that are also names of departments, a suitable name might be a Demand fulfilment process.

Both these processes need capable resources and clearly the planning, acquisition, maintenance and disposal of these resources would not be part of demand creation or fulfilment as resources is not an output of these processes. There is therefore a need for a process that manages the organization's resources and so we might as well call this the Resource management process.

Lastly, all the work involved in determining stakeholder needs, determining the mission, the vision and strategy, the business outputs and designing the processes to deliver these outputs is clearly a separate process. It is also important that the performance of the organization is subject to continual review and improvement and this is clearly a process. But neither can exist in isolation, they are in fact a continuum and when brought together would have the same stakeholder at each end. We have a choice of names for this process. We could call it a business management process but we might call the system the business management system so this could cause confusion. As the process plans the direction of the business and reviews performance against plan we could call this process the mission management process. The main classifications from the process classification framework can therefore be combined as shown in Table 6.3.

> **Process naming**
>
> Processes can be named using the verb focused convention e.g. Create demand, or the noun focused convention e.g. Demand creation. The advantage of verb focused naming is that the name of the process defines the action or process purpose whereas with the noun focused convention, the action or purpose could be obscured. It may also be confused with department names such as naming a process "Marketing".

We have identified four processes into which we could place all an organization's activities therefore there will be only four business processes in most organizations but many work processes. These are displayed diagrammatically in Figure 6.9 and the purpose of each process explained as follows with Table 6.4 showing the stakeholders.

Mission management process	Determines the direction of the business, continually confirms that the business is proceeding in the right direction and makes course corrections to keep the business focused on its mission. The business processes are developed within mission management as the enabling mechanism by which the mission is accomplished
Resource management process	Specifies, acquires and maintains the resources required by the business to fulfil the mission and disposes of any resources that are no longer required
Demand creation process	Penetrates new markets and exploits existing markets with products and a promotional strategy that influences decision-makers and attracts potential customers to the organization. New product development would form part of this process if the business were market driven
Demand fulfilment process	Converts customer requirements into products and services in a manner that satisfies all stakeholders. New product development would form part of this process if the business were order driven (i.e. the order contained performance requirements for which a new product or service had to be designed)

Table 4.3 Process classification alignment

Process Classification Framework (Main classifications)	*Business Processes*
Understand markets and customers	
Develop vision and strategy	
Manage improvement and change	Mission management
Execute environmental management program	
Manage external relationships	
Design products and services	
Market and sell	Demand creation
Produce and deliver for service organizations	
Produce and deliver for manufacturing	Demand fulfilment
Invoice and service customers	
Develop and manage human resource	
Manage information resources	Resource management
Manage financial and physical resources	

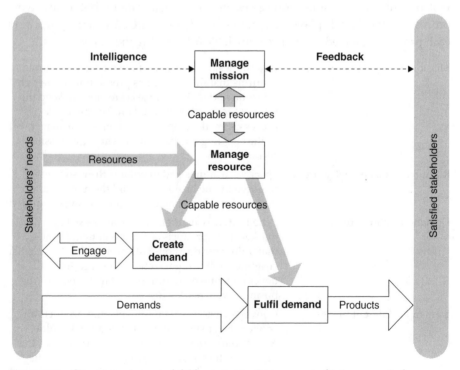

Figure 6.9 Generic system model (the organization as a set of interconnected processes)

ITEM ON HOLD

le: Quality : management
      essentials / David Hoyle.

thor: Hoyle, David.

umeration:

ronology:

py: 1

m Barcode:

0 3 6 7 6 9 3 9

em Being Held

atron: Carina L Kaiser

atron Barcode:

3 0 0 2 1 3 7 2 5

atron Phone:

old Expires: 12/14/2012

ickup At: Kelowna Circulation Desk

atron Comment

Table 6.4   Business process stakeholders

Business process	Input stakeholder (Inputs)	Output stakeholder (Outputs)
Mission management	Shareholders, Owners (Vision)	Shareholders, Owners (Mission accomplished)
Demand creation	Customer (Need)	Customer (Demand)
Demand fulfilment	Customer (Demand)	Customer (Demand satisfied)
Resource management	Resource user (Resource need)	Resource user (Resource satisfies need)

Previously we said that all work is a process but as we have seen what we regard as a process depends on our perception. If we were to ask the same question of three workers cutting stone on a building site we might be surprised to get three different answers.

We approach the first stone cutter and ask,

"What are you doing?"

"Breaking stone" he replies rather abruptly

This stone cutter appears to have no vision of what he is doing beyond the task and will therefore be blind to its impact

We approach the second stone cutter and ask,

"What are you doing?"

"I'm making a window" he replies with enthusiasm

This stone cutter sees beyond the task to a useful output but not where this output fits in the great scheme of things

We approach the third stone cutter and ask,

"What are you doing?"

"I am building a Cathedral" he replies with considerable pride

This stone cutter sees himself as part of a process and has a vision of what he is trying to achieve that will influence what he does.

If we allow ourselves to be persuaded that a single task is a process, we might well deduce that our organization has several thousand processes. If we go further and try to manage each of these nano-processes (they are smaller than micro-processes) we will lose sight of our objective very quickly. By seeing where the task fits in the activity, the activity fits within a process and the process fits within a system, we create a line of sight to the overall objective. By managing the system we manage the processes and in doing this we manage the activities. However, system design is crucial. If the processes are not designed to function together to fulfil the organizational goals, they can't be made to do so by tinkering with the activities.

So, in which process do you work?

Characteristics of a process

Process purpose

From the definitions of a process it is clear that every process needs a purpose for it to add value. The purpose provides a reason for its existence. The purpose statement should be expressed in terms of what the process does and in doing so identify what if anything is to be converted. The purpose of a sales process may be to convert prospects into orders for the organization's products. Instead of calling the process a sales process you could call it the *prospect to order process*. Similarly the purpose of a design process may be to convert customer needs into product features that satisfy these needs.

Process outputs

The outputs of a process are considered to be the tangible or intangible results such as a product or result. The principal process outputs will be the same as the process objectives.

However, for a process output to be an objective it has to be predefined – in other words it has to be something you are aiming for, not necessarily something you are currently achieving. An example may clarify this. A current process output might be 50 units/week but this does not mean that 50 units/week is the objective. The objective might be to produce only 20 conforming units/week so of the 50 produced, how many are conforming? If all are conforming the process is producing surplus output. If less than 20 are conforming the process is out of control. Therefore doing what you are currently doing may not be achieving what you are trying to do.

The outputs from business processes should be the same as the business outputs and these should arise out of an analysis of stakeholder needs and expectations. If we ask *"What will the stakeholders be looking for as evidence that their needs and expectations are being satisfied?"* the answers constitute the outputs that the business needs to produce. From this we ask, *"Which process will deliver these outputs?"* and we have now defined the required process outputs for each business process.

Process outcomes

In addition to outputs, processes have outcomes. There is an effect that the process has on its surroundings. An outcome of a process may be a detrimental affect on the environment. Satisfaction of either customers or employees is an outcome not an output. However, processes can only be designed to deliver outputs because the outputs are measured before they emerge from the process, whereas, outcomes arise long after the process has delivered its outputs and therefore cannot be used to control process performance. Any attempt to do so would induce an erratic performance. (See process measures) Outcomes are controlled by process design – i.e. you design the process to deliver the outputs that will produce the desired outcomes.

Process objectives

As the objective of any process is to deliver the required results, it follows that we can discover the process objectives from an analysis of its required outputs. All that is required is to construct a sentence out of the output. For example, if the output is growth in the number of enquiries the process objective is to grow the number of enquiries. Clearly the output is not simply enquiries as is so often depicted on process flowcharts. The process measurements should determine growth not simply whether or not there were enquiries.

In some cases the wording might need to be different whilst retaining the same intent. For example, a measure of employee satisfaction might be, staff turnover and management style may be considered a critical success factor. The output the employee is looking for as evidence that management have adopted an appropriate style is a motivated workforce. Motivation is a result but there is no process that produces motivation. It is an effect not an output. Instead of expressing the objective of the process as to motivate the workforce, it becomes "To maintain conditions that sustain worker motivation."

Process measures

Measures are the characteristics used to judge performance. They are the characteristics that need to be controlled in order that an objective will be achieved. Juran refers to these as the control subject.

There are two types of measures – stakeholder measures and process measures. Stakeholder measures respond to the question: *"What measures will the stakeholders use to reveal whether their needs and expectations have been met?"* Some call these key performance indicators. Process measures respond to the question: *"What measures will reveal whether the process objectives have been met?"* Profit is a stakeholder measure of performance (specifically the shareholders) but would be of no use as a process measure because it is a lagging measure. Lagging measures indicate an aspect of performance long after the conditions that created it have changed. To control a process we need leading measures. Leading measures indicate an aspect of performance while the conditions that created it still prevail (e.g. response time, conformity).

There are also output driven measures and input driven measures. Measures defined in verbs are more likely to be input driven. Those defined by nouns are more likely to be output driven, e.g. in an office cleaning process we can either measure performance by whether the office has been cleaned when required or by whether the office is clean. The supervisor asks, "Have you cleaned the office?" The answer might be yes because you dragged a brush around the floor an hour ago. This is an input driven measure because it is focused on a task. But if the supervisor asks, "Is the office clean?" You need some criteria to judge cleanliness – this is an output driven measure because it is focused on the purpose of the process.

The word "measures" does have different meanings. It can also refer to activities being undertaken to implement a policy or objective, e.g. a Government minister says "You will begin to see a distinct reduction in traffic congestion as a result of the measures we are taking". Clearly, traffic congestion has not been reduced by measuring it but by the provisions made to alter traffic flow.

Process measures are not the same as Stakeholder measures. Process measures need to be derived from stakeholder measures. A typical example of where they are not was the case in the UK National Health Service. Performance of hospitals was measured by waiting time for operations but the patient cares more about total unwell time. Even if the hospital operation waiting time was zero, it still might take 2 years getting through the system from when the symptoms first appear to when the problem is finally resolved. There are so many other waiting periods in the process that to only measure one of them is totally misleading. Other delays started to be addressed once the waiting time for operations fell below the upper limit set by Government but in the interim period time was lost in addressing other bottlenecks.

Process measurement methods

The integrity of the process measurement depends on the method of measurement. If we use crude measurement methods such as gut feel, perceptions or hearsay evidence the results will be suspect. Results need to be obtained using soundly based measurement methods that extract facts from the process. Some thought needs to go into:

1. Installing a sensor in the process at the appropriate stage to measure the prescribed aspect of performance.
2. Taking measurements at predetermined intervals.
3. Collecting data pertinent to the aspect of performance measured.
4. Transmitting the data to appropriate locations for analysis.
5. Analysing data to reveal meaningful information.
6. Presenting the results to the decision-makers in a format that displays with the required accuracy and precision a true measure of performance relative to the desired results.

The sensor should be accommodated as part of process design and the other stages should be a process activity.

Process targets

Measurements will produce data but not information. Managers need to know whether the result is good or bad. So when someone says "Are we on target?" the target obviously needs to be known and related to what is being measured which is why the targets are set only after determining the measurement method. Setting targets without any idea of the capability of the process is futile. Setting targets without any idea what process will deliver them is incompetence – but it is not uncommon for targets to be set without any thought

> **Targets within reach**
>
> Managers can only expect average results from average people and perhaps there are not enough extraordinary people to go round to produce the extraordinary results they demand!

being given to the process that will achieve them. Staff might be reprimanded for results over which they have no control; staff might suffer frustration and stress trying to achieve an unachievable target.

A realistic method for setting targets is to monitor what the process currently achieves, observe the variation, then set a target that on an 80:20 basis the process can deliver. There is clearly no point in setting a target well above current performance unless we are prepared to redesign the whole process. However, performance measurement should be iterative.

Process inputs

In Figure 6.9 the input is the demand placed upon the process rather than some material that needs to be transformed. If we were to look into the process activities we would probably find activities where the input was material which is transformed by the activity but this is at the micro-process level. If we take the ISO 9000 definition of a process we will see that the process transforms inputs into outputs of added value but it is not clear what the inputs are. If we regard instructions, requirements, objectives or any documents as inputs we know they are not transformed by the process. If we regard resources as inputs we know that some resources such as the people operating the process are not transformed. Therefore it is incorrect to simply say that processes transform inputs into outputs because you need to define what inputs you are referring to.

Process activators

Processes need to be activated in order to produce results. The activator or trigger can be event based, time based or input based. With an event activated process operations commence when something occurs e.g. a Disaster Recovery Process. With a time activated process operations commence when a date is reached, e.g. an Annual Review Process. With an input activated process operations commence on receipt of a prescribed input, e.g. printed books are received into the binding process.

The concept of process activators enables us to see more clearly how processes operate and better understand the realities of process management.

Process activities

Process activities are the actions and decisions that collectively deliver the process outputs. They include all the activities in the PDCA cycle. Deming's Plan, Do, Check, Act cycle is a good model with which to determine the activities needed. At a high level the sequence might be as follows:

a) On receipt of a demand there will be planning activities to establish how the deliverables will be produced and delivered.
b) There will be doing activities that implement the plans.
c) There will be checking activities to verify the plans have been implemented as intended and that the output conforms with the prescribed requirements.
d) There will be activities resulting from the checking in order to correct mistakes or modify the plans.

In principle it should be possible to place all activities needed to achieve an objective into one of these categories. In reality there may be some processes where the best way of doing something does not follow exactly in this sequence.

Depending on the level within the process hierarchy, an activity might be as grand as "Design product" or as small as "Verify drawing". There are several Activity Levels. If we examine this hierarchy in the Demand Creation Process (see Fig 6.13 on pages 146, 147) the result might be as follows:

A Level 1 Activity might be "Develop new product". If we view this activity as a process we can conceive of a series of activities that together produce a new product design. These we will call Level 2 Activities.

A Level 2 Activity might be "Plan new product development". If we view this activity as a process we can conceive of a further series of activities that together produce a new product development plan. These we will call Level 3 Activities.

A Level 3 Activity might be "Verify new product development plan". If we view this activity as a process we can conceive of a further series of activities that together produce a record of new product development plan verification. These we will call Level 4 Activities.

A Level 4 Activity might be "Select verification record blank". Now if we were to go any further in the hierarchy we would be in danger of noting arm movements. Therefore in this example we have reached the limit of activities at Level 4.

If we now examine these series of activities and look for those having an output that serves a stakeholder's needs we will find that there are only two. The Demand creation process has "demand" as its output. This serves the customer and the New product development process has "Product design" as its output and this also serves the customer. The series of New product development planning activities has an output which is only used by its parent process so remains a series of activities. The activity of "Verify product design plan" and "Select verification record blank" only have any meaning within the context of a specific process so cannot be classed as processes.

Process flow

A process is often depicted as a flowchart representing a sequence of activities with an input at one end and an output at the other. When the process activator is an input this might well be the case but it is by no means always the case. If we examine the Demand Creation process illustrated in Figure 6.13, page 147, we find that while the activity of converting enquiries follows that of promoting product, by presenting these activities as a flow it implies not only that one follows the other but the latter does not commence until the former has been completed. This is clearly not the case. Product promotion continues well after the first enquires are received and enquires may well come in before the first promotion activity has started.

Where the output depends upon work being executed in a defined sequence then it can be represented as a flowchart but when activities are activated by events or by time as opposed to inputs, there may be no flow between them.

Process resources

The resources in a process are the supplies that can be drawn on when needed by the process. Resources are classified into human, physical and financial resources. The physical resources include materials, equipment, plant and machinery but also include time. Human resources include managers and staff including employees, contractors, volunteers and partners. The financial resources include money, credit and sponsorship. Resources are used or consumed by a process. There is a view that resources to a process are used (not consumed) and are those things that don't change during the process. People and machinery are resources that are used (not consumed) because they are the same at the start of the process as they are at the end, i.e. they don't lose anything to the process. Whereas materials, components and money are either lost to the process, converted or transformed and could therefore be classed as process inputs. People would be inputs not resources if the process transforms them.

For a process to be deemed operational it must be resourced. A process that has not been resourced remains in development or moribund. There is a view that resources are acquired by the process when required and indeed, input specific resources are, but resources that are independent of the inputs such as energy, tooling, machinery, people etc. and the channel along which they flow will have been established during process development. Resources are often shared and depleted and have to be replenished but the idea that a process can exist on paper is not credible. A process exists when it is ready to be activated. Those processes that are activated infrequently need to be resourced otherwise they will not be capable of delivering the desired outputs on demand. For instance, you would not set out to acquire back-up software after there had been a computer failure unless you were managing by the seat of your pants!

Process constraints

The constraints on a process are the things that limit its freedom. Policies, procedures, codes of practices etc. all constrain how the activities are carried out. Actions should be performed within the boundaries of the law and regulations impose conditions on such aspects as hygiene, emissions and the internal and external environment. They may constrain resources (including time), effects, methods, decisions and many other factors depending on the type of process, the risks and its significance with respect to the business and society. Constraints may also arise out of the PEST and SWOT analysis carried out to determine the Critical Success Factors (see later in this Chapter). Values, principles and guidelines are also constraints that limit freedom for the benefit of the organization. After all it wouldn't do for everyone to have his or her own way! Some people call these things **controls** rather than constraints but include among them, the customer requirements that trigger the process and these could just as well be inputs. Customer requirements for the most part are objectives not constraints

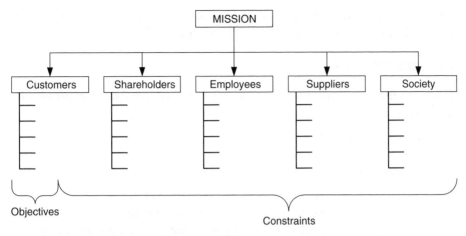

Figure 6.10 Identifying constraints and objectives

but they may include constraints over how those objectives are to be achieved. For instance they may impose sustainability requirements that constrain the options open to the designer.

To determine the objectives and constraints pass the mission through the stakeholders and ask *What are this stakeholder's needs and expectations relative to our mission?"* The result will be a series of needs and expectations that can be classified as objectives or constraints. The objectives arise from the outputs the customer requires and the constraints arise from the conditions the other stakeholders impose relative to these outputs as illustrated in Figure 6.10. The important thing to remember about constraints is that they only apply when relevant to the business, e.g. if you don't use substances hazardous to health in your organization the regulations regarding their acquisition, storage, use and disposal are not applicable to your organization.

Views differ and whilst a purist might argue that requirements are controls not inputs, and materials are inputs not resources, it matters not in the management of quality. All it might affect is the manner in which the process is described diagrammatically. The requirements would enter the process from above and not from the side if you drew the chart as a horizontal flow.

Process results

The results of a process arise out of measuring performance using the planned methods for the defined measures, at the planned frequency and against the planned targets.

If the planned measurement methods have been implemented there should be sufficient objective evidence with which to compare current performance against the agreed targets. Therefore one would expect the results to be presented as graphs, charts, and figures. These might show performance to be improving, declining or remaining unchanged relative to a particular process parameter.

The scale is important as are trends over time so that decision-makers can see the whole picture and not be led into a knee jerk reaction.

Process reviews

There are three dimensions of process performance that can be expressed by three questions:

a) *How are we doing against the plan?*
b) *Are we doing it in the best way?*
c) *How do we know it's the right thing to do?*

The first question establishes whether the objectives are being achieved in the way that had been planned to achieve them. This means that not only are planned outputs being produced but when you examine the process throughput over the last week, month, year or even longer, the level and quality of the output is consistent and these outputs are being produced in the way you said you would produce them i.e. you are adhering to the specified policies and procedures etc.

The second question establishes whether the ways in which the planned results are being achieved are best practice, e.g. optimizing resources (time, finance, people, space, materials etc.) such that they are utilized more efficiently and effectively. This would mean that you are satisfied that you are achieving your objective using no more than the allocated resources but can reduce the operating cost by optimizing the resources or using more appropriate resources such as new technologies, new materials, new working practices. These improvements arise out of doing things better not by removing waste. If planned output were being achieved there would be no unavoidable waste. A technique often used in this context is Value Engineering.

The third question establishes whether the planned outputs are still appropriate and relevant to meeting stakeholder needs and expectations. This would mean that irrespective of the planned results being achieved and irrespective of utilizing best practices we could be wasting our time if the goal posts have moved. Maybe the needs and expectations of stakeholders have changed. Maybe they no longer measure our performance in the same way. Some objectives remain unchanged for years, others change rapidly. As all our outputs are derived from stakeholder needs and expectations it is vital to establish that the outputs remain continually relevant and appropriate.

The answers to each of these questions require a different approach because the purpose, method and timing of these reviews are different. This results in there being three specific and independent process reviews.

Making the connections

It is important to visualize the complete picture when setting out to define and manage your processes. Processes exist in a context to deliver against an objective that also serves to deliver a strategic objective. As illustrated in Figure 3.3, there is a continuum from stakeholders to mission through the system to results and back to the mission. The arrows form connections so that there is a clear line of sight from the results to the mission and this will only be accomplished if those carrying out strategic planning realize that processes cause results. Processes will not cause the right results unless the process objectives have been derived from the mission. The measures employed to indicate work process performance need to relate to the measures employed in the related business process so that when all the measures indicate that the system is performing as it should, the strategic objectives are being achieved.

Process effectiveness

A process should be effective but what determines its effectiveness? How would you know whether a process is effective? Effectiveness is about doing the right things – so what should a process do? Firstly and most obviously the process should deliver the required output, namely a decision, a document, a product or a service. But there is much more. It is not sufficient merely to deliver output. Output that is of poor quality is undesirable as is output that is late. But even when the output is of good quality and on time there are other factors to be considered. If in producing the output the laws of the land are breached, the process is clearly not effective. If in producing the output, the producers are exploited, are forced to work under appalling conditions or become de-motivated and only deliver the goods when stimulated by fear, the process is again not effective. So we could fix all these factors and deliver the required output on time and have satisfied employees.

Employees are but one of the stakeholders and customers are the most important but although an output may be of good quality to its producers, it may not be a product that satisfies customers. The costs of operating the process may not yield a profit for the organization and its shareholders, and even if in compliance with current environmental laws, it may waste natural resources, dissatisfy the community and place unreasonable constraints on suppliers such that they decline to supply the process's material inputs. There is therefore only one measure of process effectiveness – that the process outcomes satisfy all stakeholders.

Developing a process-based management system

Every organization is different but has characteristics in common with others. Even in the same industry, the same market, producing the same type of products, each organization will be different in what it wants to do, how it goes about doing it and how it perceives its stakeholders and their needs. It is therefore not possible to design one system that will suit all organizations. Each has to be tailored to the particular characteristics of the organization and their stakeholders. However, just as human beings have the same organs and processes that differ in size and capability, organizations will have similar functions and processes that differ in size and capability.

In Figure 3.2 we showed that the mission is achieved by the organization that produces results that delight the stakeholders that place demands that shape the mission – and on it goes through a continuous cycle. In Figure 6.9 we showed how the organization (shown in Figure 3.2 in the cycle) could be viewed as a set of interconnected processes. These processes are present in all organizations – hence the label – Generic System Model. All organizations seek to *create a demand* – even non-profit organizations. All organizations seek to fulfil the demand, again even non-profit organizations and all organizations need resources to create and fulfil the demand and therefore have a resource management process. Finally all organizations have a purpose and a mission (even if it is not well defined) and seek to develop and improve their capability and their performance so as to achieve their mission – thus all organizations have a mission management process. This is of course at a very high level. The differences arise within the detail of each business process.

Whilst the generic purpose of these processes might be common in all organizations, the structure of them may well be different for each organization but a pattern of actions has emerged that can be used to flush out the information necessary to design these processes. Who or which function performs these activities is not important – in fact letting the function get in the way, often changes the outcome such that instead of developing a process based management system, you end up with a function-based management system that simply mirrors the organization structure.

Establishing the goals

Every organization has goals or what it wants to achieve, how it wants to be perceived and where it is going. These goals are often formed by looking both inwards and outwards and are expressed relative to the needs and expectations of stakeholders or benevolent interested parties. There are four distinct steps to establishing goals:

1. Clarify the organization's purpose, mission and vision (goals). – This is what the organization has been formed to do and the direction in which it is proceeding in the short and long term. It is the "organization purpose" that is referred to in Clause 5.3a) of ISO 9001.
2. Confirm the values and principles that will guide the organization towards its goals. – These are addressed by Clause 5.3 of ISO 9001 under the heading *Quality policy.*
3. Identify stakeholder needs relative to the purpose, mission and vision. – This is addressed by Clause 5.2 of ISO 9001 under the heading *Customer focus.*
4. Identify stakeholder satisfaction measures relative to these needs. – These are addressed by Clause 5.4.1 of ISO 9001 under the heading Quality objectives.

Purpose is clarified by top management confirming why the organization exists or for what purpose it has been established such as to exploit the gap in the market for personal communicators.

Mission is clarified by top management confirming the direction in which the organization is currently proceeding such as to provide personal communicators that are high on reliability, security, safety and data accessibility.

Vision is clarified by top management confirming what they want the organization to become in the years ahead, what they want it to be known for or known as such as being a world-class brand leader in personal communications.

Values are confirmed by top management expressing what they believe are the fundamental principles that guide the organization in accomplishing its goals, what it stands for such as integrity, excellence, innovation, reliability, responsibility, fairness etc. These values characterize the culture in the organization. It is ironic that even ENRON had values. They were: Respect, Integrity, Communication and Excellence.

Stakeholder needs

As explained previously all organizations have stakeholders, those people or organizations on which the organization depends for its success. They include customers, shareholders, employees, suppliers and society as a number of discrete groups rather than individuals. In order to identify the stakeholder needs, you need to examine the stakeholders relative to the purpose, mission, vision and values and the results will be a distinct set of needs and expectations.

Customers might need on-time delivery, high reliability, low life cycle cost, disposable product, prompt after-sales response etc. If customer focus were an organizational value (the 1st Quality Management Principle), customers might expect sales staff to frequently test their understanding of requirements.

Shareholders might need financial return on investment and above average growth. If a factual approach to decision making were an organizational value (the 7th Quality Management Principle), shareholders might expect business results to have been derived from facts and not have been massaged to make them look better than really they were.

Employees might need competitive pay and conditions, flexible working hours and crèche. If responsibility were an organizational value, the employees might expect to be delegated authority and provided with the resources for them to use as they see fit to achieve their assigned objectives and to be trusted to use the resources wisely.

Suppliers might need prompt payment of invoices, loyalty in exchange for flexibility. If mutually beneficial supplier relationships were an organizational value (the 8th Quality Management Principle), suppliers would not expect the relationship they had with the organization to be adversarial.

Society might need compliance with statutory laws and regulations, corporate responsibility, employment prospects for the local community. If inclusion were an organizational value, the local community would expect consultation before a decision was taken that affected the quality of life in the community.

Stakeholder satisfaction measures

Each of the stakeholders will be looking for certain outcomes as evidence that their needs have been met. These become the organization's performance indicators (KPIs) or outcomes and hence the corporate objectives that need to be achieved. So if customers were expecting a prompt after-sales response, how would the degree of promptness be measured? What might constitute an after-sales service? What would be the characteristics that would put the prompt after-sales service in a competitive position?

Determine critical success factors

Whatever you set out to achieve, you will not get very far unless you are conscious of the factors critical to your success. Many people do this subconsciously – always being aware of waste, relationships, customers etc. But you can be a little more scientific about this. Our question here is: *"What factors affect our ability to get it right?"* The answers identify the critical success factors – the factors upon which our success depends. They are the drivers and barriers to success. Get these wrong and you will undoubtedly fail. Drivers will help you succeed, they will propel you towards your goal. Barriers will get in the way and stop you achieving your goal. Some of these are external to the organization and out of your control. Others are internal to the organization and within your control. You can change these should there be the motivation to do so. This is where we enter the arena of the management of change. It is not only technological change but changes in attitude, behaviour, belief etc. that may be needed depending on what the goal is and the environment in which this goal is to be achieved.

These are not the same as stakeholder measures that are pertinent to what stakeholders are looking for or Key Performance Indicators. Critical success factors (CSF) are pertinent to the survival of the organization and although this does depend largely on satisfying stakeholders and meeting business objectives, there will be other factors that influence the organization's ability to do this. These factors will impose constraints on the processes established to accomplish the mission.

The CSFs can be determined simply by asking the question of the organization or a particular business proposition, *"What factors affect our ability to get it right?"* but the result might be a mixed bag of things, some of which may be more relevant to a process risk assessment. Two techniques have emerged that are more methodical, one is a PEST analysis and the other is a SWOT analysis. It is important when using these tools to:

● Identify the relevant factors that apply to your organization.

- Rate your organization relative to the factors.
- Draw conclusions from this information relative to the mission, objective or business proposition i.e. is it critical or non-critical to success.
- Validate these conclusions with others.

PEST (Political, Economic, Social and Technological) analysis measures the market relative to a particular organization or business proposition. It serves to identify what is going on in the external environment that could affect the future direction of the organization or the success of a business proposition. The significance of the four factors may vary depending on the nature of the business. Some principal factors to consider are shown in Table 6.5. More factors can be found on the Internet.

The SWOT (Strengths, Weaknesses, Opportunities and Threats) analysis looks at the organization itself or a business proposition or indeed a competitor. The PEST affects the SWOT but not vice versa. Without a clear understanding of an organization's strengths, weaknesses, opportunities and threats business plans may fail, goals will be missed and new product or service development programmes will fail to live up to their potential. The SWOT is akin to a capability assessment. The result enables management to act in a manner that does not leave the organization vulnerable. Strengths and weaknesses are internal to your organization whereas opportunities and threats are external. The results are often very subjective and will vary depending on who does the analysis. SWOT should be used as a guide but use of weighting factors can improve its validity. Some principal factors to consider are shown in Table 6.6. More factors can be found on the Internet.

Develop the processes

Having identified the organizational goals, the drivers and barriers (the critical success factors) we would then develop the business processes that are required to achieve these goals. This involves us in identifying these processes, establishing the process outputs, the units of measure and the targets that will indicate that the outputs are acceptable. This approach also goes under the name Quality Function Deployment (QFD) – a somewhat unfortunate expression as it can imply that it is about deploying people from quality departments.

Processes deliver results and effective processes achieve objectives therefore they make things happen. The key question therefore is, "Knowing the goals, the drivers and the barriers, how will we make it happen?" The relationship between all the key elements in developing the goals, the success factors and the processes is illustrated in Figure 6.11. This puts all the terms in context.

There are eight distinct steps to developing processes:

1. Identify the processes that will deliver the business outputs i.e. the *Business processes*.

Table 6.5   PEST Factors[11]

Political	*Economic*
● Environmental, health and safety and consumer-protection legislation	● Business and sales taxation issues
● Freedom of press, discrimination, trading ethics, levels of corruption	● Exchange rates, overseas economic situation, trends and potential changes
● Funding, grants and initiatives	● Impact of globalization
● Legal, ethical and law enforcement issues	● Inflation, interest rates, unemployment, immigration, GDP and trends
● Local, national and international pressure groups	● Labour availability, movement, costs and trends
● Prevailing Government values and stability	● Levels of disposable income and income distribution
● Regulation and de-regulation trends, levels of bureaucracy	● Local and global climatic issues
● Social and employment legislation, minimum wage	● Market and trade cycles, routes and distribution trends
● Strength and credibility of opposition parties	● Raw material availability, costs and trends
● Tax policy, trade and tariff controls, regional issues	● Specific industry factors

Social	*Technological*
● Brand, company, technology image, preferences	● Associated/dependent technologies
● Buying access, patterns and trends, advertising and publicity	● Consumer buying mechanisms and distribution channels
● Consumer attitudes and opinions, language differences and preferences, environmental influences	● Development of competing and replacement technologies
● Demographics, age, sex, wealth, marriage, children, location profiles and trends	● Impact and maturity of existing and emerging technologies
● Ethnic and religious influences, attitudes to work, employment patterns	● Information, communication and security
● Fashion and role models, roles of men and women within society	● Intellectual property issues
● Law changes affecting social factors	● Process maturity, capability and capacity
● Lifestyle choices, leisure time trends, mobility, health and education	● Research and development funding
● Major events and influences (natural and manmade disasters)	● Sustainability issues and emerging technological solutions
● Media views, attitudes and influences, public opinion, social attitudes and social taboos	● Technology access, transfer, licensing, patents

Table 6.6 SWOT Factors

Strengths	*Weaknesses*
● Core competences	● Data reliability and integrity
● Competitive advantages	● Gaps in capabilities, capacity and competencies
● Culture, management style, core values	● Internal communication
● Resource availability, capacity and capability	● Location of business
● Innovation, flare and imagination	● Management style, commitment, flexibility and adaptability,
● Location and geography	● Process control and capability
● Marketing – reach, expertise, brand identity	● Qualifications, certifications
● Price, quality, delivery, reputation	● Quality and delivery record
● Process capability, communications	● Resource availability, capability and capacity
● Relevant qualifications, certifications	● Timescales, deadlines and pressures

Opportunities	*Threats*
● Changes in government policy, regulations etc.	● Change in Government policy, lifestyle and trading standards
● Changes in social patterns, population profiles, lifestyle changes, etc.	● Competitor intentions, new competitors, price wars
● Competitors' vulnerabilities	● Economy – home, abroad
● Geography, export, import, grants, initiatives	● Environmental effects
● Industry or lifestyle trends	● Insurmountable weaknesses
● Information availability	● Legislative, taxation effects
● Mergers, joint ventures, partnerships or strategic alliances	● Loss of key staff, approvals, concessions, distribution channels
● New markets, developing markets	● New technologies, services, ideas
● New technologies, innovations, major government contracts	● Sustainable financial backing
● Volumes, production, economies	● Sustaining internal capabilities and capacity

2. Derive the measures of success, method of measurement and target values for each business process i.e. the *Process Control Parameters*.
3. Identify the processes that will deliver the outputs required by the business processes i.e. the *Work Processes*.

4. Determine the activities required to produce the work process outputs as measured including counter measures for eliminating, reducing or controlling risks to success i.e. detailed *Process Flow Charts and Risk assessments.*
5. Determine the competences and capabilities required to carry out the activities in a manner that will produce acceptable outputs i.e. *Resource Budgets and specifications.*
6. Equip the processes with the necessary human and physical resources to enable it to deliver the required outputs i.e. *Resourcing and installing the processes.*
7. Run the processes as designed, manage a change in the environment, eliminate special cause variation and verify and validate process performance i.e. *Process commissioning, integration and capability assessment.*
8. Monitor the interfaces between processes and verify and validate system effectiveness i.e. *System integration and acceptance.*

Identifying business processes

In Figure 6.4, we showed the organization as a set of interconnected processes, four to be precise. It is these processes that deliver stakeholder satisfaction. The names can be different for specific organizations – it matters not what they are called but it is important what they deliver.

Deriving process control parameters

We need to control the processes so that they deliver the results required,

Repeatedly – we get the same result every time we run the process with the same set up conditions.

Consistently – the results we get are those needed to meet the stakeholder needs.

Continually – the process runs as planned without unexpected interruption.

In order to do this we need to define the process parameters that need to be controlled.

By examining the objectives and constraints we identified at the stage above and asking, *"What outputs would we look for as evidence that the objectives have been achieved?"* we derive the process outputs.

If we now recall the basic principles of quality control, we addressed previously by asking, *"How would we establish that these outputs are correct?"* we reveal the units of measure and by asking, *"What criteria will indicate whether our outputs are acceptable?"* we identify the performance standard which will indicate whether our performance is good or bad.

Taking an example; customers are likely to need products that perform like the specification that are delivered on time and represent value for money. This represents three objectives. By asking the questions above we deduce that there are four outputs as shown in Figure 6.12 and that the Demand Fulfilment process can deliver these outputs. We also deduce that there are 11 different measures

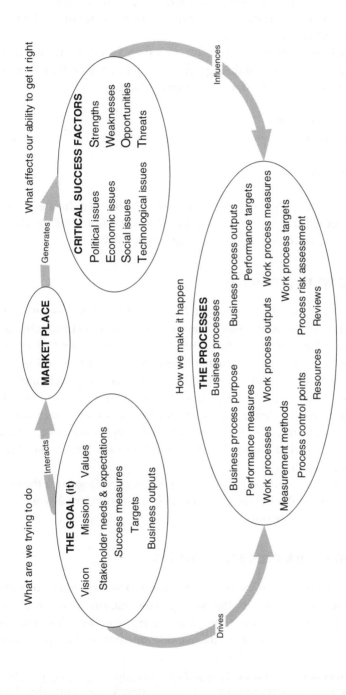

Figure 6.11 Strategic trilogy

requiring sensors or measurement methods and different standards or targets to aim for. Alternative names for the parameters are give in parenthesis.

In reality there may be hundreds of things to measure but they all need to be linked to the stakeholder outcomes.

An approach for aligning the mission, vision and values with the needs of the stakeholders and for defining appropriate performance indicators is the Balanced Scorecard[12] which covers four perspectives:

- Learning and Growth.
- Business Process.
- Customer.
- Financial Perspective.

Another approach is Stakeholder Analysis which goes further than the Balanced Scorecard and addresses all stakeholders and links stakeholder needs with the processes that deliver outputs that satisfy them.

Identifying work processes

Once we know the process outputs and how success will be measured we can determine the main work processes. The work processes can be identified from asking the question, *"What affects our ability to deliver the process outputs?"* If understanding customer requirements is key to success there will be a work process that focuses on understanding customer needs. If product innovation is key to success there will be a work process that focuses on product innovation – probably called product design. Using this method, outlines of each of the four business processes are given in Figure 6.13. Although every organization is different, the differences tend to be at the work process level rather than the business process level.

In the same way we derived the outputs, measures and targets for the business process we can take the business process objective and derive work process, outputs, measures and targets.

Determining work process activities

Once we have the defined work process parameters the next step is to determine the activities required to deliver the work process outputs. This can be accomplished by brainstorming, observation, past experience or theoretical analysis. It is also necessary at this stage to carry out a risk assessment against the process objectives and a failure modes and effects analysis on each of the identified activities. The result will be a series of process flowcharts with details of specific inputs and outputs, failure prevention provisions, checks, feedback loops and critical control points (CCP).

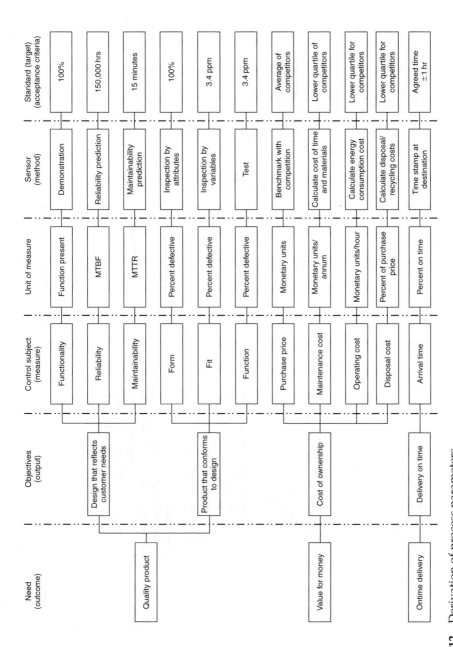

Figure 6.12 Derivation of process parameters

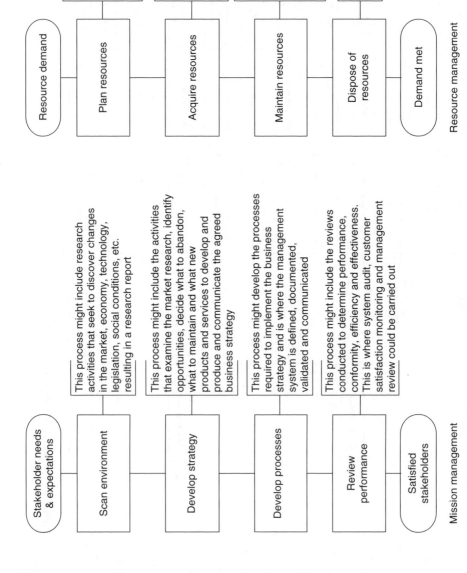

Figure 6.13 Outline business processes – 1

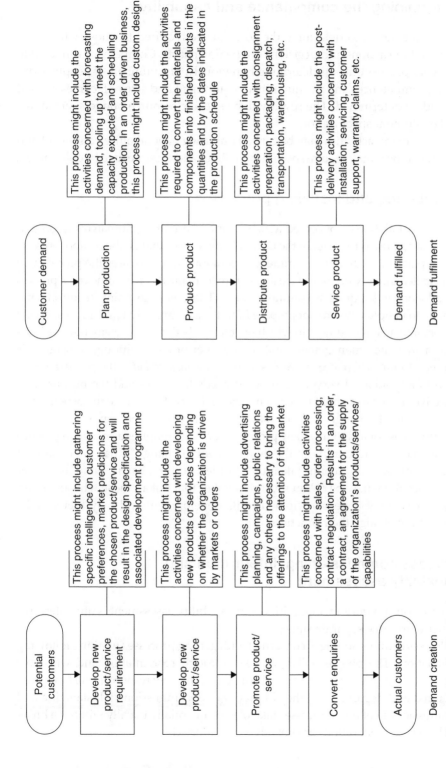

Figure 6.13 Outline business processes – 2

Determining the competence and capability

The next stage is to determine the competence required by those who are to carry out the actions and decisions on the flowcharts. Competence is related to the work process outputs determined previously. The numbers of people of differing competences and the quantity of equipment and size of facilities needed should be determined. The result will be specific resource budgets, personnel and equipment specifications.

Whilst many activities may be carried out using general office equipment and facilities, others may require specific capabilities and these need to be determined.

Resourcing and installing processes

Process installation is concerned with bringing information, human resources and physical resources together in the right relationship so that all the components are put in place in readiness to commence operation. In many cases the process will be installed already because it existed before formalization. In some cases process installation will require a cultural change. There is little point in introducing change to people who are not prepared for it. Installing a dynamic process-based system into an environment in which people still believe in an element-based system or in which management still manage performance through functions, is doomed to fail. Therefore, a precursor to *process installation* is the preparation of sound foundations. Everyone concerned needs to understand the purpose and objectives of what is about to happen – they all need to perceive the benefits and be committed to change and understand the concepts and principles involved.

The process of installing a new process or one that requires a change in practice is one that is concerned with the management of change. It has to be planned and resourced and account taken of attitudes, culture, barriers and any other resistance there may be.[13] You must remember that not all those who are to use the process may have participated in its development and may therefore be reluctant to change their practices.

Process commissioning, integration and capability assessment

Process commissioning, integration and capability assessment is often iterative rather than three separate stages.

Process commissioning is concerned with getting processes working following installation. The people will have been through reorientation and will have received all the necessary process information. Any new resources will have been acquired and deployed and the old processes decommissioned. Installation and commissioning of new processes take place sequentially usually without a break so that current operations are not adversely affected.

Process integration is concerned with changing behaviour so that people do the right things right without having to be told. The steps within a process become routine, habits are formed and beliefs strengthened. The way people act and react to certain stimuli becomes predictable and produces results that are required. Improvement does not come about by implementing requirements – it comes about by integrating principles into our behaviour. Commissioning and integration continues until the process reaches a state of readiness for verification and validation of its capability.

Capability assessment is undertaken when results indicate that performance relative to a particular process characteristic is stable and predictable. With manufacturing processes or those processes dealing with large quantities of data this can be undertaken on a preproduction run of a specific product. With other types of processes it can often only be undertaken over several months. For instance, in the mission management process the work processes may only be cycled once a year. Capability assessment in such cases becomes problematical and only reveals meaningful data after several years by which time the mission as well as the technology may have changed.

System integration and acceptance

System integration is concerned with making the interconnections between the processes, ensuring that all the linkages are in place and that the outputs from a process feed the interfacing processes at the right time in the right quality. The system will not be effective if the process linkages do not function properly. Data is gathered relative to the system goals (step 1) and a degree of effectiveness determined. As any management system is a complex entity, there probably won't be a time when it is possible to declare that all the goals are being met consistently, repeatedly and continually. For one thing, the goals might change frequently and external forces may adversely impact performance. However, an acceptable level of effectiveness will be reached so as to mark a baseline from which all system changes may be referenced.

Review performance

There are several reviews that need to take place, some during system development and others afterwards on a planned frequency.

Reviews during development

Performance reviews are necessary to verify that development is proceeding to plan and the correct outputs have been generated for each of the stages above.

Risk assessments are necessary to verify that each of the process designs reflect a safe and cost effective way of producing the required process outputs in a manner that satisfies the constraints with adequate failure prevention features inherent in the design.

Reviews after development

Output reviews are necessary to establish whether the required outputs are being produced.

Process reviews are necessary to establish whether the process outputs are being achieved in the most effective way.

Effectiveness reviews are necessary to establish whether the outputs, measures and targets remain relevant to stakeholder needs.

Improve capability

Following each review, changes need to be made as necessary to bring about improvement by better control, better utilization of resources and better understanding of stakeholder needs.

Summary

In this Chapter we have examined process management concepts, explored the terminology, the various types of processes and we have introduced a system model that put processes in context relative to the business cycle. We have concluded that any organization has only four business processes but lots of work processes.

We have analysed various process models from the simple to the complex and drawn the conclusion that processes deliver results and effective processes achieve objectives so that any model that simply shows a process to take inputs and transform them into outputs is misleading. Using a more complex model, we have shown that people and other resources are part of the process as are the constraints rather than being inputs to it. From this model we have explained the characteristics of processes and provided key questions to tease out essential information for managing processes effectively.

We have introduced a set of principles on which effective process management can be based and shown how these can be used to test the robustness of processes. We have introduced a strategic trilogy that puts into context goals, critical success factors and processes and shown how to gather vital information relative to these elements using three simple questions – *What are we trying to do, what affects our ability to get it right and how do we make it happen?*. We go on to show how the various elements of a process-based management system can be developed top down from answers to these questions and finally we explained the various reviews needed during and after system development to keep the project on course and the system improving in performance, efficiency and effectiveness.

Throughout we have used some questions that will enable us to discover the process characteristics. These are put together in Table 6.7 to provide a handy reference.

Table 6.7 Process design questions

To discover the:	Ask:	Notes
Vision	What does the organization want to become or be known for?	This is the long term goal
Mission	What is the organization trying to do (right now)?	This is the journey currently being undertaken – the medium term goal
Values	What principles will guide us on our journey?	These are corporate values not personal values – i.e. These values characterize the culture in the organization
Stakeholders	For whom is the organization doing it? (the mission)	Primarily this will be customers and shareholders but ultimately if employees, suppliers and society do not want it, the organization will not survive.
Business outcomes	What do the stakeholders want from the organization?	These are the stakeholder needs and expectations
Stakeholder success measures (Key performance indicators)	What will the stakeholders look for to assess if their needs have been met?	Obtained by filtering the mission through each stakeholder's needs and expectations
Critical success factors	What factors affect our ability to accomplish our goals?	Ask this question of the mission to reveal factors that might be turned into a set of corporate values and strategic objectives
Business outputs	What outputs will deliver successful outcomes?	You can't control a process by measuring outcomes as they arise long after the process has delivered its output
Performance targets	What criteria will indicate whether our performance is acceptable?	These are the standards you need to achieve
Business processes	What processes deliver the business outputs?	There are probably only 4 of these so if you discover more, it is likely that two or more have a common output
Process purpose	What is the main function of this process?	Derived from an assessment of what the process outputs have in common – the essence

(Continued)

Table 6.7 *(Continued)*

To discover the:	Ask:	Notes
Process activities	What affects our ability to deliver process outputs?	If you are doing something that does not affect your ability to deliver a successful output – stop doing it
Risks	How could this process fail to achieve its objectives?	These are the failure modes or hazards inherent in the process that need to be eliminated, reduced or controlled
Process output	What outputs would we look for as evidence that the process objectives have been achieved?	Must match a stakeholder need
Process measures	What parameters will we control to ensure delivery of the process outputs?	These are the subjects for which you apply the universal steps of quality control
Process constraints	How do the expectations of the other stakeholders impact (influence or constrain) the process for achieving customer expectations?	The other stakeholders are shareholders, employees, suppliers and society
Competence	What skills, knowledge and behaviours are needed to produce these outputs?	The results that people can deliver under the stipulated conditions are more important than what people say they know or can do or once did
Performance review	How do we know we are doing things right?	Process outputs are reviewed resulting in improvement by better control
Efficiency review	How do we know we are doing things in the best way?	Practices are reviewed resulting in improvement by better utilization of resources
Effectiveness review	How do we know we are doing the right things?	Objectives are reviewed resulting in improvement by better understanding of stakeholder needs

Chapter 7

Making the case for managing quality more effectively

There's only one corner of the universe you can be certain of improving, and
that's your own self.

Aldous Huxley (1894–1963), English author

Identifying the need

There will always be a case for managing quality more effectively simply
because we can always do things differently or do different things in order to
yield better results, but not everyone will be motivated to change. Many will
disagree that the evidence for change is convincing or if it is convincing that it
should be given a priority or if it is a priority that action needs to be taken
immediately. There will be resistance to change and even when change has
been acknowledged as being necessary there will be further resistance to how
the change is to be made and who is to be involved. There will be lots or barriers to cross and allies to win but it all starts with one individual identifying a
need for change. Whether the organization decides to manage quality more
effectively will depend upon how well the case for change is made. Here we
look at four scenarios to illustrate different motivators.

Alan's story

Alan was a sales executive and his job was to meet his sales targets for the period.
He had done well these last few months since he had passed his target with no
trouble. He felt this was due to his company's excellent product, and so it was. The
new model was indeed a breakthrough in technology and surpassed anything the
competition could rival. It had been in production now for over a year and was
selling well.

<table>
<tr><td>

Process Maturity

If you have adopted the process approach you will have:

- Clear & measurable business objectives
- Derived these objectives from Stakeholders' expectations
- Designed the processes to achieve these objectives
- Policies, values or principles that will guide the organization in achieving these objectives
- Connectivity between stakeholder needs, process objectives, activities, measures and the business results
- Determined the competences and capabilities required to achieve these objectives
- Conducted reviewing and be improving performance against these objectives
- Conducted reviews and be improving the efficiency of the processes
- Reviewed the relevance of the objectives against stakeholder needs

If your organization has not done any of these you have identified an opportunity for improvement.

</td></tr>
</table>

Then one day, a customer called to say his machine was faulty. It was only three months old and was therefore covered by the warranty. Alan told the customer to return it. We will repair the product in five days or replace it he told the customer (this was company policy). Alan had always put the customer first. He was not the kind of sales executive who would try to win a sale by cheating the customer. He believed in the win-win situation and would never fool a customer into believing that he was getting a bargain when he wasn't.

Five days later the customer called again to say that a replacement had not been supplied. Alan called the servicing department and was informed that there had been a backlog of repairs and it would be another two days before they could get around to that particular machine. He notified the customer who was not at all pleased as no replacement was offered as promised. Alan apologized and said he would get back shortly. He began to think about the company policy of "We will repair the product in five days or replace it". He knew of no mechanism in place that would guarantee a replacement within the five-day period. Meanwhile another of Alan's customers had a faulty machine so he started an investigation to find out whether the two machines had a common fault. He found that in both cases a fault was discovered in the same component. Further investigation established that a batch of machines had been assembled by a new employee who had misunderstood the part numbers and consequently fitted the wrong part. In fact it was the right type of component but did not have the latest modifications. In discussing the problem with the production manager, they agreed that all new employees would be given training in the company's numbering system. Alan was puzzled as to why it should be possible for employees to select the wrong component on a production line, but as he was in sales he held his tongue.

The second customer had bought the machine over 12 months prior and it had had the older part fitted – it was one of the first production machines. However, that machine was no longer covered by the warranty so Alan had to explain that there would be a repair charge. The customer was not pleased as the warranty period had only just expired, and enquired as to the nature of the fault. Alan explained that the model had been modified (on reflection he thought he shouldn't have told the truth, but that was not his nature). The customer naturally was upset and demanded a no charge repair since the fault was not due to fair wear and tear. Alan checked with his superior and was told that a charge would have to be made since they could not have one law for one customer and another for someone else. Needless to say the customer was very dissatisfied and threatened to take his business elsewhere next time.

Alan's first customer was on the phone again. Two days elapsed and no replacement machine had been delivered. Alan again investigated the problem and found that several people in the servicing department had gone sick and the backlog was increasing.

"Why can't we use the production line technicians?" Alan asked Bill, the production manager.

"Well we could," replied Bill "but they are working flat out to meet their quota."

"Why can't we take in contractors to move the backlog?" enquired Alan.

"You'll have to take that up with Tony the servicing manager," said Bill. "I am only responsible for production; not servicing."

Alan went into the servicing department and put the problem to Tony.

"We can't move production staff into servicing," said Tony "because they won't understand the way we do things around here."

"But haven't we got written procedures or something that they can follow?"

"Hell no!" said Tony. "I haven't time to write things down and anyway it would always keep changing. You know how lean we are. The slightest change and everything is affected."

Alan began to reflect on his week so far. There had not been so many problems in a single week before. There were the faulty machines, although they had tracked down the fault and hopefully taken adequate corrective action by training all new employees. Then there was the resource problem in the servicing department. We couldn't solve that until either we had more technicians or could use contract labour. If we had documented procedures, Alan thought, new staff and contractors could quickly learn our methods so he undertook to speak to the CEO about this. The CEO told Alan that *his* job was to satisfy customers and not to worry about operations as *they* will write procedures if they believe *they* need them. He also made it clear that Alan was not to interfere in the work of other departments.

Satisfy customers – Alan thought. Well we haven't done very well this week and he started to list the incidents.

- Delivered several faulty machines.
- Didn't meet the response time promised.
- Didn't provide the replacement we were committed to.
- Made a customer pay for something that was our fault.
- Inadequate resources in the servicing department.

- Inadequate training of new employees.
- No written procedures.

Alan began to think about customer satisfaction. What satisfies the customer? He came to the conclusion that it is more than supplying product that is ordered. The products have to be reliable and if they do happen to fail then the customer expects this to be put right at our cost if it's our fault. But it's not only that, the customer also expects a prompt service and if we make promises, we should keep them.

Later the following week Alan checked the problems previously encountered to see if the agreed actions had been taken. He was pleasantly surprised to find that both the faulty machines had been repaired and dispatched. He called the first customer and was told that the machine was delivered but not in the five days promised. However, the machine worked so the customer was relatively satisfied. In the second case the customer was livid. Not only was a charge made for labour but for a new part as well. Alan said he would withdraw the invoice and passed a memo to Accounts to execute it.

A few weeks later Alan received yet another complaint from a customer with a faulty machine. Alan's chance meeting with Bill in the canteen, prompted him to ask whether the training of the new employee has been initiated. Bill was puzzled by Alan's question since as far as he could recall the training was scheduled for only one person. Alan was puzzled by Bill's response. Surely Bill had installed a training plan that would be implemented on every new employee. As it turned out, no such plan was implemented because at the time, Bill had only one new employee in the production department. However since then Bill had replaced one of his staff as a sick employee had not returned to work. When Alan looked into the problem he found that the last machine that was returned had been assembled not by a new employee but by a worker who had transferred from the servicing department. On further investigation it transpired that an operator had again misunderstood the company's part numbering system. Alan burst into Bill's office and demanded an explanation. Bill told Alan that the numbering system was inherently troublesome as it was not logical.

"Anyway I expected one of Tony's servicing staff to understand the numbering system," replied Bill to Alan's outburst.

Alan asked why a new system had not been developed and was told to his dismay that there were more important things for the development engineers to do. "But its loosing customers," said Alan.

"Well you had better go and tell the chief designer because every time I mention it I am criticised for employing idiots," said Bill.

A month later the CEO announced that the repair group in the servicing department was transferring into production in order to overcome the resource problems and provide greater flexibility. On hearing the news, Alan went to see Bill and asked him what he intended to do about training the new staff. Bill told Alan that he hadn't got the time and anyway, as he had said previously, "These people know the job!"

"I wouldn't have agreed to the transfer if I thought I had to train them," said Bill. Alan could see he was not going to get a commitment from Bill so left his office.

Alan believed that no one seemed to be interested in preventing errors and came to the conclusion that each person was only interested in his/her own department's performance. He began to think about how the company could ensure these failures didn't recur and started doing some research on the Internet. He came across some stuff on "systems thinking" and immediately saw it as the way of the future. What was really needed was for some joined-up-thinking. If everyone saw him or herself as part of a system that existed to enable the organization to satisfy its customers and other stakeholders, and derived their goals from the organizational goals, none of this would have happened – but how is he going to convince the others that this is what is needed?

Brenda's story

Brenda had just waved goodbye to the ISO 9000 auditors following another surveillance visit. It had all gone well. A few minor nonconformities; nothing to worry her boss about and a couple of improvement actions. While there had been some difficulty in showing the relationship between quality objectives and the results being achieved, Brenda had convinced the auditor that all the graphs, charts and action plans demonstrated that they had a process for continually improving the effectiveness of the quality management system. However, she did not like ducking and diving to avoid giving a direct answer to the auditor's questions and perhaps this had shown up in her behaviour and resulted in the request for "improvement action".

The company has always had a commitment to quality and was one of the first to register to ISO 9001 way back in 1987, but this had often appeared more intent than reality. Brenda had inherited the management system, developed by her two predecessors although she had managed the transition to ISO 9001:2000 with the help of the certification body. They recommended an audit against the new requirements before they had started; a sort of gap analysis, which would identify the changes they needed to make. Apart from turning the top-level procedures into flowcharts and adding a few additional "processes" it was not as difficult as Brenda had been led to believe from the literature she had downloaded from the Internet. However, she had become increasingly disturbed by what was going on. It was as though they were paying lip service to the standard. There was evidence of compliance but it was often like pulling teeth to get the managers to reveal it. If the auditor had only challenged the managers to show how the results were being achieved, the house of cards would have collapsed. It's not as though procedures are not followed – they are, but from what Brenda had read, processes are different – they are the enablers of results and she was quite confident that the procedures in no way described how the processes are supposed to be managed and the results were to be achieved. They only described how to perform discrete tasks and the results were often achieved by hard work, overtime and firefighting.

After work one night, Brenda went to a lecture on business excellence hosted by the local Chamber of Commerce. The speaker was a CEO of a company that had recently won a Business Excellence Award. He spoke of the benefits that such an award brings in terms of staff motivation and increased marketability but although it had taken quite a long time and a lot of effort to change the culture and improve performance he remarked upon how satisfying it was to work in a company that did what it said it did. In their submission they made statements showing how they met the award criteria. Subsequently, along came the assessors to verify the statements and in all cases they were congratulated on the accuracy of their submission. One of the things they had done was to define the processes that produce the business results. They were able to demonstrate to the assessors the clear linkage between the enablers and the results using a web-based file structure with a dynamic user interface. Brenda thought she might be onto something here as this concept was at the heart of the Excellence Model so she managed to corner the speaker to talk with him when his talk ended.

"Yeah! that's right," said the speaker, "Its easy to navigate through the information although you have to be pretty disciplined and stop changing things on the fly, but that's no hardship, all our review processes include system updates. It's a real breeze. Just click on an objective and up pops the latest performance data. I have a monitor on my desk that is switched on all day and I can see what is going on. It's like having a dashboard in front of you as you drive towards your goals."

"I am really impressed, "said Brenda." I am looking into ways in which I can get our organization system focused and I wondered if it would be possible for me to pay you a visit to learn more about the way you have done this."

John Penfold was a busy executive with little time to spare but welcomed Brenda's request and suggested he contact his Business Systems Manager who had masterminded the web-based solution.

"Unfortunately I will be out of town," said John. "But I will inform my Business Systems Manager and she will show you around. Her name is Claire Hughes. She's on the ball and knows how it all works."

Brenda arrived at the plant the following morning and met Claire. Enthusiastic to show off the new system, Claire showed Brenda to her office where she sat down at her PC, clicked on an icon on her desktop and brought up the home page of what she called the Business Management System. Brenda was impressed.

"Is this it," said Brenda. "I didn't realize it was literally like a car dashboard."

"That's the way John Penfold wanted it, "replied Claire." We have virtually a paperless system. In fact things change so often, it would be out of date before you had collected your stuff from the printer so we wanted something that was as real time as we could get it. We got some help from a local consultant who provided some templates but it is largely all our own work," said Claire. "Let me show you around our business management system."

Claire proceeded to navigate through what looked like a web site, page after page, showing Brenda first the Mission statement, then a diagram identifying the processes and how they fit together. She then passed her mouse over one of the shapes and immediately a flowchart was displayed. "This is what our Resource Management Process looks like Brenda. If you want to know anything about this process you just click on one of these boxes." On the screen along side the flowchart were links to Objectives, Measures, Activities, Resources, Results, Reviews and Improvement plans. Claire clicked on the Results button and up popped a page showing the key objectives and along side charts showing corresponding performance trends.

"This is fantastic," said Brenda. "You mean to say that instead of scouring manuals looking for a policy, procedure or report, all you need to do is click on links and follow a path to where you will find what you are looking for."

"Well, more or less," said Claire. "But we still have lots of files on other servers and stopping people saving their files to their PC instead of the main server is becoming a real problem. It's a whole new ball game but we have got people looking at using one system. Also the main benefit is that we can not only look at the results we are achieving but can also view the process that is delivering the results. Managers can no longer hide behind the mystery of the process. If the results are poor, we look at the process and debate what we should change. We make the change, prove it works then sit back and in no time performance will get back on track."

"I like this," said Brenda. "This is just the kind of system we need. It looks more dynamic than those manuals of procedures we have."

"Oh, we still have procedures," said Claire. "They are of course all electronic files now and take up less space but instead of collecting dust on a shelf, they sit on a server which is just a mouse click away."

"How much did all this cost?" asks Brenda.

"I don't know off hand, but I could put you in touch with the consultant we used," said Claire. "Apart from the front end this is not a bespoke product. We used tools that we already had. The applications that generate the reports, drawings and procedures are just the same as we used before."

"I would like to investigate this further," said Brenda. "I need to prepare a case for our senior management so I will probably be back in touch when I have spoken to the consultant you used."

"Thanks OK, glad to be of help," said Claire. "If you would like to bring over your management team to show them what I have shown you, just let me know."

Brenda now had a vision of what she wanted the management system to look like but how was she going to convince her peers that this was a realistic and worthwhile path to take?

Catherine's story

Finding out customer's needs and expectations was Catherine's primary responsibility. She was the commercial manager of an electronics company and knew that in this fast moving business, if she did not keep her ear to the ground her company would go under. At a recent meeting with one of the key accounts Roger, the Purchasing Manager, pulled Catherine to one side and whispered into her ear.

"Catherine, I want to give you some advanced warning about a change in our procurement policy. It's not finalised yet, but we are coming under increasing competition from South East Asia. They can beat us on price because of the low labour costs and their quality is also second to none because they pay great attention to process capability. Our R & D is where we have the competitive edge but we need real confidence that our suppliers can deliver to our requirements."

"But we always do meet your requirements, Roger" said Catherine forcefully.

"Yes I know," said Roger. "But I am not talking about the standard products you supply. I am referring to some really new stuff, right at the forefront of technology. We have taken on some wiz kids from Silicon Valley and they are pushing us in a different direction, so the specifications we will be inviting you to tender against might well stretch your capability."

"We have a very innovative team in our design department," said Catherine with pride in her voice. Her father was the Chief Designer so she knew only too well the capability of his team.

"It's not just design capability we are after but production capability," said Roger. "We will be asking your organization to meet ISO 9001 – you know, the international quality system standard. But I want you to understand, we are not imposing ISO 9001 simply as a way of reducing our vendor control. We believe that by demonstrating compliance with ISO 9001 you will be giving us an assurance of product and service quality."

"OK I think I know where you are coming from," said Catherine. "But from what I have heard about ISO 9001 I am not so sure you will get anymore confidence than you get now."

Roger was sensing a little resistance from Catherine and quite understandably since her company had been a good supplier for over 15 years. "I agree," said Roger. "There are those that have implemented this standard and not improved quality, but the standard was revised in 2000 and it is more results focused," said Roger. "I think you will find the new approach is more in tune with what your senior management would consider good business practice. There is much less focus on paperwork and more on the processes to deliver customer satisfaction."

"Right, I'll get our Quality Manager to take a look at it," replied Catherine.

"If your Quality Manager is on the ball Catherine, he will already know what it's about," said Roger dryly. "Anyway, I though I'd give you the benefit of an early warning. You will find the new requirement in tenders going out in the second quarter of next year. Now lets look at the current delivery schedules."

When Catherine got back to the office, she made a point of calling in on Bill, the Quality Manager and asking him about this new version of ISO 9000. "What's it all about Bill," said Catherine. "Is it going to cost a lot to get certified?"

"Well, it all depends," said Bill. "Depends on what," said Catherine. "It depends on whether or not Tolland will make third party ISO 9001 certification mandatory or whether we can present their vendor control people with sufficient evidence that they accept we have a system that has the capability of delivering product that meets their requirements, because that what it's all about – capability."

"Yes, Roger mentioned capability," said Catherine. "But he also talked about wanting an assurance of product and service quality."

"ISO 9001 is all about demonstrating to either customers or third parties that we have the capability to meet the requirements of customer and other stakeholders," said Bill. "In essence it means giving an assurance of product and service quality. Quality and meeting requirements is the same thing."

"So I guess I need to get back to Roger to confirm whether they will require certification," said Catherine.

"That's right," said Bill "then come back to me and we can sit down and plan an appropriate strategy."

Catherine later contacted Roger who confirmed that Tolland was intending to require ISO 9001 certification because they didn't want to have multiple requirements. He also said that they were going to use their vendor control people to do product specific audits rather than general audits. Relying on third party certification for an assurance of compliance with common requirements would enable them to make better use of their resources, although Roger admitted it would have little impact on overall costs.

When Catherine met with Bill a while later, she was able to confirm that they needed to get ISO 9001 certification. However, Bill had said that it was important their senior management understood Tolland's rationale otherwise they might perceive it simply as a badge on the wall.

Catherine now understood what was needed but convincing the senior management that they needed to demonstrate they had the capability to meet customer requirements by satisfying ISO 9001 was going to be difficult.

Daren's story

Daren was Quality Manager in an organization providing traffic management services to local authorities and he had received three letters from different authorities concerning ISO 9001 certification.

"What does this mean?" said Daren to his contact in the council.

"We sent these letters out to all suppliers of primary services requiring them to get ISO 9001 certification by next December otherwise they will no longer be invited to tender for council contracts," said Bob, a Purchasing Manager with a local authority.

"But has our performance record over the years given you any reason to doubt our commitment to quality," Daren asked Bob in a questioning tone.

"Not at all," replied Bob. "We want to create a level playing field and it is in no way a reflection of your past performance. I expect you should have no trouble getting ISO 9001."

"You do realise that it will increase our costs. We will incur additional costs for certification and continual surveillance audits which we will have to recover somehow so it is likely that you will be paying more for the same services in future," said Daren, rather irritated by Bob's apparent disregard for the cost of it all.

"No it won't," said Bob. "We will only select suppliers that have ISO 9001 certification in future and as I say it will create a level playing field. It will save us a lot of time and push the responsibility for verifying compliance with our requirements onto our suppliers where it ought to be. So on balance we don't believe costs will increase, and in any case it will improve your profile and get you more contracts."

"So we have no option," said Daren.

"Not if you want to remain on our list of preferred suppliers," replied Bob.

Daren was left in no doubt as to what the council wanted. However, whether they knew what they were asking for, he wasn't as certain. He thought he ought to check with Sales and picked up the phone to call Peter, the Sales Manager.

"Peter, I have three letters from local authorities stating that we need to get ISO 9001 certification by next December otherwise we will be removed from the tender list. I have just been talking with our local authority's Purchasing Manager and he confirms that all local authorities have adopted the same policy. Have you heard anything, what are your contacts saying?"

"Oh, I did hear something but I don't think there is anything to worry about. As far as I understand it, you just have to write some procedures and some guy comes in and checks they meet the standard, that's all."

"Well, I think its far more than that, Peter. If we want to do the job properly, we will have to put in a lot of effort," replied Daren.

"You are making a mountain out of a mole hill," said Peter. "Look, no one in the council has complained. They all seem pretty happy with the quality of the stuff we provide – after all it's not rocket science is it."

"But it's only awarded to organizations that have a system that delivers products and services that satisfy customer requirements," replied Daren.

"Exactly," retorted Peter. "We do satisfy our customers and therefore it should be a doddle."

"Yes, but we don't do all those things required by the standard do we?" suggested Daren.

"Look, I know companies that are far worse than we are and they have the certificate so stop worrying and get on with it. I'll give you some stuff you can use and I'm sure Dave in Operations will have some forms and notes you can turn into the fancy documents to satisfy the auditors."

Daren decided it wasn't worth arguing with Peter. He obviously had made up his own mind on the subject and that was that. He decided to examine the standard to try and understand what the implications would be and having looked at ISO 9001 to get an idea of what they would be assessed against, then at ISO 9000 to get a clear understanding of the fundamental concepts and principles he came to the conclusion that there was no way that certification would be won simply by producing a few procedures. Perhaps Peter was thinking about the 1994 version which was dominated by requirements for documented procedures. This latest version appeared to be more about a system of processes that achieved customer focused objectives that was also subject to continual improvement and this would require far more work than simply writing a few procedures.

So it seemed Daren had to convince his boss that he needed some resources to help him get the company through ISO 9001 certification. But getting certification is one thing – keeping it might well be another. He would therefore surely need some additional staff to maintain certification.

Summary

Four different stories; each from a person who had identified a problem and discovered a way of resolving it.

In Alan's story the organization operated as a number of discrete functions each doing its own thing and having little regard for the other but collectively having a detrimental impact on customers. The company did not have ISO 9001 certification nor was there a customer requirement for certification to our knowledge but there appeared to be no system in place that would ensure work went to plan and people kept their promises. Alan identified the problem as a lack of systems thinking and although he was a Sales Executive, he was motivated to cause change as it was his customers that were complaining and he felt responsible.

In Brenda's story the organization had a system that passed the scrutiny of the external auditors but it wasn't very effective because there was no connectivity between the formally documented procedures and the results. Results were achieved but through unpredictable processes. Having been shown a process-based system that had been designed with this connectivity in mind, Brenda was motivated to cause change as it would bring about a degree of certainty that had so far alluded her management.

In Catherine's story, her company did not have a formal management system but was delivering customer satisfaction, at least with the current range of products, and saw no need to change. However, the market was changing and their customers were seeking confidence that they had the capability to meet more challenging requirements and required they gained ISO 9001 certification. Catherine was motivated to cause change because it was a question of survival in their chosen market.

In Daren's story, the customer was about to impose a requirement for ISO 9001 certification not because they lacked confidence in the quality of the service provided but because of a change in procurement policy. Daren was motivated to make changes to keep his job.

These four stories show how needs are often identified. It is usually one person in the right place at the right time that is observant enough or passionate enough to be motivated by the circumstances in which they find themselves. Sometimes, the motivation comes from a single incident and in other cases it develops over many incidents until there is a compelling desire to take action as in Alan's story. The stories also reveal another common trait that the motivation arises after meeting others that have made improvements. This gives the originator of change someone to bounce ideas off, someone with whom to confirm beliefs and also an outsider to show the direction in which others are going.

> **Decisions – decisions**
>
> "I see it all perfectly; there are two possible situations – one can either do this or that. My honest opinion and my friendly advice is this: do it or do not do it – you will regret both".
> *Soren Kierkegaard (1813–1855), Danish philosopher*

But identifying the need for change is only the first step. Changes are not made in a vacuum. In all the above cases, it was not the originator of the change who needed to change, but the system of processes whether formal or informal that enabled the organization to achieve its objectives. That system included the managers and the staff so everyone in the organization might become affected by the change and many of these same people might need to be convinced of the need to change and be persuaded to carry through the changes.

When trying to convince anyone of the need for change, it is important to define the reason or objective for change and this is our next step.

Defining the objective

In all four cases a need for change had been identified. In Alan's case, there was a need to improve product and service quality. In Brenda's case there was a need to improve the way the business processes were being managed. In both Catherine's case and Daren's case there was a need to get ISO 9001 certification, but are these the objectives? We do know it's not the whole story.

Alan's company needed to improve product and service quality but the reason why product and service quality was poor was that there was no effective system place to make it happen. So if the objective is stated simply as "To improve product and service quality" one might get many different solutions none of which actually address the root cause. Therefore we make the objective include the reason for change by stating it thus: "To establish a system that enables the organization to satisfy its customers with the quality of products and services it provides." We have not said what this system is but we have defined what it needs to achieve and how we will measure that achievement i.e. by measuring customer satisfaction.

Brenda's company needed to improve the way the business processes were being managed but the reason why the processes appeared that they were not being managed effectively was because the documented procedures didn't describe the means by which the results were being achieved. The link between enablers and results could not be demonstrated with the present procedure-based system. So one might expect many different responses if the managers were told to manage their processes more effectively. Including the reason for change and the measure of success in the objective it can be stated thus: "To establish a process-based management system that enables the organization to demonstrate it is managing its processes effectively by providing a clear line of sight between results and enablers."

Catherine's company needed to get ISO 9001 certification, which meant establishing a formal management system in place of the present informal system. But the reason for getting ISO 9001 certification was not simply for marketing purposes but a means of demonstrating they had the capability of meeting continually changing requirements to their customers' satisfaction. Therefore the objective, reason and measure might be: "To establish a system that will provide customers with confidence that the organization has the capability to meet their requirements and satisfy the requirements for ISO 9001 certification."

Daren's company also need to get ISO 9001 certification but for entirely different reasons to Catherine's company. Here it was simply a matter of getting on to an approved suppliers list and the passport was ISO 9001 certification. Provided they maintained ISO 9001 they would continue to be invited to tender for local authority contracts. Therefore the objective, reason and measure might be: "To establish a system that enables the organization to achieve and retain ISO 9001 certification."

In all cases, the objectives included the words "To establish a system . . . " This is because, as we learnt in Chapter 3, systems exist to achieve objectives, so if objectives need to be achieved and there is no system in place, one has to be established.

Proving the need

Before senior management is approached with a reason to change, proof of the need is required. A singer always sounds more appealing if there is a well-orchestrated accompaniment. Up to this point only one person has identified the need. Alan in his role as sales executive has experience of dissatisfied customers and thus is convinced of the need for change. Brenda has herself witnessed an entirely new way of describing business processes that will overcome the disconnect between results and enablers. Catherine has been given advanced warning about impending changes so unless she convinces her peers quickly, this competitive advantage will be lost. Daren has no option. The organization will have to get ISO 9001 certification but getting it and keeping it are two different things in his view so he needs to convince his boss to provide additional resources not only to get certification but also to retain it.

Before managers will take action, they need answers to specific questions. It will not be enough simply to go before management and tell them that they need to change or ask them for resources. They will want to know the what, why, when, where and how of the change and the consequences of doing nothing including justification for any claims made.

If we put these questions into a matrix together with typical answers for each of our four cases it might look like Table 7.1.

Table 7.1 only contains a summary of the information that is likely to be needed to convince management they need to act. There may well be much more information that one could and should provide but remember, senior management doesn't like to be bombarded with information. They assimilate information if it is conveyed in small amounts with the salient facts being prominent.

Establishing feasibility

The objective for change is defined, the reason for change is clear and proof has been gathered but is the change feasible?

- Is the timing right for this change?
- Do we have the capability to make this change?
- What are the barriers or obstacles to change?
- What are the drivers for change?

These are some of the questions you need to address and collect data that will demonstrate that change is feasible before approaching the senior management.

Timing

In all four cases above, timing is fairly critical as revenue will be lost unless the objectives are achieved. However, there might be some leeway. It could be the best of times or the worst of times but unlike in Dickens' *The Tale of Two Cities*, it is doubtful that revolution will follow.

The best of times might be represented by customer pressure that may just be what is needed to drive the organization out of the doldrums. A common enemy is sometimes a motivating force that will focus everyone on improving performance. The impetus for change might also arise from within the particular industry sector, bad press, litigation, government regulation, a new initiative etc. that

Table 7.1 Proving the need

Questions to which management will expect answers	Alan's story	Brenda's story	Catherine's story	Daren's story
What is the issue?	Our customers complain about the quality of the products and services we provide	The link between enablers and results cannot be demonstrated with the present procedure-based system	We can't demonstrate to our customers' satisfaction that we have the capability of meeting their requirements	We need to get ISO 9001 certification
Where is the evidence for this?	This report I have prepared on our performance following several customer complaints	This report I have prepared prompted by the results of the last external audit	This report I have prepared on a meeting with Tolland Computers	These letters from our customers
Why is this an issue?	No effective system in place to ensure product and service quality	The current procedures don't describe how the processes are managed and the results are being achieved, therefore we are not managing our processes effectively	We have not pursued ISO 9001 registration	Local authorities have changed their procurement policy and all are requiring suppliers of primary services to be ISO 9001 registered
What is this costing us?	Current performance shows an upward trend in customer complaints and a downward trend in orders	Current performance shows an increasing inspection and failure cost on the production line over the last 6 months	Currently nothing, but by the second quarter of next year we will cease to get contracts from Tolland Computers unless we are ISO 9001 registered.	Currently nothing to our knowledge
What should we do about it?	Establish a system that enables the organization to satisfy its customers with the quality of products and services it provides	Establish a process-based management system that enables the organization to demonstrate it is managing its processes effectively by providing a clear line of sight between results and enablers	Establish a system that will provide customers with confidence that the organization has the capability to meet their requirements and satisfy the requirements for ISO 9001 certification	Establish a system that enables the organization to achieve and retain ISO 9001 certification

(Continued)

Table 7.1 (Continued)

Questions to which management will expect answers	Alan's story	Brenda's story	Catherine's story	Daren's story
What will the impact of this be?	We will have to fundamentally change the way we manage the organization	We will have to identify our processes and manage them more effectively	We will have to document our processes and demonstrate their capability	We will have to define objectives that are customer focused and employ processes for meeting these objectives that are subject to continual improvement
How much will it cost?	Approx 5% of turnover	Approx 1% of turnover	Approx 2% of turnover plus an annual certification cost of about £5K	Approx 1% of turnover plus an annual certification cost of about £2K
Where are the resources going to come from?	The investment will be recovered inside 3 years from the resultant increase in turnover	The investment will be recovered inside 2 years from the resultant decrease in failure costs	The investment will be recovered inside 2 years from the profit made on contracts from Tolland Computers	Out of profits
When do we need to act?	As soon as possible	As soon as possible	It will take us a good 18 months so the sooner we start the better	Immediately
What are the alternatives and their relative costs?	Diagnose and fix individual problems and hope others don't arise elsewhere. Much cheaper but not a long term solution	Do nothing, fudge the audit and wait until customers find a more competitive source of supply	There is no alternative if we wish to retain Tolland as a customer. They are a key customer, but this could be the start of a trend in our market sector	There is no alternative as all local authorities will require ISO 9001 certification
What are the consequences of doing nothing?	Customers will eventually take their business elsewhere resulting in a further decline in revenue	Failure costs will continue to vary and reduce profitability therefore profit targets in the years ahead will not be met	We won't receive any invitations to tender from Tolland after the second quarter next year	The present business will fold up

is receiving increased attention. There might have been some changes in senior management and a project like this could give a particular manager a means to show true leadership.

The worst of times might be represented by financial pressures. Perhaps all available funds are being applied to restructuring, breaking into new markets or new product development so there will be insufficient funds to spare for any additional projects. These types of project tend to be long term. They do not deliver immediate results except where all that is needed is an ISO 9001 certificate as in Daren's case. In fact a company in this situation is likely to grab the chance to get ISO 9001 with the minimum of expenditure as it will be wrongly perceived as no more that a paperwork exercise. Getting ISO 9001 certification under these circumstances makes it very difficult to associate ISO 9001 with improved quality.

If you look into the future, say 1–6 months, there might be a window of opportunity. A project consuming resources might be coming to a close and this quality improvement project might be welcomed as the next challenge. Or, a new CEO might be in place and it might be better handled by him or her rather than the retiring CEO.

On the micro scale there will also be timing issues as to when to approach the senior management. It might be prudent to avoid approaching them after a particular acrimonious board meeting, or just before the summer holidays or annual festivals. Approaching the CEO after he or she has been berated by a series of irate customers might be a good time because it will appear that you had already detected the deterioration in performance and conceived a cunning plan to get the company back on track. However, if the CEO thinks you are responsible for upsetting these customers (whether he or she is correct or not is irrelevant), it might be the worst of times and keeping a low profile might be a better strategy!

Capability

None of the four cases we are studying would require a rocket scientist but they will require people with skills in the management of projects, change and processes. In Catherine's and Daren's case there is a need for someone with an in depth understanding of the ISO 9000 series of standards and in Brenda's case probably Intranet design skills might also be needed. Current goals might not be being achieved because of a lack of capability or capacity either in the equipment and facilities or in the people employed. Some investigations will therefore be needed to qualify any gap in capability and identify the options available for closing this gap. One option is to recruit new people possessing the requisite competences but this will take several months. Another is to train existing staff but this might not be feasible if the jobs these people currently do cannot be assigned to others. A third option is to engage consultants but this can be expensive. However, unlike recruitment, it is a cost that is non-recurring. Often the solution is to do all three but not all at once. Engage a consultant to kick-start the project, train the people and then transfer the skills by which time you will know if you need additional staff or different staff.

Barriers

The barriers are the factors that might delay, impede, retard or stop the project such as:

- Refusal to accept the need for change.
- Contentment with the status quo or a belief that current performance is acceptable.
- Agreement to the need but objection to solution.
- Disagreement as to the priorities for change.
- An absentee CEO or MD – comes in two days per week so is ignorant about the local pressures.
- Shortage of funds.
- Having a monopoly in the market.
- Instability (frequent changes in leadership, structure and location).
- Too many distractions (meetings, exhibitions and unplanned events).
- Too ambitious goals (the scope may be too big, the targets too tight).
- Being the first to pursue this objective.
- A culture in which there is a fear of failure, an environment of secrecy or an absence of praise for achievements.
- A belief that we don't have the capability so should not do it.

There is no doubt that if the goal is too ambitious, a project may fail. Even if the ultimate goal is to bring everything and everyone into a dynamic system that delivers never ending stakeholder satisfaction you might be more successful if you set less ambitious targets and work towards your ultimate goal gradually. It is said that the best way to eat an Elephant is one bite at a time!

Drivers

The drivers are the factors that might create success such as:

- Having a strong or visionary leader.
- Having an enthusiastic and competent goal driven project champion.
- Having a receptive management team.
- A culture in which change is the norm.
- A target driven culture.
- A competitive market.
- Having people willing to pick up a challenge and run with it.
- Having other organizations in the same sector that have achieved this objective.

- External pressures that may threaten the business if nothing is done.
- Having the support of the board and/or the parent company.
- Leaders who are dissatisfied with the status quo.
- A culture where achievements are recognized whatever the outcome.
- A culture in which people are honest, open and free to speak their mind.

There will always be inhibitors who are opposed to change, those who fear the unknown, the conservatives who hold back until they have confidence that it is the right thing to do and the innovators who will charge fearlessly ahead in spite of the warnings and prefer any change rather than continue what they are doing now.[1]

The best approach if it can be used, is to make an ally of an innovator, make some progress that will impress the conservatives and leave the inhibitors out in the cold so that they too will come on board eventually rather than face the future alone.

Securing the commitment

If you find yourself in a similar position to Alan, Brenda, Catherine or Daren you will need to prepare your case well. Even if your manager is not the one that will make the decision, he or she may champion your cause, but more than likely will ask you to prepare the case for presentation to senior management. You might be the one making the presentation or supporting your manager, either way you need to do your homework and recognize that there is a road to commitment (Table 7.2) along which many of the people from whom you need support will follow. Your task is to move them along this road but the difficulty you will face is that you won't be sure which stage each of them is at until long after you have moved past that stage. Some people will appear to understand but don't and others will tell you they have taken action but they haven't.

> **Commitment**
>
> Some men are born committed to action: they do not have a choice, they have been thrown on a path, at the end of that path, an act awaits them, their act ...
> *Jean-Paul Sartre (1905–1980), French novelist & philosopher*

There are several ways in which you might progress from Stage 0 to Stage 2 just as there are several ways in which people learn.

Determining your audience

When you have to make a presentation to a group of people with the objective of getting a commitment to action you need to take account of the different ways in which people take in information, understand the message and draw conclusions. These are what we call learning styles of which there are four.

Table 7.2   The road to commitment[2]

Stage	Level	Meaning
0	Zero	I don't know anything about it.
1	Awareness	I know what it is and why I should do it.
2	Understanding	I know what I have to do and what I need to do it.
3	Investment	I have the resources to do it and I know how to deploy them.
4	Intent	This is what I am going to do and how I am going to do it.
5	Action	I have completed the first few actions and it has been successful.
6	Commitment	I am now doing everything I said I would do.

Feelers, thinkers, watchers and doers. Once they have reached their conclusions, if appropriate they will proceed to make a decision and once again people make decisions in different ways and these are what we call decision styles of which there are a further four: decisive, flexible, hierarchical and integrative. Effective presentations will be those that accommodate all of the styles.

The learning process is a four-stage process.[3] It starts with a concrete experience followed by reflective observation that leads to the formulation of abstract concepts and generalizations. These can be developed into hypotheses to be tested in the future, which leads to new experiences. People continuously pass through this process, test concepts, and new experiences and modify them as a result of observation and analysis of the outcomes. Some people are more comfortable with different stages of the learning process. Some are *feelers*, who learn better by experiencing situations. They are unlikely to accept a hypothesis unless they have actual experience of a situation. They prefer examples not theory. Others are *thinkers,* who are more comfortable with abstract conceptualizations relying on logic, theory and abstract analysis. They crave facts and often want to be left alone to work things out for themselves. They are less inclined to be influenced by examples and will often find the exception that makes the example inappropriate. Then there are *doers* who learn better by experimentation. They want to get their hands dirty and get on with it. They don't need to have worked it out before rolling up their sleeves. They learn best in groups and don't relish instruction or theory. Lastly there are the *watchers* who take a reflective, somewhat detached view. They come to their conclusions from careful observation and analysis. They don't need to get involved and can learn from audio-visual aids.

If there is one thing that senior management will not be interested in, it is the detail of ISO 9001 or lots of statistical data. So it is not a case of getting senior management to understand the requirements or the statistical theory. More importantly, it is a case of getting senior management to understand the need for action and getting their commitment to take the action on the basis of providing not only additional resources but also committing their time to steering the project and doing the things only they have authority to do. The last thing you want is for senior management to provide the funds and let you get on with it, issuing monthly reports that they scan but don't understand. If it gets to this stage, then you have failed to grab their attention. If we look at the bottom line in Table 7.1, we will see that in every case the business is adversely affected if the project is not a success. Therefore permitting senior management to take a back seat is not an option.

Alan, Brenda, Catherine and Daren might only be the messengers. They might not be the generals or captains and therefore someone else has to pick up the batons and lead the project.

Designing the presentations

Depending on the size of the management team and its availability one or more presentations may be needed. There are a number of aspects to be agreed:

Problem definition

Problem definition is the definition of the issues requiring resolution, their cause and their impact on the business. The presentation needs to address the questions given in Table 7.1. If there is no consensus on these matters, it is pointless proceeding to the next stage. At this stage a project sponsor needs to be identified – someone who will own the problem and be responsible for its resolution.

Feasibility

Feasibility looks at the options for resolving the issues, their credibility, budgetary cost and their impact on performance. Include drivers and barriers for each so that management may assess feasibility. Only put forward viable options. It is pointless proposing a solution that would not be taken seriously by the management.

Project definition

Project definition is the definition of the chosen option and its impact on current policies, practices and processes. The purpose here is to create awareness, understanding and commitment to the solution. There has to be clarity in management's expectations. There is no point getting agreement if management don't fully understand what is expected of them before, during and after the new system has been established.

Project planning

Project planning defines the project objectives, timescales, resources and responsibilities. Outline the project management strategy and identify the major tasks and work packages. Identify the key roles and responsibilities, the project team and Steering Committee. Outline the planning, communication and system design processes and present the bar chart indicating the key milestones and when the major task will commence and finish. If possible at this stage provide an effort profile and identify any external resources needed.

Presentation content

There is often a temptation to fill a presentation with lots of content i.e. dozens of slides showing text and graphics. There will obviously be some facts that need to be transmitted and slide presentations are good for this providing the slide it lightly populated. Too dense and it won't be read from the back of the room. Too brief and the message may not be received and understood. Remember you are trying to communicate so use verbal and non-verbal, visual and non-visual techniques to good effect. Slides are simply an aid to communicating the message, they give the message more lasting impact but should never be a substitute for verbal delivery. The diagrams in this book can be adapted for use in presentations but be careful of using material you don't fully understand which is why it is often better to create your own slides. Animation can be used to good effect as it enables you to feed the audience at the pace you are talking and is better at getting over new concepts.

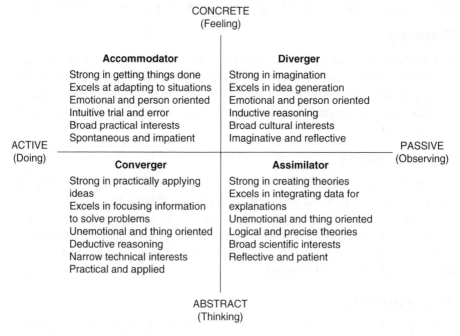

CONCRETE
(Feeling)

Accommodator
Strong in getting things done
Excels at adapting to situations
Emotional and person oriented
Intuitive trial and error
Broad practical interests
Spontaneous and impatient

Diverger
Strong in imagination
Excels in idea generation
Emotional and person oriented
Inductive reasoning
Broad cultural interests
Imaginative and reflective

ACTIVE
(Doing)

PASSIVE
(Observing)

Converger
Strong in practically applying
ideas
Excels in focusing information
to solve problems
Unemotional and thing oriented
Deductive reasoning
Narrow technical interests
Practical and applied

Assimilator
Strong in creating theories
Excels in integrating data for
explanations
Unemotional and thing oriented
Logical and precise theories
Broad scientific interests
Reflective and patient

ABSTRACT
(Thinking)

Figure 7.1 Learning Styles

To some extent you are attempting to educate the management team because they have not experienced the issues that have brought you to this point. You need to accommodate all learning styles. (See Figure 7.1)

- Accommodators – learn from concrete experience and active experimentation.
- Convergers learn through abstract conceptualization and active experimentation.
- Divergers learn through concrete experience and reflective observation.
- Assimilators learn through abstract conceptualization and reflective observation.

Therefore your presentation needs a mixture of:

1. *Tell sessions* where you transfer information. These suit the Assimilators. So if it is facts that you need to get across, simply use a "tell session". The text needs to be broken with graphics and animation will grab the attention of the Convergers providing it is not over done. However, facts might emerge after a Discovery session so for the Assimilators among your group you need to recap and conclude on the findings of any group work in case they were asleep! Accommodators and Convergers might well fall asleep during tell sessions if they are too long so keep them short and interwoven with discussion and pull sessions.
2. *Pull sessions* where you ask questions and pull answers from the audience. These suit the Divergers but to appease the Assimilators who might not answer any questions, write the question on a slide and the answers on a flipchart or overhead foil. Accommodators are usually happy with pull sessions because they are spontaneous and the Convergers follow up with responses from their experience or which they have deduced from previous dialogue.
3. *Discovery sessions* where two or more people discuss a topic, question or observation and draw out opinions, beliefs and comments. These suit the Accommodators and Convergers who will lead the discussion. The Assimilators will probably take a back seat, thinking and reflecting upon what is going on in the group. The Divergers may provide suggestions, ideas and participate but not lead the discussion. These sessions are very important and a presentation that does not have them may fail to achieve the level of commitment expected. This is because most managers like to get involved and don't like being talked at.

The content will differ depending on what you are trying to achieve but in general it might include some or all of the following:

1. **Introduction.** A brief session identifying the project sponsor, defining the objectives of the presentation and the reasons why these objectives need to be addressed at this time.
2. **Background**. A session on the background should explain the circumstances that have led to the discovery of the problem or opportunity. At the end of this

session the audience should be nodding in agreement that there is a problem to be solved or an opportunity to be grasped. This can be accomplished by a *tell session* but might be more effective if run as a *discovery session* – the agreement you get will be more emphatic with this approach.

3. **Causes and effect/impact.** A session devoted to determining the cause and effect of the problem on the business is needed before proposing solutions. This can be accomplished by a *pull session* or form part of the previous session on Background.

4. **Project objectives.** A session devoted to deriving an objective or series of objectives from the foregoing is needed so there is a clear link between the project and the problem/opportunity. Remember this is what the project aims to achieve and when it intends to be completed. Also define the success criteria – what will/won't be happening in the organization after project completion. These must be measurable. This can be accomplished by a discovery session but a pull session may work just as well.

5. **Feasibility**. This session will address the timing, drivers, barriers and capabilities associated with the objectives. This will require a study of what else is going on that may impede progress should the project go ahead and from a historical perspective, what success the organization has had with similar change initiatives. Research is needed here but once again a *discovery session* followed by a *pull session* might reveal some interesting facts.

If it is anticipated that sessions 1–5 are enough for management to absorb in one sitting, this may be a convenient point at which to break and resume after a suitable project strategy has been developed. Before breaking at this point, it is necessary to have reached agreement on the project objectives and measures of success for without such an agreement any strategy that is subsequently developed might be futile.

There is simply no point in pursuing a change initiative knowing that there are significant barriers in the way. If this is the case, you need to establish the best way forward because the original problem remains and loss of revenue might continue. If it is timing then you can plan ahead, if it is capability, you might be able to introduce additional training as part of the programme. If the barriers are cultural or ideological you may have to shelve the project while you work on the individuals concerned. Although there will always be a number of inhibitors in any organization you can't proceed if they are in the majority. Just because other organizations have successfully made the change does not mean your organization is either ready for change or needs to change.

6. **Project strategy**. A session devoted to the overall approach taken to achieve the agreed objectives as measured. You may of course discuss alternatives but if you do you need to say why you are rejecting others. This can be accomplished by a *tell session* but keep testing understanding so that there is no confusion as to what is meant. Use case studies from other organizations or published literature to reinforce the strategy. Define any new terms you use by

way of examples. Translate any definitions you use from external standards into a language understood by those present.

7. **Benefits.** A session devoted to explaining the benefits to be derived from adopting this strategy. Again quote from other organizations where possible to give credibility to the strategy but beware of the NIH syndrome. The Not Invented Here (NIH) syndrome is prevalent in many organizations particularly those at the forefront of technology in their sector and can be a barrier to change. Managers of such organizations tend to reject innovations they have not discovered or invented and they also tend to dismiss examples from other industry sectors as having no relevance to their organization. If your organization is one of these, presenting your solution as unique (even if not entirely true) may give you an advantage. This will be a *tell session* but you can augment it with a *pull session*.

8. **Programme of work.** A session covering the work to be carried out to achieve the project objectives. Parcel the work into stages or phases – each with a defined objective. Define the major tasks and responsibilities. Make a point of identifying the contributions required from the management. If you don't do it at this stage, you might get a rough ride later on. This session might be better presented as a handout as the detail could be too much for a slide but a summary is necessary to capture attention.

9. **Project organization.** A session covering the key appointments and project management structure. Nominations for Project Manager and the composition of the Steering Group and Project Team need to be defined. This will likely be a *tell session* resulting from some prior consultation with the project sponsor.

10. **Costs and timescales**. A session addressing the costs and timescales together with any assumptions. Timescales could be presented as a bar chart and the costs presented against the Stages or major tasks and totaled. If you need external help, separate the costs to clearly show what you expect from the external consultants. A summary slide plus a handout might be the better solution here. Don't take this too lightly as many a project has been abandoned once the managers have realized what the costs will be. There is of course the drip feed approach. By withholding the full costs, you get agreement to proceed one stage at a time. Stage 1 being fully costed with only ball-park estimates for the other stages. After stage 3 you reveal further costs which might be accepted on the basis of, *"We have gone too far to stop now"*. Cross reference the session on benefits in a way that clearly shows the payback from the investment.

11. **Action plan**. This session needs to identify the actions immediately following the presentation together with completion dates and responsibilities.

Giving the presentation

Fail to plan and your plan will fail, therefore pay great attention to detail and divide each event into a Before, During and After.

Before the event

- Ensure the invitation to attend goes to the people whose commitment is essential for project success.
- Ensure they are made aware of why they have been invited and been given sufficient background information for them to judge how important it is that their contribution is needed.

> **The traffic light method**
>
> Go down the list of attendees and mark the inhibitors red, the innovators green and the conservatives yellow.
>
> Ensure the innovators and conservatives outnumber the inhibitors.

- Ascertain which of the attendees are likely to be innovators, conservatives or inhibitors and ensure there is a bias towards the positive. You can do this either using personal knowledge or from consultation with an insider. Too many inhibitors will spell disaster and may result in the presentation coming to a halt within 30 minutes. If there are no inhibitors among senior management you are very lucky, but try to get at least one of the senior managers wholly on your side – someone to whom you can address a question in the knowledge that you will receive an answer supporting your case. If you have to get commitment from an audience about which you know nothing, postpone the presentation until you clearly understand who you are dealing with – to do otherwise will result in a disaster unless you are an exceptionally skilled communicator.
- Ensure the date and time for the presentation is suitable and not one where it is likely that managers will be diverted to other duties.
- Avoid Friday afternoons and Monday mornings. Arrange an external venue if possible.
- Try to predict the needs and expectations of the attendees and ensure your plans will satisfy them as well as possible.
- Develop an Event Plan that identifies the timing and objectives of each section, the slides, handouts and/or group work sessions.
- Test the presentation, projectors, floppy disks, pen drives, software etc.
- Don't go in for fancy wizardry – remember KISS (keep it simple and straightforward).
- Have a back-up plan in the event of computer failure, bad weather, building works or other emergencies.
- Always arrive early and arrange the room to give you the best chance of success. Try to avoid boardroom tables and opt for a more relaxed layout where you can approach the attendees.

During the event

- Start on time even if the CEO or MD has not arrived unless you have been forewarned of a delay.
- Make a note of who is present.

- Open with an "icebreaker", something to break the tension, and initiate a rapport but avoid anything that is not relevant to the presentation and anything that is controversial – you don't want to set them against you before you start. Perhaps a pertinent news story, a current incident in the factory that most people present know about, or perhaps a story about the successes of a competitor or partner.

> **Opinions**
> New opinions are always suspected, and usually opposed, without any other reason but because they are not already common.
> *John Locke (1632–1704), British philosopher*

- Introduce yourself and your colleague if you are not alone. If you are an external consultant and have not met the group previously you may want to ask those present to introduce themselves.
- Before presenting the objectives of the day it is often useful to illicit the views of those present as to what they hope to get out of the event. This does not mean you need to return to this at the end and prove you have or have not met their expectations, but it gives you the opportunity to clarify any ambiguity before you start.
- Stick to the plan and don't be persuaded to cut it short. Remember you have designed it for this audience and determined what they need to know before giving a commitment. Attendees who leave early will not take with them the key messages and consequently will not have a full appreciation of what is involved. If managers must leave early, tell them that you will contact them to arrange a date when they can complete the presentation.
- Use a language the managers will understand as they can be turned off by jargon. Also don't go into detail unless asked to do so as it rarely resolves issues of principle.
- Test understanding several times. Go back to parts where a fundamental point was made and repeat it.
- Elicit questions. Provoke responses – be controversial if necessary to get a discussion underway for it is with discussion that others might change their perceptions.

> **Understanding**
> "I know you believe you understand what you think I said. But I am not sure you realise that what you heard is not what I meant."
> *Alan Greenspan (1926- American economist*

- At break times when asked how you think it is going, be noncommittal. Remember the objective will not be met half way through – if it could the presentation would be half as long. People learn at different rates so the most you can admit is that it is going to plan.
- Be prepared for managers to challenge your observations and conclusions. Do your homework – be sure of your facts. Don't make things up on the spot. A good ploy before accepting a challenge is to ask what others think. If it looks like you might be mistaken accept the point and follow it up later rather than draw attention to the conflict by continuing to justify your position.

- Another approach to challenges is to try to understand where the other person is coming from – the facts that bring them to the position they are taking. You are dealing with perceptions often created through experiences or the influence of others having strongly held views, e.g. a person's dislike of ISO 9000 might have arisen from being exposed to a very dogmatic auditor or an arrogant consultant, or they might have read a powerful article on the subject. They don't share the views of the auditor, consultant or author and infer that the views are consistent with ISO 9000 when in reality a close reading of ISO 9000 would lead one to a different conclusion. Politely exploring the origin of their perceptions may get to the root cause of their beliefs which you can then deal with objectively.
- Remember, when you get yourself in a hole, stop digging. You won't win any allies for embarrassing a manager in front of his/her peers even if you are right.
- When a person asks a question be careful not to go on the defensive – it is simply a question not a challenge. Answer the question truthfully without being negative.
- Make a note of the innovators, conservatives and inhibitors – are they the same as you predicted beforehand? Also make a note of those who give the impression of changing their perception as these can often be your strongest allies.
- Don't close without getting agreement to the next stage.

After the event

- Try to get immediate feedback and note where it comes from relative to it being negative or positive.
- Follow-up on those who departed the event early and obtain their agreement or disagreement to the objectives, strategy programme and action plan.
- Progress actions promptly because the project will not be taken seriously if there is a long delay before it commences.
- Establish the communication mechanisms for getting funding approved, work planned, executed and reviewed.
- Establish benchmarks (if not done already) for measuring achievement. Remember such projects are intended to bring about change and improved performance. It is wise therefore, to record the performance before work commences so that improvement can be measured after the planned work is reported as having been completed.

> **Leadership**
>
> For if the trumpet give an uncertain sound, who shall prepare himself to the battle?
> *St. Paul, in 1 Corinthians, 14:8*

- Don't change the goal posts without agreement of both the Steering Group and Project team.
- Keep testing understanding and reinforcing the key messages from the presentation at every opportunity because the slightest

difference in belief can jeopardize success. It is vital that everyone has a common understanding of the goal and the strategy for achieving it.
- Keep control. Don't allow others to take over unless you relinquish control to them. Having two leaders will give others the opportunity of driving a wedge between you and the other person.

Summary

In this Chapter we have examined four different situations where a need had been identified for changing the way quality was being managed. We concluded that in each case there was a root cause that was deeper than initially identified. We showed how to express the objectives for change in terms of the objective, the reason for change and the measure of success and demonstrated that in each case a system needed to be established to resolve the issues from which the need for change arose.

We then set about proving the need by anticipating what top management would look for and examined the factors that need to be considered in determining the feasibility of change. Having gathered the information needed to commence the journey towards a better way of managing quality, the next stage is to gain the commitment of management and here we examined the factors to be considered in determining our audience and designing a successful presentation. We identified different learning styles that need to be taken into account so that our presentation has multiple ways of getting across the key messages. We learnt that commitment rarely comes about by telling and that most people need to experience or witness situations for themselves before they feel comfortable with what is being said.

We covered several elements of the presentation, and emphasized the importance of problem definition and objectives because without a clear understanding of what the project is intended to accomplish, support and commitment will be patchy and detrimental to project success. We explained that there is more to a successful presentation than delivery. Care needs to be taken before, during and after the event and guidance is given to help presenters through this process.

Securing the commitment of management to change the way quality is managed is never a pushover. It does require careful planning and execution and it is important to recognize that you are selling ideas to people who may not see the opportunities or the problems as you see them. They will have their own problems and of course their own objectives so anything that gets in the way of enabling them to achieve these objectives they will side step. Your task, should you choose to accept it, is to use persuasion, influence, reason, logic, peer pressure and anything else providing it's legal to enable them to realize that their interests will be served best by undertaking a commitment to improve the way quality is managed in your organization.

Appendix A
Food for thought

1. Without a set of principles, achieving a common understanding in the field of quality management would be impossible.
2. In supplying products or services there are three fundamental parameters that determine their saleability – price, quality and delivery.
3. Organizations exist because of their ability to satisfy their customers and other stakeholders.
4. It is quite possible for an organization to satisfy its customers and fail to satisfy the needs of the other stakeholders.
5. The needs of all parties have to be satisfied in order for *quality* to be achieved.
6. Products or services that do not possess the right features and characteristics either by design or by construction are products of poor quality.
7. A gold-plated mousetrap that does not fail is not a success if no one needs a gold-plated mousetrap!
8. The more prescription we have the more we get immersed in the detail and lose sight of our objectives.
9. Customer focus means putting your energy into satisfying customers and understanding that profitability or avoidance of loss comes from satisfying customers.
10. People naturally concentrate on what they are measured – it is therefore vital that leaders measure the right things.
11. Processes are dynamic – they cause things to happen.
12. The behaviour of any part of a system has some effect on the behaviour of the system as a whole.
13. Everyone in the organization should be continually questioning its performance and seeking ways to reduce variation, improve their methods and seeking better ways of doing things.
14. The factual approach leads us to control activities based on fact rather than opinion or emotion.
15. Organizations depend on their suppliers as much as they depend on their customers.
16. Does ISO 9000 mean different things to different people?

17. If ISO 9000 is perceived rightly or wrongly, as a badge on the wall, a system, a label, a goal or a set of documents, is that what it is?
18. If any set of rules, rituals, requirements, quantities, targets or behaviours that have been agreed by a group of people could be deemed to be a standard – is ISO 9000 a standard?
19. Do managers think of the organization as a system? – if so how come they don't manage the organization as a system?
20. Was ISO 9001:1994 simply a matter of documenting what you do and doing what you document?
21. Do quality systems only exist to assure customers that product meets requirements?
22. Do you believe that if it's not documented it doesn't exist and that's why your quality system is a set of documents?
23. Do you believe that you can write instructions that don't rely on the user being trained?
24. Can a faulty product delivered on time, within budget and with a smile be anything other than a faulty product?
25. If your organization chooses not to pursue ISO 9001 certification or not to retain the certificate, will it make any difference to the way the organization is managed?
26. Did *you* cheat to get the ISO 9001 certificate?
27. Did your application of ISO 9000 prevent you from producing nonconforming product or did it simply prevent you from producing product?
28. Is your organization one of those that coerced its suppliers into seeking ISO 9000 certification because it was believed that the standard required it?
29. Did you establish a quality system to ensure that product met your customer's requirements or did you simply use it to ensure you met your own requirements?
30. If you were to take away the ISO 9001 certification would there be a business need for all the procedures?
31. Did your third party auditor establish your organization's readiness for the audit by the closeness with which the quality manual addressed the requirements of the standard?
32. Did you focus on the things the auditor looked for and not on the things that mattered?
33. Were your management more interested in surviving the ISO 9000 audit than improving performance?
34. Were those producing the documentation focusing on meeting ISO 9000 or achieving quality?
35. Did your management believe the system was effective if it conformed to the standard?
36. Do you believe there are real benefits from managing organizations as a set of interconnected processes focused on achieving objectives that have been derived from an understanding of the needs of all stakeholders?

Appendix B
Glossary

This list includes some of the terms and common words that have acquired a special meaning in the field of quality management. Some first appeared in other books by the same author, others have been compiled for this book or taken from books already mentioned in the bibliography.

3 Ms. These are three Japanese words associated with lean production
    M1   Muda (Waste).
    M2   Muri (Overburden).
    M3   Mura (Unevenness).

5 Why's. These typically refer to the practice of asking, five times, why a failure has occurred in order to get to the root cause.

5 Ss. These Japanese words apply to the visual management of a workspace
    S1   Seiri (straighten up). Differentiate between the necessary and unnecessary and discard the unnecessary.
    S2   Seiton (put things in order).
    S3   Seido (clean up). Keep the workplace clean.
    S4   Seiketsu (personal cleanliness). Make it a habit to be tidy.
    S5   Shitsuke (discipline). Follow the procedures, adhere to the policies and exemplify the values.

6 Ms. These are the six words that are used to title the arms in a fishbone diagram. The words vary but the most commonly used Ms are:
    M1   Machines.
    M2   Methods.
    M3   Materials.
    M4   Measurements.
    M5   Milieu (Surrounding Environment).
    M6   Manpower.
One could also add Money, Management.

7 Wastes. These

> W1 Overproduction.
> W2 Excess inventory.
> W3 Waiting time.
> W4 Unnecessary transportation.
> W5 Unnecessary movement.
> W6 Over processing or incorrect processing.
> W7 Defects.

8D. A problem solving method that is structured into eight disciplined steps. The 8 basic steps are:

> D1 Establish a team.
> D2 Describe the problem.
> D3 Develop interim containment.
> D4 Define and verify root cause.
> D5 Choose permanent corrective action.
> D6 Implement corrective action.
> D7 Prevent recurrence.
> D8 Recognize and reward the contributors.

> (Note: some of these terms are not consistent with ISO 9000 definitions for corrective and preventive action)

Acceptance Authority. The organization having the right to decide on the acceptability of something, typically products, services, designs, projects or proposals for changing a design or project. Also referred to as Design Authority and Project Authority.

Acceptance criteria. The standard against which a comparison is made to judge conformance.

Accreditation. A process by which organizations are authorized to conduct certification of conformity to prescribed standards.

Activity. An element of work that produces an output required by a process. Activities comprise tasks or operations.

Adequate. Suitable for the purpose.

Appropriate. Means suitable for its purpose or to the circumstances and requires knowledge of this purpose or circumstances. Without criteria, an assessor is left to decide what is or is not appropriate based on personal experience.

Approved. Something that has been confirmed as meeting the requirements.

Assessment. The act of determining the extent of compliance with requirements.

Assurance. Evidence (verbal or written) that gives confidence that something will or will not happen or has or has not happened.

Audit. An examination of results to verify their accuracy by someone other than the person responsible for producing them. (See also ISO 9000 Clause 3.9.1)

Authority. The right to take actions and make decisions.

Authorized. A permit to do something or use something that may not necessarily be approved.

Autonomation. Automation with the human touch. The purpose is to free equipment from the necessity of constant human attention, separate people from machines and allow workers to staff multiple operations. In Japanese the word is Jidoka. (See also *Error proofing*)

Balanced Scorecard. A strategic planning and review methododology that enables organizations to clarify their vision and strategy and translate them into action. It provides feedback around both the internal business processes and external outcomes in order to continuously improve strategic performance and results.

Benchmarking. A technique for measuring an organization's products, services and operations against those of its competitors resulting in a search for best practice that will lead to superior performance.

Business management system. The set of interconnected and managed processes that function together to achieve the business objectives.

Business objectives. Objectives the business needs to achieve in order to accomplish its mission. These are usually derived from an analysis of stakeholder needs and expectations.

Business process. A process that is designed to deliver outputs that satisfy business objectives.

Calibrate. To standardize the quantities of a measuring instrument.

Capability index C_p. The capability index for a stable process defined as the quotient of tolerance width and process capability where process capability is the 6σ range of a process's inherent variation.

Capability index C_{pk}. The capability index which account for process centring for a stable process using the minimum upper or lower capability index.

Certification body. (*See Registrar*)

Certification. A process by which a product, process, person or organization is deemed to meet specified requirements.

Class. A group of entities having at least one attribute in common or a group of entities having the same generic purpose but different functional use.

Clause of the standard. A numbered paragraph or subsection of a standard containing one or more related requirements such as 7.2.2. Note: Each item in a list is also a Clause.

Codes. A systematically arranged and comprehensive collection of rules, regulations or principles.

Commitment. An obligation a person or an organization undertakes to fulfil i.e. doing what you say will do.

Common cause. Random variation caused by factors that are inherent in the system.

Competence. The ability to demonstrate *use* of education, skills and behaviours to achieve the results required for the job.

Competence-based assessment. A technique for collecting sufficient evidence that individuals can perform or behave to the specified standards in a specific role (Shirley Fletcher).

Competent. An assessment decision that confirms a person has achieved the prescribed standard of competence.

Concession. Permission granted by an acceptance authority to supply product or service that does not meet the prescribed requirements. (See also ISO 9000 Clause 3.6.11)

Concurrent engineering. (See also *Simultaneous engineering*)

Continual improvement. A recurring activity to increase the ability to fulfil requirements. (ISO 9000)

Contract loan. An item of customer-supplied property provided for use in connection with a contract that is subsequently returned to the customer.

Contract. An agreement formally executed by both customer and supplier (enforceable by law) which requires performance of services or delivery of products at a cost to the customer in accordance with stated terms and conditions. Also agreed requirements between an organization and a customer transmitted by any means.

Contractual requirements. Requirements specified in a contract.

Control charts. A graphical comparison of process performance data to computed control limits drawn as limit lines on the chart.

Control methods. Particular ways of providing control which do not constrain the sequence of steps in which the methods are carried out.

Control procedure. A procedure that controls product or information as it passes through a process.

Control. The act of preventing or regulating change in parameters, situations or conditions.

Controlled conditions. Arrangements that provide control over all factors that influence the result.

Core competence. A specific set of capabilities including knowledge, skills, behaviours and technology that generate performance differentials.

Corrective action.   Action planned or taken to stop something from recurring. (See also ISO 9000 Clause 3.6.5)

Corrective maintenance.   Maintenance carried out after a failure has occurred that is intended to restore an item to a state in which it can perform its required function.

Criteria for workmanship.   Acceptance standards based on qualitative measures of performance.

Critical success factors (CSFs).   Those factors on which the achievement of specified objectives depend.

Cross-functional team.   (See *Multidisciplinary team*)

Customer complaints.   Any adverse report (verbal or written) received by an organization from a customer.

Customer feedback.   Any comment on the organization's performance provided by a customer.

Customer supplied product.   Hardware, software, documentation or information owned by the customer which is provided to an organization for use in connection with a contract and which is returned to the customer either incorporated in the supplies or at the end of the contract.

Customer.   An organization or person that receives a product from another organization and includes Consumer, client, end user, retailer, beneficiary and purchaser.

Cusum Chart.   A type of control chart (cumulative sum control chart) used to detect small changes between 0–0.5 sigma. Cusum charts plot the cumulative sum of the deviations between each data point (a sample average) and a reference value, T. Unlike other control charts, one studying a cusum chart will be concerned with the slope of the plotted line, not just the distance between plotted points and the centreline.

Data.   Information that is organized in a form suitable for manual or computer analysis.

Define and document.   To state in written form, the precise meaning, nature or characteristics of something.

Demand creation process.   A key business process that penetrates new markets and exploits existing markets with products and a promotional strategy that influences decision-makers and attracts potential customers to the organization.

Demand fulfilment process.   A key business process that converts customer requirements into products and services in a manner that satisfies all stakeholders.

Demonstrate.   To prove by reasoning, objective evidence, experiment or practical application.

Department. A unit of an organization that may perform one or more functions. Units of organization regardless of their names are also referred to as functions (see *Function*).

Design and Development. Design creates the conceptual solution and development transforms the solution into a fully working model. (See also ISO 9000 3.4.4)

Design of experiments. A technique for improving the quality of both processes and products by effectively investigating several sources of variation at the same time using statistically planned experiments.

Design review. A formal documented and systematic critical study of a design by people other than the designer.

Design. A process of originating a conceptual solution to a requirement and expressing it in a form from which a product may be produced or a service delivered.

Disposition. The act or manner of disposing of something.

DMAIC. Define, Measure, Analyse, Improve and Control – the problem solving technique at the heart of Six Sigma programmes.

Documented procedures. Procedures that are formally laid down in a reproducible medium such as paper or magnetic disk.

DPMO. Defects per million opportunities – the units of measure for process capability.

Effectiveness of the system. The extent to which the system fulfils its purpose.

Embodiment loan. An item of customer-supplied property provided for incorporation into product that is subsequently supplied back to the customer or a party designated by the customer.

Employee empowerment. An environment in which employees are free (within defined limits) to take action to operate, maintain and improve the processes for which they are responsible using their own expertise and judgement.

EMS. Environmental management system. The set of interconnected and managed processes that function together to achieve the organization's environmental goals.

Ensure. To make certain that something will happen.

Establish and maintain. To set-up an entity on a permanent basis and retain or restore it in a state in which it can fulfil its purpose or required function.

Evaluation. To ascertain the relative goodness, quality or usefulness of an entity with respect to a specific purpose.

Evidence of conformance. Documents which testify that an entity conforms to certain prescribed requirements.

Executive responsibility. Responsibility vested in those personnel who are responsible for the whole organization's performance. Often referred to as top management.

Fagan inspection. A software inspection technique in which someone other than the creator of a product examines it with the specific intent of finding errors. Software Inspections were introduced in the 1970s at IBM, which pioneered their early adoption and later evolution. Michael Fagan helped develop the formal software inspection process at IBM, hence the term "Fagan inspection".

Failure mode effects analysis (FMEA). A technique for identifying potential failure modes and assessing existing and planned provisions to detect, contain or eliminate the occurrence of failure. (See also *Risk assessment*)

FIFO. First in first out. A term used to describe a method of inventory control.

Final inspection and testing. The last inspection or test carried out by the organization before ownership passes to the customer.

Finite element analysis. A technique for modelling a complex structure.

First party audits. Audits of a company or parts thereof by personnel employed by the company. These audits are also called Internal Audits.

Follow-up audit. An audit carried out following and as a direct consequence of a previous audit to determine whether agreed actions have been taken and are effective.

Force majeure. An event, circumstance or effect that cannot be reasonably anticipated or controlled.

Function. In the organizational sense, a function is a special or major activity (often unique in the organization) which is needed in order for the organization to fulfil its purpose and mission. Examples of functions are design, procurement, personnel, manufacture, marketing, maintenance etc.

Geometric dimensioning and tolerancing. A method of dimensioning the shape of parts that provides appropriate limits and fits for their application and facilitates manufacturability and interchangeability.

Grade. Category or rank given to entities having the same functional use but different requirements for quality; e.g. hotels are graded by star rating and automobiles are graded by model. (See also ISO 9000 Clause 3.1.3)

Hazard. Anything that may cause harm to people, product, property or the natural environment.

Hazard analysis. The process of collecting and evaluating information on hazards and conditions leading to their presence to decide which are significant for food safety and therefore should be addressed in the HACCP plan. (ISO 15161)

HACCP. Hazard Analysis and Critical Control Point. A technique used particularly in the food industry for the identification of hazards and control of risks.

The CCP is a step at which control can be applied and is essential to prevent or eliminate a food safety hazard or reduce it to an acceptable level. (ISO 15161)

Hoshin kanri. A Japanese term for a systems approach to goal achievement. *Hoshin* means a course, a policy, a plan or an aim. *Kanri* means administration, management, control, charge of or care for. Also known as policy deployment but it goes further than this.

IAF. International Accreditation Forum.

Identification. The act of identifying an entity, i.e. giving it a set of characteristics by which it is recognizable as a member of a group.

Implement. To carry out a directive.

Implementation Audit. An audit carried out to establish whether actual practices conform to the documented quality system. Note: Also referred to as a Conformance Audit or Compliance Audit.

Importance of activities in auditing. The relative importance of the contribution an activity makes to the fulfilment of an organization's objectives.

Indexing. A means of enabling information to be located.

In-process. Between the beginning and the end of a process.

Inspection authority. The person or organization that has been given the right to perform inspections.

Inspection, measuring and test equipment. Devices used to perform inspections, measurements and tests.

Inspection. The examination of an entity to determine whether it conforms to prescribed requirements. (See also ISO 9000 Clause 3.8.2)

Installation. The process by which an entity is fitted into a larger entity.

Integrated management. The understanding and effective direction of every aspect of an organization so that the needs and expectations of all stakeholders are justly satisfied by the best use of all resources. (IQA – Integrated Management Special Interest Group)

Integrated management system. A management system that enables the organization to achieve all its objectives in a manner that satisfies the needs and expectations of all stakeholders. Synonymous with Business Management System. Often perceived to be the amalgamation of quality, environmental, health and safety management systems and other similar systems.

Intellectual property. Creations of the mind: inventions, literary and artistic works, and symbols, names, images, and designs used in commerce. Intellectual property is divided into two categories: Industrial property and Copyright.

Interested party. Person or group having an interest in the performance or success of an organization which normally includes: Customers, owners, employees, contractors, suppliers, investors, unions, partners or society. However, interested parties can be benevolent or malevolent and the latter group might include terrorists, criminals and competitors whose only interest is to harm the organization. (See also *Stakeholder*)

ISO. International Organization for Standardization.

Issues of documents. The revision state of a document.

Just-in-time. A method of lean production where the demand comes from the end of the process through to the beginning so that the only parts that are delivered are those that are needed at the time they are needed.

Kanban. A Japanese word for "tag" or "ticket" or "sign board". These tickets are used as a means of picking up and receiving the right quantity of parts required by a process thus ensuring parts are delivered just-in-time by preceding processes.

Key performance indicators (KPI). The quantifiable characteristics that indicate the extent by which an objective is being achieved. (See also *Stakeholder success measures*)

Lagging measures. Measures that indicate an aspect of performance long after the conditions that created it have changed (e.g. profit and return on capital).

Leading measures. Measures that indicate an aspect of performance while the conditions that created it still prevail (e.g response time, conformity).

Lean production. A method of production that is demand driven (pull) rather than supply driven (push) as with mass production. There is zero waiting time, zero inventory, line balancing and reduction in process time with less space required for materials and finished product. This results in product being produced only to satisfy a demand. In lean production the person goes to the job and performs multiple tasks.

Line balance. Balancing the resources in a process or number of processes by optimizing speeds, feeds, batch size, number of workstations, operators, idle time, changeover time, cycle time and process yield.

Manage work. To manage work means to plan, organize and control the resources (personnel, financial and material) and the tasks required to achieve the objective for which the work is needed.

Management representative. The person management appoints to act on their behalf to manage the management system.

Management system. The set of interconnected and managed processes that function together to achieve the organization's goals. A qualifying prefix would describe a management system that achieves the organization's goals relative to this qualifying prefix (e.g. a quality management system achieves the organization's quality goals).

Mass production. A method of production that is supply driven based on sales forecasts rather than firm orders. It produces large amounts of standardized products on parallel production lines that stretch from raw materials to finished product (vertical integration). In mass production the job comes to the worker who passes it on to the next worker to perform the next operation on the line.

Master list. An original list from which copies can be made.

Measures. The characteristics by which performance is judged. They are the characteristics that need to be controlled in order that an objective will be achieved. They are the response to the question *"What will we look for to reveal whether the objective has been achieved?"*

Measurement capability. The ability of a measuring system (device, person and environment) to measure true values to the accuracy and precision required.

Measurement uncertainty. The variation observed when repeated measurements of the same parameter on the same specimen are taken with the same device.

Mission management. A key business process that determines the direction of the business, continually confirms that the business is proceeding in the right direction and makes course corrections to keep the business focused on its mission.

Modifications. Entities altered or reworked to incorporate design changes.

Monitoring. To check periodically and systematically. It does not imply that any action will be taken.

Motivation. An inner mental state that prompts a direction, intensity and persistence in behaviour.

Muda. The Japanese term for waste.

Multidisciplinary team. A team comprising representatives from various functions or departments in an organization, formed to execute a project on behalf of that organization.

Nationally recognized standards. Standards of measure that have been authenticated by a national body.

Nature of change. The intrinsic characteristics of the change (what has changed and why).

Objective evidence. Information that can be proven true based on facts obtained through observation, measurement, test or other means. (See also ISO 9000 Clause 3.8.1)

Objective. A result to be achieved usually by a given time.

Obsolete documents. Documents that are no longer required for operational use. They may be useful as historic documents.

OEM. Original Equipment Manufacturer.

Operating procedure. A procedure that describes how specific tasks are to be performed. (Might be called a *Work instruction*)

Organizational goals.   Where the organization desires to be, in markets, in innovation, in social and environmental matters, in competition and in financial health.

Organizational interfaces.   The boundary at which organizations meet and affect each other expressed by the passage of information, people, equipment, materials and the agreement to operational conditions.

Performance index P_{pk}.   The performance index accounts for process centring and is defined as the minimum of the upper or lower specification limit minus the average value divided by 3σ.

Performance indicators.   Quantifiable measures of performance related to specific objectives. They respond to the question *"What would we expect to see happening if this objective had been achieved?"* (See also *Measures*)

Plan. Provisions made to achieve an objective.

Planned arrangements.   All the arrangements made by the organization to achieve the customer's requirements. They include the documented policies and procedures and the documents derived from such policies and procedures.

Poka-yoke.   Japanese term that means "mistake proofing", a concept introduced by Shigeo Shingo to Toyota in 1961. It is a device that prevents incorrect parts from being made or assembled, or prevents correct parts being assembled incorrectly. Previously the term baka-yoke was used but as this means fool proofing and is rather offensive it was discontinued. Even mistake proofing has evolved into "error proofing" to avoid the personal implications. Error proofing is one of the two pillars of the Toyota Production System (TPS).

Policy.   A guide to thinking, action and decision.

Positive recall.   A means of recovering an entity by giving it a unique identity.

Positively identified.   An identification given to an entity for a specific purpose which is both unique and readily visible.

Potential nonconformity.   A situation that if left alone will in time result in nonconformity.

Predictive maintenance.   Work scheduled to monitor machine condition, predict pending failure and make repairs on an as-needed basis.

Pre-launch.   A phase in the development of a product between design validation and full production (sometimes called pre-production) during which the production processes are validated.

Prevent.   To stop something from occurring by a deliberate planned action.

Preventive action.   Action proposed or taken to stop something from occurring. (See also ISO 9000 Clause 3.6.4)

Preventive maintenance. Maintenance carried out at predetermined intervals to reduce the probability of failure or performance degradation; e.g. replacing oil filters at defined intervals. Also referred to as Planned maintenance.

Procedure. A sequence of steps to execute a routine activity. (See also ISO 9000 Clause 3.4.5)

Process. A set of interrelated activities that use behaviours and resources to produce a result. An effective process would be one in which the interrelated activities use behaviours and resources to achieve a prescribed objective. (See also ISO 9000 Clause 3.4.1)

Process approach. An approach to managing work in which the activities, resources and behaviours function together in such a relationship as to produce results consistent with the process objectives.

Process capability. The inherent ability of a process to reproduce its results consistently during multiple cycles of operation.

Process description. A set of information that describes the characteristics of a process in terms of its purpose, objectives, measures, design features, inputs, activities, resources, behaviours, outputs, constraints, measurements and reviews.

Process management. The management of organizations as a series of interconnected processes that function together to achieve the goals of the organization.

Process measures. Measures used to judge the performance of processes. They are generally a response to the question *"What will we look for to reveal whether the process objectives have been met?"*

Process parameters. Those variables, boundaries or constants of a process that restrict or determine the results.

Product realization. All those processes necessary to transform a set of requirements into a product or service that fulfils the requirements.

Product. Anything produced by human effort, natural or manmade processes. Result of a process. (ISO 9000-2)

Production. The creation of products.

Proprietary designs. Designs exclusively owned by the organization and not sponsored by an external customer.

Prototype. A model of a design that is both physically and functionally representative of the design standard for production and used to verify and validate the design.

Purchaser. One who buys from another.

Purchasing documents. Documents that contain the organization's purchasing requirements.

Qualification. Determination by a series of tests and examinations of a product, and its related documents and processes that the product meets all the specified performance capability requirements.

Quality. The degree to which a set of inherent characteristics fulfils a need or expectation that is stated, generally implied or obligatory. (ISO 9000)

Quality assurance. Part of quality management focused on providing confidence that quality requirements will be fulfilled. (ISO 9000)

Quality characteristics. Any characteristic of a product or service that is needed to satisfy customer needs or achieve fitness for use.

Quality circles (or QC Circles). A group of volunteers who perform activities within a process participating continuously together for the purpose of self-development, mutual development, control and improvement of the process. (Derived from the texts of Kaoru Ishikawa)

Quality conformance. The extent to which the product or service conforms to the specified requirements.

Quality control. A process for maintaining standards of quality that prevents and corrects change in such standards so that the resultant output meets customer needs and expectations. (See also ISO 9000 Clause 3.2.10)

Quality costs. Costs incurred because failure is possible. The actual cost of producing an entity is the no failure cost plus the quality cost. The no failure cost is the cost of doing the right things right first time. The quality costs are the prevention, appraisal and failure costs.

Quality function deployment. A technique to deploy customer requirements (the true quality characteristics) into design characteristics (the substitute characteristics) and deploy them into subsystems, components, materials and production processes. The result is a grid or matrix that shows how and where customer requirements are met.

Quality improvement. Part of quality management focused on increasing the ability to fulfil quality requirements. (ISO 9000)

Quality management system requirements. Requirements pertaining to the design, development, operation, maintenance and improvement of quality management systems.

Quality management system. The set of interconnected and managed processes that function together to achieve the organization's quality goals. (See also ISO 9000 3.2.3)

Quality objectives. Those results which the organization needs to achieve in order to improve its ability to meet the needs and expectations of all the stakeholders.

Quality planning. Provisions made to achieve the needs and expectations of the organization's stakeholders and prevent failure.

Quality plans.   Plans produced to define how specified quality requirements will be achieved, controlled, assured and managed for specific contracts or projects.

Quality problems.   The difference between the achieved quality and the required quality.

Quality requirements.   Those requirements which pertain to the features and characteristics of a product, service or process which are required to be fulfilled in order to satisfy a given need.

Quarantine area.   A secure space provided for containing product pending a decision on its disposal.

Registrar.   An organization that is authorized to certify organizations. The body may be accredited or non-accredited.

Registration.   A process of recording details of organizations of assessed capability that have satisfied prescribed standards.

Regulator.   A legal body authorized to enforce compliance with the laws and statutes of a national government.

Regulatory requirements.   Requirements established by law pertaining to products, services or processes.

Remedial action.   Action proposed or taken to remove a nonconformity (see also *Corrective and Preventive action*).

Representative sample.   A sample of product or service that possesses all the characteristics of the batch from which it was taken.

Resources.   Something of which there is an available supply that can be called on when needed. Resources include time, personnel, skill, machines, materials, money, plant, facilities, space, information, knowledge etc. Resources are used by processes resulting in some being reusable and others changed, lost or depleted by the process.

Resource management.   A key business process that specifies, acquires and maintains the resources required by the business to fulfil the mission and disposes of any resources that are no longer required.

Responsibility.   An area in which one is entitled to act on one's own accord or able to respond by virtue of having caused an event.

Review.   Another look at something.

Rework.   Continuation of work on a product to make it conform to the specified requirements without additional procedures or techniques.

Risk.   The likelihood of something happening that could have a positive or negative effect. Also: the combination of the probability of an event and its consequences. (ISO/IEC Guide 73)

Risk assessment. A study performed to quantify potential risks associated with a particular event or situation. It identifies hazards or failure modes, their effect on people, product, property or natural environment, the probability of their occurrence and detection and the severity of their effect in order to identify provisions taken or needed to eliminate, control or reduce the root cause. (See also *FMEA, HACCP*)

Risk management. The process whereby organizations methodically address the risks attaching to their activities with the goal of achieving sustained benefit within each activity and across the portfolio of all activities. (A Risk Management Standard IRM 2002)

Scheduled maintenance. Work performed at a time specifically planned to minimize interruptions in machine availability; e.g. changing a gearbox when machine is not required for use (includes predictive and preventive maintenance).

Shall. A provision that is binding.

Should. A provision that is optional.

Simultaneous engineering. A method of reducing the time taken to achieve objectives by developing the resources needed to support and sustain the production of a product in parallel with the development of the product itself. It involves customers, suppliers and each of the organization's functions working together to achieve common objectives.

Six sigma. Six standard deviations.

SMS. Safety management system.

Special cause. A cause of variation that can be assigned to a specific or special condition that does not apply to other events.

Specified requirements. Requirements prescribed by the customer and agreed by the organization or requirements prescribed by the organization that are perceived as satisfying a market need. Such requirements may or may not be documented.

Stakeholder. A person or an organization that has freedom to provide something to or withdraw something from an enterprise. (See also *Interested party*)

Stakeholder measures. Measures used to judge the performance of an organization. They are generally a response to the question, *"What measures will the stakeholders use to reveal whether their needs and expectations have been met?"* (See also *Key performance indicators*)

Statistical control. A condition of a process in which there is no indication of a special cause of variation.

Status of an activity (in auditing). The maturity or relative level of performance of an activity to be audited.

Status. The relative condition, maturity or quality of something.

Subcontract requirements. Requirements placed on a subcontractor that are derived from requirements of the main contract.

Subcontractor. A person or company that enters into a subcontract and assumes some of the obligations of the prime contractor.

System. An ordered set of ideas, principles and theories or a chain of operations that produce specific results.

System audit. An audit carried out to establish whether the quality system conforms to a prescribed standard in both its design and its implementation.

System effectiveness. The ability of a system to achieve its stated purpose and objectives.

Targets. The level of performance to be achieved, e.g. Standard, specification, requirement, budget, quota, plan.

Task. The smallest component of work. A group of tasks comprise an activity.

Technical interfaces. The physical and functional boundary between products or services.

Tender. A written offer to supply products or services at a stated cost.

Theory of constraints. A thinking process optimizing system performance. It examines the system and focuses on the constraints that limit overall system performance. It looks for the weakest link in the chain of processes that produce organizational performance and seeks to eliminate it and optimize system performance.

TQM Total quality management. A management philosophy and company practices that aim to harness the human and material resources of an organization in the most effective way to achieve the objectives of the organization. (BS 7850: 1992)

Traceability. The ability to trace the history, application, use and location of an individual article or its characteristics through recorded identification numbers. (See also ISO 9000 3.5.4)

Unique identification. An identification that has no equal.

Validation. A process for establishing whether an entity will fulfil the purpose for which it has been selected or designed. (See also ISO 9000 3.8.5)

Values. The fundamental principles that guide the organization in accomplishing its goals. They are what it stands for such as integrity, excellence, innovation, inclusion, reliability, responsibility, equality, fairness, confidentiality, safety of personnel and property etc. These values characterize the culture in the organization.

Value engineering. A technique for assessing the functions of a product and determining whether the same functions can be achieved with fewer types of components and materials and the product produced with fewer resources. Variety reduction is an element of value engineering.

Verification activities. A special investigation, test, inspection, demonstration, analysis or comparison of data to verify that a product or service or process complies with prescribed requirements.

Verification requirements. Requirements for establishing conformance of a product or service with specified requirements by certain methods and techniques.

Verification. The act of establishing the truth or correctness of a fact, theory, statement or condition. (See also ISO 9000 Clause 3.8.4)

Waiver. (See *Concession*)

Work breakdown structure. A structure in which elements of work for a particular project are placed in a hierarchy.

Work environment. A set of conditions under which people operate and include physical, social and psychological environmental factors. (ISO 9000:2000)

Work flow. A method of manufacture whereby value is added to the product in each process as it moves along a production line. Invented in 1910 by Charles Sorensen, first President of Ford Motor Company.

Work instructions. Instructions that prescribe work to be executed, who is to do it, when it is to start and be complete and if necessary how it is to be carried out.

Work packages. An assembly of related work elements.

Workflow system. A method of manufacture whereby value is added to the product in each process as it moves along a production line. Invented in 1910 by Charles Sorensen, first President of Ford Motor Company.

Workmanship criteria. Standards on which to base the acceptability of characteristics created by human manipulation of materials by hand or with the aid of hand tools.

Zero defects. The performance standard achieved when every task is performed right first time with no errors being detected downstream.

Bibliography

Chapter 1

1. Maslow, Abraham, H., (1954). Motivation and Personality, New York, Harper and Row
2. http://http-server.carleton.ca/~jchevali/STAKEH2.html
3. Crosby, Philip, B., (1979). Quality is Free, McGraw-Hill
4. Rollinson, D., Broadfield, A. and Edwards, D. J., (1998). Organizational behaviour and analysis, Addison Wesley Longmans. Based on Table 14.3

Chapter 2

1. Juran, J. M., (1992). Juran on Quality by Design, Free Press
2. Juran, J. M., (1974). Quality Control Handbook Section 21, McGraw-Hill, Third Edition
3. Hoyle, David and Thompson, John, (2001). ISO 9000:2000 Auditor Questions, Transition Support
4. ISO Geneva, (1997). ISO/TC/176/SC2/WG15/N130 Quality Management, Principles McGraw-Hill (1995)
5. Boone, Louise, E. and Kurtz, David, L., (2001). Contemporary Marketing 10th Edition, Harcourt College Publishers, pp. 11–13. Chapter 1 Customer-driven marketing
6. Juran, J. M. Managerial breakthrough
7. Deming, W. Edwards, (1982). Out of the crisis, MITC
8. Pyzdek, Thomas, (2001). The Complete Guide to Six Sigma, McGraw-Hill
9. Liker, J. K. The Toyota Way. McGraw-Hill 2004
10. General Electric web site http://www.ge.com/sixsigma/sixsigstrategy.html (2005)
11. Deming, W. Edwards, (1982). Out of the crisis, MITC. Juran as observed by Edwards Deming
12. ISO/TS 16949:2002
13. Watson, Gregory. H, (1994). Business Systems Engineering, Wiley

Chapter 3

1. Shannon, R. E., (1975). Systems Simulation, Prentice-Hall
2. Seddon, John, (2000). The case against ISO 9000, Oak Tree Press
3. Concise Oxford English Dictionary

Chapter 4

1. Unknown, (© 1994–1999). *Britannica® CD 99 Multimedia Edition*, Encyclopaedia Britannica, Inc.

Chapter 5

1. ISO Management systems October 2001 Edition
2. Department of Trade and Industry, (1982). *White Paper on Quality, standards and competitiveness*, HMSO
3. Selection and Use of the ISO 9000:2000 family of standards available from http://www.iso.ch/iso/en/iso9000-14000/iso9000/selection_use/selection_use.html
4. International Organization of Standardization, (2000). *The ISO Survey of ISO 9000 and ISO 14000 Certificates Ninth cycle 1999*, ISO
5. Seddon, John, (2000). *The case against ISO 9000*, Oak Tree Press

Chapter 6

1. Drucker, Peter. F., (1977). Management: Tasks, Responsibilities, Practices. Pan Business Management
2. Drucker, Peter. F., (1977). Management: Tasks, Responsibilities, Practices. Pan Business Management
3. Hammer, Michael and Champy, James, (1993). Reengineering the corporation, Harper Business
4. Juran, J. M., (1992). Juran on Quality by design, The Free Press
5. Hammer, Michael and Champy, James, (1993). Reengineering the corporation, Harper Business
6. Davenport, T. H., (1993). Process Innovation: Reengineering work through Information Technology, Harvard Business School Press
7. Total quality management BS7890:1992. Part 1 guide to management principles. BSI London.
8. ISO/TC 176/SC2 N544R
9. ISO/TC 176/SC2 N544R2 available on www.iso.org
10. Juran, J. M., (1992). Juran on Quality by design, The Free Press. Based on Figure 11-1

11. Adapted from http://www.businessballs.com and http://www. marketingteacher.com
12. Kaplan, Robert and Norton, David, (1992) The Balanced Scorecard– Measures that Drive Performance," Harvard Business Review
13. Juran, J. M., (1995). Managerial Breakthrough, Second Edition, McGraw-Hill.

Chapter 7

1. Juran, J. M., (1995). Managerial breakthrough, Second Edition, McGraw-Hill.
2. Hoyle, David and Thompson, John, (2000). Converting a quality management using the process approach., Transition Support
3. Hunsaker, P. L. & Alessandra, A. J. (1966) The art of Managing People, Simon & Schuster

Index